Head of Hadrian.
In Bronze.

ILLUSTRATIONS

OF

ROMAN LONDON.

BY

CHARLES ROACH SMITH,

AUTHOR OF "COLLECTANEA ANTIQUITIES OF RICHBOROUGH, RECULVER,

LONDON:
PRINTED FOR THE SUBSCRIBERS; AND
M.DCCC.LIX

Gough's London 4° 168.

to be amicably settled, as again[st] [the?]
factory state, and war as probable
A letter of the 18th from Turi[n]
ceeding from an opponent of the [?]
tains the following passages :—

"A ship full of German volunteers h[?]
But it must be remembered that the I[?]
only one which at the commencemen[t]
found volunteers. In Austria corps [?]
greater part of them set out to fight u[?]
in Italy. The sudden Peace of Villafr[?]
ment to them. They had mustered to [?]
not return to their universities wit[h?]
Some have enrolled themselves und[er]
house of Este, and are at Mantua ; [?]
the defence of the Holy See. The br[?]

ILLUSTRATIONS

OF

ROMAN LONDON.

BY

CHARLES ROACH SMITH,

AUTHOR OF "COLLECTANEA ANTIQUA;" "ANTIQUITIES OF RICHBOROUGH, RECULVER, AND LYMNE," ETC.

LONDON:

PRINTED FOR THE SUBSCRIBERS; AND NOT PUBLISHED.

M.DCCC.LIX

LONDON :
T. RICHARDS, 37, GREAT QUEEN ST

PREFACE.

THE present volume is, for the most part, the result of personal investigations made during my residence in Lothbury and in Liverpool Street, in the City of London.

The excavations, which led to those researches, were made for sewerage, for what is commonly termed "city improvements," and for deepening the bed of the Thames to facilitate navigation.

A wide space in the area of the Roman city has, consequently, been penetrated in various directions, by deep longitudinal cuttings in the centre of streets; and, occasionally, by transverse channels. Where new streets were formed, the foundations of the houses required greater width of excavation; but the sections were not so deep as those for sewers. Extensive as these operations were, they left untouched by far the most considerable part of the site, or level, of the Roman city. The excavations were, in fact, but so many channels, cut here and there, sometimes penetrating through and below the bed of the ancient city, sometimes superficially entering it; and, not unfrequently, so comparatively shallow that they did not pass through the *débris* of buildings of the middle ages.

b

Such circumstances were not of themselves the most congenial
to an antiquarian explorer. The excavations, moreover, were conducted with rapidity by large bodies of workmen. As regards the
sewers, tunnelling was often adopted, relays of labourers working
through the night. Even if the corporation of London had thought
fit to employ a dozen antiquaries or an archæological society to
watch the excavations, with full power to protect and to preserve, the
watchers would have been severely tasked. But the corporation
was not embarrassed by any such solicitude. It was compelled to
undertake and prosecute these public works; but beyond this it was
not propelled by public opinion; and on such a subject as the antiquities of the City, it had no opinion of its own. Volunteers were not
encouraged: at the best, they only received a precarious toleration
to inspect the excavations; and usually they were denied access to
them.

In the meantime, under these disadvantageous circumstances,
several collections of antiquities were formed by purchases from the
workmen. The principal were those made by Mr. Kempe, Mr. John
Newman, Mr. George Gwilt, Mr. Price, Mr. Chaffers, and myself.
With the exception, probably, of Mr. Gwilt's, which, for the present,
I believe, remains in the possession of his family, exertions were
made to secure these collections in some proper receptacle in the city
of London; but in vain. My own, as is well known, after having
been rejected by the corporation, has found a safe resting-place in the
British Museum. The rest are all dispersed. Mr. Chaffers, however,
has preserved a faithful manuscript record of his collection, with good
sketches of the more remarkable objects; and the Guildhall Library,
through my own interference, contains the monumental inscription,
fig. 1, pl. ii, of this volume, and the fragment of sculpture engraved in

p. 33 (which for a long time remained neglected in the City stone-yard).
In it are, also, some of the antiquities dug up on the site of the New
Royal Exchange, collected by the vigilance of Mr. Russell, clerk of
the works. The Guildhall gave a temporary shelter to the inscribed
stone represented in p. 29 ; but where this important fragment now
is, I cannot say: it was not to be found in the Guildhall very recently,
and there is every reason to believe it has been destroyed.

The citizens must share the opprobrium which attaches to the
corporation for this indifference to the antiquities of the metropolis ;
for when, a few years since, an attempt was made, in a large and
stormy meeting, to establish in the City a free library and a museum,
they scouted the proposal, under the pretext that the funds of the
corporation were adequate for the purpose without the new impost
proposed, which would probably have amounted to about one half-
penny in the pound ! It is, however, not agreeable to me to be ever
censuring ; and I therefore forbear entering into long details in
justification of general charges, contenting myself with an appeal to
one grand fact, patent to the world, and which no one will attempt to
deny. It is, that the City of London has no museum of collections of
its antiquities. The severest condemnation of the corporation is in
the fact itself.

In the arrangement of this volume I have omitted much which,
I think, is often introduced into similar works without any benefit to
archæology or to the general reader ; and I have endeavoured, as far
as it was practicable, to convey a notion of Roman London from the
antiquities themselves. If I had been warranted in so doing I should
have chosen to give more plates ; but while studying to show grati-
tude to my subscribers, I find it necessary to be just to myself. To
them I am deeply obliged, because they have contributed to enable

me to bring together into one view more engravings of the antiquities of London than I had, on former occasions, been able to obtain or to afford.   Like all works which I have printed, being my own property, the few unsubscribed copies of the *Illustrations of Roman London* will be retained with proper consideration for the compact which tacitly exists between an author and his subscribers.

To the Society of Antiquaries of London my thanks are offered for the loan of the plates which accompanied my communications printed in the *Archæologia.*

Temple Place, Strood, Kent.
June 1st, 1859.

ERRATUM.

Page 48, line 5 from the bottom, for " figs. 2 to 8" read " figs. 2 to 5."

ILLUSTRATIONS OF ROMAN LONDON.

THE fate of towns and cities closely resembles that of the kingdoms and empires of which they form part. It would, indeed, be out of the natural order and sequence of things, if the mutations and decay to which nations and countries have been subjected, should not be shared by the habitations of the people ; and, if our knowledge of the one is very limited, all we can know of the other must be equally confined. The most copious histories of the most civilized states of antiquity afford but scanty information in comparison with their extent. In one year the daily press of a free country prints more than is contained in the entire works of the most voluminous writer. The provincial journals furnish local histories of the places in which they are published, such as are not to be found in any literary legacy bequeathed to us by past ages ; and to these may be added the numerous works of collectors of medieval records of towns and countries, frequently illustrated with views of streets and buildings, since destroyed or totally changed in character. The antiquary of the present day has no such materials to work upon as the historical inquirer of a remote futurity will possess in abundance.

Of the most renowned cities of antiquity but few traces can now be discovered, except in the ruins of walls or of remarkable buildings, which, here and there, from their extraordinary stability or extent have escaped the general devastation, or which, from their abundant stores have supplied, without complete exhaustion, the pillagers of many ages. The private dwellings, the workshops of the artisan and manufacturer, and all the various humble structures which make up the bulk of cities and towns, have long since disappeared ; and with them almost every clue to their disposition and arrangement. This change is more complete in those towns which, with all the vicissitudes to which they have been subjected, have never succumbed to the worst disasters of war, but have continued to flourish without any permanent check to their commercial prosperity. In such towns it is often difficult to recognize a vestige of antiquity. But the change is less complete when, at some comparatively remote period, the tide of progress has been impeded, and the towns have declined in trade and in population. In the former class may be instanced London and Paris ; in the latter, Treves, Orange, Fréjus, etc. Pompeii stands in a class by itself, in having been preserved to us, in a great measure, in the condition in which it was eighteen hundred years since, by an extraordinary natural catastrophe. As a rule, we shall find, that the prosperity of towns has been the most fatal cause of the loss of their ancient configuration and of their monuments ; and, on the contrary, that where remains of antiquity abound, there we may find evidence of some important change having taken place in the middle ages, prejudicial to commerce and to the increase of local population. Paris and London, the capitals of Gaul and of Britain, are good illustrations of this rule. In both, population has for centuries gone on increasing. In spite of temporary mischances, their peculiar situations and other causes have maintained them as the centres of the civilization and commerce of their respective countries ; and they have both so outgrown their pristine garb, and every feature of remote antiquity, that scarcely a ruin or relic of their earlier days can be found even by the most plodding antiquary ; and the busy multitudes which daily throng their streets, never care to inquire about what does not concern them, or if prompted to inquire, resign themselves to scepticism ; for all around them speaks of the present and not of the past.

It is the same with all great commercial cities which have succeeded Roman towns. Population, extending rapidly in successive ages, has demanded new boundaries, and occupied every available rood of ground ; and buildings which could not be made applicable to purposes of trade were, from time to time, doomed to destruction. The close packing of ancient streets, and the wooden superstructures of most of the houses, were ever fertile causes in the middle ages of destruction by fires, one of the most fatal instruments in subverting the plans of arrangement of the streets of old towns. The worth of land in flourishing towns caused every spot from which a building had been removed to be reoccupied. Every stone had its value ; and the sculptured column and cornice, the inscribed slabs which recorded the building or restoration of temples and other public edifices, were estimated only as quarried material for houses or structures adapted to the wants of generations with habits and feelings totally different from those of their predecessors ; and void of that sentiment which, in modern times, among educated persons, tends to the preservation of the monuments of past ages.

So thoroughly is the ancient character of most of our towns effaced, that it is difficult, if not impossible, to conceive what they may have been. The former boundaries of many can only be traced at the present day by the help of tradition and old plans. We can tell what changes three centuries have produced, from the houses of the sixteenth century which yet remain, and from drawings and engravings; but if the imagination attempt to stretch backwards three centuries further, it will not so readily nor so truly realize a picture of the towns of the thirteenth century; and from the thirteenth to the fourth or third century the interval is long and almost impenetrably obscure. When the traveller approaches cities which have not entirely outgrown their ancient limits, such as Treves, Nismes, Autun, he sees before him evidences of their former greatness, and he admits they must have been grand and noble cities. But in most towns of ancient origin nothing of the kind is presented; and, if he think at all on the subject, he finds it difficult to allow their claim to antiquity. The Londoner, tied for life to his counting-house or his shop, and knowing no London but that which he has threaded to and fro from his boyhood, is incredulous when told of what was the probable condition of the city fifteen hundred years ago : he sees nothing to help him to realize the description; his mind pictures nothing beyond the visible present ; and he dwells only upon the scene before him, which comprises his present, his future and his past.

But although war, the various accidents of time, and especially the increase of population and commerce, have tended to denude England of the monuments which attested her greatness as a Roman province, those who would underrate the prosperity of Britain must have studied both history and existing remains to very little purpose. At the lowest computation, when the Roman legions were finally withdrawn, Britain possessed more than fifty walled towns, united by roads upon which, at stated intervals, were stations for resting and relays of horses and carriages, or as they may be called, inns and posts, but which are in no way reflected in our modern establishments bearing those names. Exclusive of the towns, there were numerous military walled stations, to which frequently, in the process of time, had become attached extensive suburbs. These towns and stations possessed public buildings, baths and temples within and without their walls. Many of the towns were of large extent ; and even if we may only judge from the remains discovered in our own time, were adorned with edifices of considerable grandeur and of architectural importance, and their public places were often embellished with statues. One bronze equestrian statue, at least, decorated Lincoln ; a bronze statue of the tutelary deity of the place, stood in a temple at Bath ; a statue in bronze, of Hadrian, of heroic size, was one of the public ornaments of London ; one of the temples at Colchester bore an inscription in large letters of bronze ; and Verulam possessed a theatre for dramatic representations, capable of holding some two to three thousand spectators.[1] It is accident alone that, in very recent times, has revealed to us these and other remains which speak of former luxury and magnificence. Verulam now presents to the eye nothing but fields, a church, and a dwelling-house, surrounded by thick walls overgrown with trees : Bath has nothing beyond other large modern cities ; and Colchester and Lincoln, however the antiquary may esteem them, would exhibit nothing very impressive to the casual visitor or to the untutored observer : their inhabitants, for the most part, are quite unconscious of the *indicia* of antiquity which yet remain. The spacious villas which were spread over Roman Britain, are only known to us from their splendid pavements casually laid open under cornfields and meadows, from time to time, deprived of the superstructures which would be indispensable in conveying a proper notion of the extensive and commodious edifices of which they once formed the flooring. These are among the most striking remains we possess of the domestic luxury of Roman Britain ; and we owe them entirely to the abandonment of the sites by those who succeeded the Romano-British population. It is from these villas a notion may be gained of the character of many of the buildings of the more important cities, in which, from obvious circumstances, they are but seldom found except in a very shattered condition ; or when met with cannot be uncovered, owing to the great depth of soil and the superincumbent houses. The plans of rural villas have in some cases been made capable of restoration, as, for instance, that of Bignor. The plans of some of the castra or military towns in the north of Britain have also been partially recovered by careful excavation. This is entirely owing to the absence of the cause which is so obstructive to any systematic investigation of the buried remains of our great cities, the deep accumulation of soil and its covering of modern buildings. The rural villas and the castra referred to, man has for ages ceased to occupy ; and what his destroying hand spared nature has preserved. In some towns, which have not greatly increased their old bounds, such as Chichester, Rochester, Colchester, Chester, Lincoln, etc., the original Roman plan can be defined, so far as to ascertain the chief entrances and the courses of the main streets corresponding to them ; but beyond this, it is almost impossible to form any reliable idea of the filling up of the angles or quarters intersected by these streets. Even the position of the side entrances or postern gates can seldom be ascertained, and their sites are not to be established from the courses of modern streets.

The modern fortunes of great cities are also made at the sacrifice of another class

---

[1] See Mr. Grove Lowe's " Description of the Roman Theatre of Verulam," printed for the St. Alban's Architectural Society: London, 1848. This should be perused together with the account given by Matthew Paris of discoveries made at Verulam in the eleventh century.

of antiquities, the most valuable of all, and which must rank next to written history. This is, lapidary inscriptions, or records, public and private, cut upon stone. They are, indeed, so many little histories. Frequently brief, and sometimes formed with words abridged even to obscurity, they nevertheless afford a mass of curious local information unattainable from any other source. They often throw much light upon the civil and political constitution of cities, their government and governors; the observances of religious ceremonies and the forms of worship peculiar to particular places; public games and festivals; the trades and professional occupations of the inhabitants; corporate bodies; military affairs; the erection of public buildings and their restoration; sepulchral memorials; and occasionally they preserve the name of a street or of some other locality. Unfortunately this class of ancient monuments, from its nature, has been the most exposed to mutilation and destruction. Even the Romans themselves did not always spare these records of their ancestors, as is proved by the fact that many of them have been extricated from the masonry of Roman buildings. But, in after ages, all that were above ground and accessible, being valued only for the material, were broken up whenever stone was wanted for any purpose to which it was applicable. The monuments of the latest times, being the more apparent, were less liable to elude the searcher's eye; and this may account for the comparative rarity of Roman inscriptions of a very late date. These important antiquities are also found more plentifully among the ruins of deserted towns and localities, and are but sparingly discovered in our chief towns and cities, where they must have been abundant.

There was yet another cause of destruction of works of art; and one, to some particular classes, especially calamitous. This was the exuberance of religious zeal, which aimed at the annihilation of every object of pagan worship, or which was likely to perpetuate or recall tendencies to paganism. The Christian ministers and missionaries had to encounter a deeply rooted superstition, reflected every-where in the productions of the sculptor, the engraver and the painter, in the highways, in the byways, in the public temples and in the private dwelling. While they inculcated the worthlessness of the images and the evil nature of the beings these works were supposed to represent, they felt that reason and persuasion were but of little avail while the images and symbols of the popular belief were everywhere familiar to the eye; and they preached and practised the utter destruction of every-thing that could possibly imply paganism. The choicest productions of renowned sculptors equally with the rude cuttings of the village masons fell before this sweep-ing extermination. The sepulchral monuments which stood upon the sides of the highways in the suburbs of towns, were similarly condemned as the works of Satan,

especially when, as was often the case, they were accompanied by effigies, or ornamented with mythological representations and scenes illustrative of the profession or
avocations of the defunct. Those only who have made the monuments of antiquity
a special study, can at all form a notion of the extent to which, in the earlier days of
Christianity, iconoclasm was carried. The writings of the old ecclesiastical authors
are filled with narratives of this spiritual warfare; and these curious recitals are
confirmed by the enormous number of mutilated works of pagan art recovered in
modern times in a condition of disfigurement, which proves how systematically and
effectually the iconoclasts laboured.

When we consider, lastly, the total absence, in the middle ages, of that feeling for
the remains of antiquity which prevails among the better educated of the present
day, the general indifference with which they are still regarded, and the natural consequences of this apathy, we have reviewed the main causes which have combined to
efface in so many great towns all vestiges of the grander works of antiquity; vestiges
which serve to create, when they do exist, an impression of their entirety, and permit
the mind to renovate monuments from their ruins and picture them in their days of
youth and glory.

London must be placed in the category alluded to in the foregoing remarks.
Once the capital of the rich and fertile province of Britain; occupying a larger extent
of ground than any other town in the island; and renowned for commerce, even in
her early days, the ancient city has not retained the ruins of one of the public
edifices which, we may suppose, must have been provided for so important a place;
and the sites only of one or two can be reasonably conjectured. Even her walls,
usually the last to fall before the levelling spirit of trade, have almost disappeared,
reduced to misshapen, huge blocks of masonry, to be found with difficulty here and
there, doing service as the walls of warehouses, stables, and cellars. Her citizens
have ever been perfectly indifferent, with a very few exceptions, to such matters, so
inconvertible to pecuniary profit; and they seem rather pleased to find some daring
champion who will decry the glory and honour of Roman London, because he helps
to shield them from their share of reproach, under the pretext that what never existed
could never have been destroyed. The fragments rescued from the general wreck,
which it is the object of this volume to collect together, will be viewed with an
additional interest, from the very fact of the vast destruction that has befallen so
many of the monuments which would have supplied us with some connective links
towards the history of Londinium. If the remains which have been gathered from
out of the grave of the ancient city could be seen in connexion with what has passed
away, if they could be associated, in a restored view, with the place and its inhabitants,

then they might seem almost insignificant and worthless; but as the imagination alone can form such a picture, they must be accepted in their present condition as valuable evidence on the state of the population, of the arts, the industry, the manners and customs of Roman London.

The ancient writers who have in any way been called upon to speak of Britain, are singularly void of topographical information; and even the professed geographers, with the exception of Ptolemy, do not seem to have considered the remote province demanded more than a brief notice; and special localities are seldom mentioned. To Ptolemy, to the *Itinerary* of Antoninus, and to the *Notitia*, we are indebted for almost all we know respecting the Roman geography of Britain. It is to the historian Tacitus we are indebted for the earliest mention of London. From the invasion of Julius to the period at which Tacitus wrote, occurs an interval of a hundred and fifty years. We are introduced to Londinium, not as being then the capital of Britain, or even as a town endowed with the privileges and political rights of a colony, as Camulodunum, or of a *municipium*, as Verulamium, towns mentioned in connexion with Londinium. These three towns, in the reign of the emperor Nero (A.D. 61), were among the most distinguished in the province of Britain, if not the most eminent. Seventeen years previous, the emperor Claudius had reduced Britain into the condition of a Roman province. Nearly a century had elapsed since the invasion of Julius. During this long period, the island remained as Julius found it, under the government of petty kings or chiefs of tribes; nominally free, but in reality not wholly independent of the Romans who, during the reign of Augustus, had added Gaul to the provinces of the empire; and who, in all probability, derived advantages from Britain, if not in the form of a fixed and certain tribute, at least from mercantile intercourse. The inscription at Angora,[1] in Asia Minor, which is a summary of the public acts of Augustus during his reign, supplies, among other valuable information, that of British kings seeking the protection or countenance of the emperor, and confirms a statement to the same effect made by Strabo. Suetonius[2] relates that Adminius, a son of Cunobeline, on being defeated in an insurrectionary movement, fled to Caligula, then in Belgic Gaul; and on another occasion, Bericus, under similar circumstances, urged the Romans to espouse his cause.[3]

These occurrences, which transpired previous to the invasion of Claudius, prove that the British princes, or reguli, ever at war among themselves, were accustomed to rest upon Roman patronage, and in their domestic quarrels did not hesitate to

[1] For an elaborate account of this inscription consult the Rev. Beale Poste's "Coins of Cunobe- line and of the Ancient Britons." London, 1853, J. R. Smith.
[2] Caligula, 44.
[3] Dion Cassius LX, 30.

invoke it as a last resort under difficulties. The treaties and friendship which the British princes readily secured from their powerful ally, contributed to foster Roman influence and civilization, and ultimately led the way to permanent subjugation.

To this period belong the coins, struck by order of the British kings. The importance of these minute but faithful monuments is well appreciated by the numismatic student, but it is not generally taken into proper consideration by the historian. It is a received axiom, that no work of art so fully sets forth the civilization of a country as the coinage ; and ancient and modern times can furnish many examples of the truth of this proposition. The British coins are numerous, and many of them bear favourable comparison, in design and execution, with the contemporary productions of the Roman mint. They are, in fact, obviously founded upon Roman models; but at the same time they are by no means slavish imitations, as they evince in many respects originality of conception. A coinage such as the Britons issued during the reigns of Augustus, Tiberius, and Caligula, is a remarkable evidence of the beneficial results of the intercourse which followed the invasion of Julius. In the absence of any historical notices (and there are but few) the coins alone supply materials to enable us to form a conception of the progress made by the Britons in one of the greatest results of civilization. The establishment of a monetary system such as the Britons possessed, and the mechanical and artistic requirements which were indispensable to it, imply a well-founded policy at home and friendly relations with the imperial court at Rome. The British mints were, there is every reason to suppose, superintended by Romans ; at all events it would be difficult to suppose the coins were not designed and engraved by Roman artists.

Of the three towns in Britain mentioned by Tacitus, two, namely, Verulamium and Camulodunum, were, as appears by the coins, places of mintage ; but Londinium was not thus distinguished : the former were seats of regal power, the latter derived consequence solely from its commercial relations. If from the negative testimony of coins we thus draw conclusions as to the early condition of Londinium, in later times, from the same source, we deduce evidence of an opposite tendency. Before the reduction of Britain into a province, Londinium does not appear to have been dignified by a mint : under the Romans it is the only town in Britain in which this distinction is to be noticed, if we except the reigns of Carausius and Allectus. So far, then, as the evidence of coins goes, it is quite in accordance with the statement of Tacitus, that while in the reign of Nero, Verulamium was entitled a *municipium*, and Camulodunum had the distinction of being a *colonia*, Londinium was eminent as the chief place of trade. In the course of time the advantages of her situation appear to have led the way to her supremacy, not only over her early rivals, but also over the whole of the towns of the province. The mint established in the reign of Constantine is almost of itself a conclusive proof of her claims to superiority; but other evidence will arise as we proceed.

In estimating the extent and condition of these three towns at the period in which Tacitus introduces them, it will be necessary to consider that in the course of the century which had elapsed since the invasion of Julius, they could not have remained in the state of towns such as those in Gaul and Britain are described to have been when the Romans first became acquainted with these countries. It is quite impossible to conceive that the southern Britons could institute a system of coinage, and engrave and strike elegant coins in huts: the manipulatory processes and the requisite establishments would necessarily demand, among other appliances, that of stone buildings. But a century is a long period of time for a people such as the Britons to advance towards civilization and refinement, unless we may suppose them far inferior in capabilities to the New Zealanders of the present day; and no one will imagine this to have been the case. When the emperor Claudius founded a municipium at Verulamium and a colony at Camulodunum, he must have found the towns of the Trinobantes already of considerable consequence; and it is hardly to be conjectured that Londinium, unless it had already advanced to some degree of consequence, could well have risen, in a comparatively brief space of time, to be spoken of as *copia negotiatorum et commeatuum maxime celebre ;* and as contributing, in conjunction with Camulodunum and Verulamium, no less than seventy thousand citizens and allies to the fatal vengeance of the insurgent Britons. The historian divides the slaughtered inhabitants into *cives* and *socii*, or those who possessed the rights and privileges of Roman citizenship, and those who, whether Britons or foreigners, were in friendly alliance, and probably, for the most part, permanently settled, but not in all respects holding the full civic rights of the *cives*. It is probable that among the *socii* were many veterans, military allies, and numerous persons visiting Londinium from the continent for the purposes of trade and commerce.

Ptolemy, the geographer, who lived in the reigns of Trajan, Hadrian, and Antoninus Pius, places Londinium in the region of the Cantii. Recent discoveries have proved that the Roman city extended over what is now known as Southwark. In the time of Ptolemy communication with Britain was accelerated by the great military operations in the north of the province, and it is probable he was assisted in the compilation of his work by maps or surveys recently prepared. A person travelling through the territories of the Cantii, on arriving at the habitations and buildings on the south bank of the Thames might consider he was in Londinium. In the early Saxon period London seems to have been partly dependant on the kingdom of Kent. c

The *Itinerary* of Antoninus is a document more satisfactory in relation to our subject, as it shows, in a direct and unquestionable manner, that many of the routes are regulated and arranged with reference to Londinium, either as a starting point or as a terminus. It is made the central or chief station to which the main military roads converge; and a map of Roman Britain based upon this *Itinerary* resembles one of modern England : in both the direction and tendency of the roads reveal the metropolis of the country. The third iter proceeds from Londinium to the Portus Dubræ (Dover) ; the fourth, from Londinium to the Portus Lemanæ (Lymne) ; the fifth, from Londinium to Luguvallium (Carlisle) ; the sixth, from Londinium to Lindum (Lincoln); and in the seventh, eighth, and ninth iters, Londinium is the terminus from Regnum (Chichester) ; Eburacum (York) ; and Venta Icenorum (Caister, near Norwich). In the rest of the fifteen iters, Calleva (Silchester) is the only town which is similarly distinguished : twice it commences a route, and twice it occurs as the terminus. The *Itinerary* of Antoninus may be considered to have been drawn up at some period not anterior to the reign of Antoninus Pius nor later than that of Caracalla; and to have received additions in after times.

In the reign of Diocletian and Maximian, Londinium was plundered by the Franks and other foreign mercenaries in the army of Allectus, after its defeat by the generals of Constantius. Eumenius, the orator, who gives a rather circumstantial account of the recovery of Britain after its seven years separation from the Roman empire, terms the city *oppidum Londiniense*.[1] The Franks and other barbarians (as Eumenius designates them), who seem to have constituted the main strength of the military establishment of Allectus, had no difficulty in gaining access to Londinium ; when, foreseeing the consequences of the victory gained by the Romans, they loaded themselves with pillage and prepared for flight. Their intention was prevented by the sudden appearance of Constantius himself, who appears to have sailed up the Thames and disembarked under the walls of the city, taking the Franks by surprise and slaughtering them in the streets ; thus affording to the citizens, as the writer expresses it, protection and the exhibition of a gladiatorial spectacle.

Under the dominion of Carausius and Allectus, gold, silver, and brass coins were struck in Britain, in great abundance and in a good style of art, with the exception of some which may be regarded as the hastily executed work of less experienced artists in the earliest days of the rebellion of Carausius. The places of mintage appear to have been Londinium (M.L.) ; Rutupiæ (R.S.R.) ; and Colonia or Clausentum[2]

---

[1] Panegr. Constantio. Cæs., cap. xvii.

[2] It is more probable that the coins of Carausius bearing c. or m.c. in the exergue, and those of Allectus with c. and q.c., belong to Colonia. Those of the latter emperor bearing c. l., may indicate Londinium rather than Clausentum.

(c. or M.C.) Under Allectus, the second of these (presumed Rutupiæ) does not appear. Of all these coins, the mint mark ascribed to Londinium occurs most frequently. The coins of Maximian in middle brass, with the exergual letters LON, were, most probably, struck at Londinium after the recovery of Britain by Constantius Chlorus. A short time subsequently, under Constantine and his family, we find numerous coins with the exergual letters P. LON., *Pecunia Londiniensis:* namely, of Constantine, Helena, Fausta, Crispus, Constantine the Younger, and Constantius the Younger.[1] Upon the coins of subsequent emperors the mint of Londinium is not to be recognised, although it is possible its functions may not have wholly ceased. In the *Notitia*, the mint of Londinium is not mentioned as a separate and distinct establishment, as the mints of Gaul, each of which is entered as under the management of a procurator. Londinium, however, takes a place among the capitals of the provinces, under the title of Augusta, as the seat of the treasury of Britain controlled by a special officer : *præpositus thesaurorum Augustensium in Britannis.*

The historian Ammianus Marcellinus, who wrote about A.D. 380, in the reign of Gratian, states that Londinium (he calls it *Lundinium*) was in his days called Augusta.[2] From him we learn that Lupicinus, who was sent by Julian to repress the inroads of the Scots and Picts, made Londinium his head quarters, and there concerted the plan of the campaign. In the reign of Valentinian Britain was again disturbed, not only by the northern barbarians, but also by the Franks and Saxons. Theodosius, who was appointed commander of the legions and cohorts selected for this service, came from Boulogne, by way of Rutupiæ, to Londinium, the same route taken a few years previously by Lupicinus, and there he also matured his plan for the restoration of the tranquillity of the province. It is on this occasion that Marcellinus speaks twice of Londinium as an ancient town, then called Augusta. By the anonymous chorographer of Ravenna it is called Londinium Augusta ; and it is in this sense, a cognomen or distinguishing appellation, as applied to a pre-eminent town or capital, that we must probably understand the term as used by Marcellinus in relation to Londinium.

Such are the few and brief sources of all the historical information bequeathed us which can strictly be brought to bear upon Roman London ; and they arise, almost wholly, from events which belong more legitimately to the history of the island itself, upon which they throw a light scarcely suspected, certainly not fully appreciated, by most of the writers on the early history of our country. The

---

[1] A description of these coins is given in Mr. Akerman's "Coins of the Romans Relating to Britain." To it may be appended a few additional varieties more recently discovered.

[2] Vetus oppidum, quod Augustam posteritas appellavit. Lib. xxvii.

illustrations of Roman London to which this volume is restricted belong to a different class of materials, being the visible and tangible remains of objects which once formed a part and parcel of the city itself, emanating from its inhabitants, the result of their industry and skill, and administering to their social wants, comfort and luxury.

The extent of Londinium, from Ludgate on the west to the Tower on the east, was about a mile, and about half a mile from the wall on the north (London Wall) to the Thames, giving dimensions far greater than those of any other Roman town in Britain.   These were the limits of the city when the Romans relinquished the dominion of the island.   Recent discoveries have revealed the fact that, at a more remote period, the bounds of the city were far more confined.   Sepulchral deposits, which have been brought to light in such situations as Bow Lane, Moorgate Street, Bishopsgate Within, and in other localities within the wall, demonstrate that when these interments were made the sites chosen were beyond the city enclosure. The extensive cemeteries in the neighbourhood of Smithfield, in Whitechapel, in the Minories, and in Spitalfields, are of comparatively late dates, and must be referred to times subsequent to the erection of that wall the remains of which are yet standing.   A discovery of a very different kind, made during the excavations for the New Royal Exchange, confirms the conclusions deduced from the burials.

As the excavations advanced to the centre of the area of the old Royal Exchange, foundations of well constructed walls were laid open, together with a solid mass of masonry, six feet square, composed of tiles and mortar.   Two sides of this mass, which formed part of a room belonging to a Roman building, still retained considerable portions of the paintings with which the walls had been decorated.   They were laid upon a thick coat of compact and smooth stucco, the ground a pale pink colour, bordered by the egg-and-tongue pattern, surmounted by an elegant scroll.   Beneath this masonry was a layer of gravel, two feet thick, which at first I considered to be the native undisturbed stratum, as it lay nineteen feet below the modern street level ; but upon its removal, the subsoil was found to be wholly foreign to the locality.   It was composed, almost entirely, of animal and vegetable matter, which, from its character, appeared to be refuse carried out from adjoining shops and houses and thrown into what had been a gravel pit.   In one part were loads of oyster shells ; in another, dross from the smith's forge, bones of cows and oxen, sheep, and goats, broken pottery, leather, old sandals, glass, lamps, implements of iron, fibulæ, a strigil, coins, and a variety of other objects, which, though now regarded with interest by the antiquary, had in their day been thrown away with the sweepings of streets and houses.   This pit extended fifty feet by forty, and was nineteen feet deep.[1] It was not until it had been fully cleared out, that the origin and nature of this pit could be properly understood. It was then discovered to be a gravel pit, excavated, probably, in the infancy of the Roman settlement, for the purposes for which gravel was required. As this material is common in all parts of the neighbourhood, the pit, in the course of time, was abandoned, and served as a receptacle for rubbish. The site in after days, being required for building, the cavity was completely filled in and covered over with a thick layer of gravel, for the houses the ruins of which were descried on the occasion above mentioned.

The coins alluded to are of importance in this discovery, as affording some notion of the period when the pit was covered in and built upon. They are chiefly of Vespasian and Domitian, with one of Severus. As none were noticed subsequent to the reign of the last-named emperor, it may be supposed that the ground upon which the building or buildings were erected was on the outside of the city until at least the early part of the third century. The coins prove that the pit was not covered over and made level and fit for houses before the time of Severus; but they convey no such decisive testimony on any posterior occurrence; for this coin of Severus may have been in circulation long after the death of that emperor, although the absence of any coins of later princes may support a conjecture that the extension of Londinium thus far towards the north took place before the middle of the third century.

In estimating the extent of the Roman city, it must be considered that its bounds were not confined to the northern banks of the Thames. Ptolemy, as I have before remarked, places Londinium in the territories of the Cantii. Discoveries have proved there was some reason for this geographer's thus fixing its position, even if it be assumed that the river strictly separated the Cantii from the Trinobantes. In making the approaches to the new London Bridge, and in subsequent very extensive excavations for foundations of buildings in various parts of Southwark, substantial remains of Roman houses were laid open, particularly on both sides of the High Street, up to the vicinity of St. George's church, in which district the wall paintings and other remains indicated villas of a superior kind. Nearer the river, where the ground had been exposed to inundations, the houses were built upon piles of timber, over which layers of chalk and rubble and tiles cemented together were laid, to ensure a solid foundation. One of the cemeteries of this part of Londinium bordered the Kent Road, and from the numerous interments it contained, fully corroborated

---

[1] Its existence was made known by Mr. Russell, clerk of the works; but for his sagacity, being covered by gravel, it would probably have been a very insecure foundation for the heavy pile about to be erected upon it.

the populousness of the neighbourhood.[1] There have never been noticed any traces of a mural enclosure of the town on the south bank of the Thames.

If there be difficulty in recovering the plan of the internal arrangements of Londinium in its enlarged and full extent, as indicated by the wall yet partially standing, there are still more serious impediments to a satisfactory comprehension of the bounds of the primitive town. Here and there during the late excavations for sewerage, for new streets and for other purposes, walls of great thickness, such as may be referred to a circumvallation, were intersected ; but as no effort was made on the part of the Corporation to ascertain their course, the favourable opportunities thus afforded of making research were lost; and the question remains a matter of speculation, unsolved by any conclusive facts. The extraordinary substructures which were cut through in Bush Lane and in Scot's Yard (an account of which I printed in the *Archæologia*, vol. xxix), may indicate a south-eastern boundary wall with a flanking tower. In Cornhill, another thick wall, which seemed to point towards the Bank of England, was met with. Now if we assume, as probably with reason we may, that old London Bridge marked the centre of the earlier Londinium, the top of Fish Street Hill, at its junction with Gracechurch Street, Eastcheap, and Cannon Street, may have been that centre. There is greater difficulty in fixing the limits ; and without the assistance of remains, and of any historical notices such as can be relied upon as bearing upon the question, every attempt must be almost wholly speculative. I should be inclined to place the northern wall somewhere along the course of Cornhill and Leadenhall Street : the eastern, in the direction of Billiter Street and Mark Lane : the southern, in the line of Upper and Lower Thames Street ; and the western, on the eastern side of Walbrook.[2] This suggested plan will give the form of an irregular square, in about the centre of each side of which may be placed the four main gates corresponding with Bridge Gate, Ludgate, Bishopsgate, and Aldgate.

The course of the boundary wall of Londinium, in its enlarged and widest extent, is yet capable of being traced on the eastern, northern, and western sides ; but nowhere is any fragment now visible which will convey any notion of its original character. Within the memory of man huge masses, with trees growing upon them,

---

[1] For details of the discoveries made in Southwark, see papers by Mr. Corner, Mr. Kempe, and myself, in vols. xxv, xxvi, and xxix of the *Archæologia*.

[2] Mr. Arthur Taylor's papers on the original site of Roman London, printed in the *Archæologia*, vol. xxxiii, are worthy of every attention in regard to this difficult question : particularly so are his remarks on Walbrook, Dowgate, and Bishopsgate. While I agree with him in most of his views, it will be seen I am disposed to assign much wider bounds to the original town. Discoveries made under favourable circumstances can alone determine which of the two opinions is the more correct.

were to be seen at London Wall, opposite what is now Finsbury Circus. They were probably, like what may still be seen opposite Sion College, and in various places within warehouses, in obscure courts, and in cellars, from opposite the Tower to Cripplegate, merely the core of the wall denuded of the facing stones, affording no architectural character, and being, in fact, so many large blocks of shapeless masonry. In the autumn of 1852, however, I was enabled to examine a portion which had fortunately escaped the general fate, in consequence of a buttress having been built against it at some early period in the middle ages. This formed part of the City Wall at Tower Hill, which, some few years ago, the Corporation had given up to the Church Building Society to be pulled down ; but which was saved solely from a representation I made to the late Sir Robert Inglis, the chairman of the society, who, at once, upon understanding the historical importance of the fragment, induced the society to decline being a participator and agent in its destruction. It was then, I believe, claimed by the Commissioners of the Woods and Forests and taken out of the hands of the Corporation. But although the wall was thus saved from imminent destruction, it could not be preserved from the effects of the prevailing spirit of the day, which cannot recognize the utility of ancient monuments except in the ratio of their applicability to the necessities of trade, and the common, practical purposes of life ; and the wall is now a side wall for stables and out-houses, and, of course, is hidden from public view. As, I believe, not a dozen persons who took the least interest in such a discovery, saw this interesting example of the external facing of the Roman Wall, the subscribers to this volume will receive an engraving from a careful sketch made by Mr. Fairholt, as a somewhat unexpected and acceptable addition to our scanty examples of the architecture of Roman London. The buttress which chiefly concealed the facing of the wall was, in a great measure, composed of stones which had belonged to Roman buildings of importance, and to sepulchral monuments, which will be presently described.

The wall was laid open quite to its foundation, which could be well examined and understood. In the first place, a trench was dug between two and three feet deep. This trench was filled in, or " puddled in", as it is termed, with a bed of clay and flints. Upon this were laid boulders and concrete to about a foot thick. The view in the plate (1), represents the ground excavated somewhat deeper than the foundation ; and the level of the ground before the excavation is shown in the left hand corner of the plate. Upon the foundation was placed a set-off row of large square stones ; upon them four layers of smaller stones, regularly and neatly cut ; then a bonding course of three rows of red tiles, above which are six layers of stones separated, by a bonding course of tiles as before, from a third division of five layers of stones :

the bonding course of tiles above these is composed of two rows of tiles ; and in like manner the facing was carried to the top. The tiles of the third row are red and yellow ; and they extend through the entire width of the wall, which is about ten feet, the height having been apparently nearly thirty feet. The core of the wall is composed of rubble cemented together with concrete, in which lime predominates, as is usual in Roman mortar. Pounded tile is also used in the mortar which cements the facing. This gives it that peculiar red hue, which led Fitzstephen to imagine the cement of the foundations of the Tower to have been tempered with the blood of beasts.[1]

I am enabled to give another representation of the character of the external facing of the wall, from a drawing made by Gough in 1763, which Mr. Fairholt

copied some years since. It was not accompanied by any description further than that of its being a sketch of a Roman tower in Houndsditch. It shows the courses of stones and tiles at a somewhat higher elevation than they appeared at Tower Hill; and may be relied upon as a careful and faithful copy of a part of the wall as it appeared nearly a century since, but which has now disappeared. Fitzstephen, who wrote his description of London in the reign of Henry II, states that the wall on the north was fortified with towers at intervals.[2] From Gough's sketch we may infer that these towers were square, such as are yet to be traced at Richborough, in Kent. They were built solid at the bottom, hollow in the centre, and united to the main wall again at the top, the cavity being probably intended for a small room provided with loopholes for watchers.[3] The construction of the square towers at Richborough is clearly to be understood, although the towers themselves are destroyed. That of Houndsditch

---

[1] " Habet ab oriente arcem Palatinam, maximam et fortissimam, cujus et area et muri a fundamento profundissimo exurgunt; cæmento cum sanguine animalium temperato."—*De situ et nobilitate Londini.* This description is as inapplicable to Norman mortar as it is characteristic of the Roman.

[2] " Muro urbis alto et magno, duplatis heptapylæ portis, intercontinuante ; turrito ab aquilone per intercapedines. Similiterque ab austro Londonia, murata et turrita fuit."

[3] " Antiquities of Richborough, Reculver, and Lymne," pp. 41 and 42.

had been appropriated in after times as a chamber, and a window occupied, it would seem, the place of a loophole. The towers at the angles of the castrum at Richborough, it should be mentioned, were circular ; and such they appear to have been at London, if we may judge from the bastion in St. Giles's churchyard, at Cripplegate, which, although externally modern, doubtless takes its form from encased Roman work. The facing of the London wall may be considered as satisfactorily exhibited by the remains at Tower Hill and by Gough's sketch. It may be accepted as a good example of the prevailing style of mural architecture of the Roman towns and stations in England and in France.

In the spring of last year (1857), excavations, for the foundation of houses on the north-eastern side of Aldermanbury Postern, laid open a portion of the wall, of peculiar construction, being composed of a series of blind arches, as shown in the annexed cut, prepared from a sketch made on the north of London Wall looking towards the street, the present level of which is indicated by the horizontal line below the temporary paling upon the pavement. The view shews the wall as it appeared while being cut through and excavated up to the street. At first it was supposed there had been openings in the wall ; but as the work advanced, it was ascertained that the

Excavations at Aldermanbury Postern.

arches were merely constructional, as they formed, throughout, part of the solid masonry.

The course of the Roman Wall on the western, the northern, and the eastern sides of London, is ascertained from the position of the gates, from discoveries, of which there are well-authenticated accounts, and from remains yet extant. It runs in a straight line from the Tower to Aldgate, where, making an angle, it takes again the straight line to Bishopsgate : from Bishopsgate it runs eastward to St. Giles's churchyard, where it turns to the south as far as Falcon Square ; and at this point again pursues a westerly direction by Aldersgate, running under Christ's Hospital towards Giltspur Street, near which it forms an angle, and proceeds directly south by Ludgate towards the Thames. Throughout the greater extent on the north and east, the precise line of the wall is indicated by the streets which flank the inner side; and which have obviously been formed and regulated in reference to the wall: thus, throughout what is called London Wall, the houses of the north side stand upon the lower courses of the Roman wall, or upon the site where the masonry has been wholly removed; and a person may walk from Cripplegate to Tower Hill upon the pavement of streets, and, with some few breaks, keep close to the line of the ancient wall throughout the entire distance. This is easily explained by the ground immediately adjoining the inner side of the wall in the Roman times having been left open, and having continued unoccupied by houses a long time subsequent. From Ludgate the Roman wall did not take a direct line towards the Thames. It traversed the ground now occupied by Printing-house Square and the office of *The Times* newspaper; and about that spot diverged towards St. Andrew's Hill, passing to the south of St. Andrew's church, where, although not a stone of it is visible, its course is clearly indicated by the abrupt ascent. At Rutland Place, in particular, a flight of no less than twenty steps, is to be explained by no other cause than that of subterranean masonry upon which the houses have been partly built, as at Colchester, where precisely the same peculiarities exist, and where they admit of being more clearly understood.

From this point the wall appears to have crossed Addle Street, and to have taken a course along the upper side of the Upper and Lower Thames Streets towards the Tower. Its exact line it is difficult to determine; but a discovery, made a few years ago, seems to confirm the testimony of Fitzstephen, who states that, although in his time the southern wall no longer existed, the city had been formerly enclosed by a mural defence on that side as well as on the others. The workmen employed in excavating for sewerage in Upper Thames Street, advanced without impediment from Blackfriars to the foot of Lambeth Hill, where they were obstructed by the remains of a wall of extraordinary strength, which formed an angle at Lambeth Hill and Thames Street. Upon this wall the contractor for the sewer was obliged to excavate to the depth of about twenty feet; and the consequent labour and delay afforded me an opportunity of examining the construction and course of the wall. The upper part was generally met with at the depth of about nine feet from the level of the present street, and six from that which marks the period of the great fire of London; and as the sewer was constructed to the depth of twenty feet, eight feet of the wall in height had to be removed. In thickness it measured from eight to ten feet. It was built upon oaken piles, over which was laid a stratum of chalk and stones; and upon this a course of hewn sand-stones, each measuring from three to four feet, by two, and two and a half feet, cemented with the well-known compound of quick lime, sand, and pounded tile. Upon this solid substructure was laid the body of the wall formed of rag-stone, flint, and lime, bonded at intervals with courses of plain and curved-edged tiles. This wall continued, with occasional breaks where at some remote time it had been broken down, from Lambeth Hill as far as Queenhithe. On a previous occasion I had noticed a wall precisely similar in character in Thames Street, opposite Queen Street. I have no doubt of its being part of the ancient city wall; and that it was not noticed during excavations made in Lower Thames Street merely shews, either that contractors for public works are not the persons to be expected to understand and report upon such matters, or that it is not at all improbable substantial mural foundations might have been ' rooted up and carted away, as those in Upper Thames Street were, in perfect silence on the part of the contractors and their employers.

One of the most remarkable features of this southern wall remains to be described. Many of the large stones which formed the lower part were sculptured and ornamented with mouldings, denoting their use in the friezes or entablatures of edifices, at some period antecedent to the construction of the wall. Fragments of sculptured marble, which had also decorated buildings, and part of the foliage and trellis work of an altar or tomb, of good workmanship, had also been used as building materials. In this respect the wall resembles those of many of the ancient towns on the continent, which were partly built out of the ruins of public edifices, of broken altars, sepulchral monuments and such materials, proving their comparatively late origin, and showing that even the ancients did not at all times respect the memorials of their ancestors and predecessors, and that our modern vandalism sprang from an old stock.

Stowe terms Bridgegate, Aldgate, Aldersgate, and Ludgate the four principal gates of the city, and the most ancient. The topographical contour would warrant our considering Bishopsgate also as one of Roman origin. The others which were standing in his time, and which make up the number seven, as stated by Fitzstephen, were probably originally Roman postern gates. The chief gates were constructed of double portals, with side entrances for the foot passengers; and if we may judge from the uses to which they were applied in the middle ages, were of great strength and very spacious. The gates in the southern wall, with the exception of the Bridgegate, were probably only postern entrances.

It is hardly to be expected, when ancient writers have remained almost silent respecting Londinium, that mention should have been made of its architectural

details. If there be difficulty in describing the walls from the fragments yet
standing or recently extant, it is quite impossible to convey any notion of the
character of another almost equally important appendage to the city, namely, the
bridge ; but, at the same time, there is an equal difficulty in attempting to deny
the existence of a bridge across the Thames at Londinium, at any period during the
Roman occupation. No great stress can be laid upon the reference made by Dion
Cassius (lib. xx, c. 20) to a bridge over the Thames, as the locality is not stated to
have been at or near Londinium, although the inference is it could not have been
far from it. In recording the invasion of Britain by Claudius, this writer says the
Britons, knowing the shallows, crossed the Thames near its mouth, while the Romans
in pursuing them were brought into great danger ; but some of the Gauls, having
passed over by a bridge higher up the river, attacked the Britons, etc. Whether
this were a temporary bridge thrown across the river by Claudius, or a permanent
structure ; and wherever it may have been, there can be but little doubt that the
erection of a bridge at Londinium closely followed the conquest of Britain. It is
impossible to avoid coming to this conclusion when we consider, that the building
of bridges formed a part of the construction of the military roads, which would have
been incomplete without this essential provision for the marching of troops and the
general purposes of travelling without interruption. The stations in Britain named
from bridges, as *Pontes, Ad Pontium, Tripontium, Pons Ælii,* and *Durolipons,* and
the existing remains of bridges at other stations, sufficiently prove that the foresight
and genius of the Romans, which spanned the Rhine and the Danube, easily
subjugated the rivers of Britain.

In one of the divisions of this volume will be given numerous objects of Roman
art discovered in the bed of the Thames, upon the site of old London Bridge, together
with many thousands of coins extending from Augustus to Honorius, a selection
from which will also be found among the engravings. They were found by the
ballast-heavers or workmen employed in dredging up the gravel and silt from the
bed of the river to deepen the channel, after the removal of the old bridge, at a
considerable depth in the gravel, extending across the Thames. Very many of these
coins are as sharp as when issued from the mint ; and the majority of those in bad
condition appear to have been detrited more from the friction of the gravel by tidal
action than from circulation ; for it is not unusual for one side of a coin to be well
preserved and the other almost illegible. The coins of the Higher Empire were particularly abundant ; especially those of Claudius, Nero, Vespasian, Titus, Domitian,
Trajan, and Hadrian. I observed that they used to be frequently dredged up, as it
were, in chronological series, as if they had been deposited in sequences at intervals,

the latest in date being the most superficial, the earliest in the deepest bed.[1] Among
them are medallions of Marcus Aurelius, Faustina, and Commodus. The erection
and reparation of bridges were held by the Romans to be works of such public
utility as to require the sanction of religious ceremonies. It is probable that on
such occasions, in connection with the building and repairing of the bridge of
Londinium, most of the coins and other medallions alluded to were deposited as
commemorative memorials, precisely as such objects are used for similar purposes at
the present day.

If there be difficulty in recovering the precise courses of the main streets, of the
subordinate ones no traces whatever are left. The oldest arrangement of the
thoroughfares with which we are acquainted affords no guide to their more remote
disposition ; and while the recent excavations have proved that most of the streets
of the present day run upon the ruins of Roman houses, they have not been of a
nature to help us to any plan of the Roman city that can at all be relied upon ;
neither have we been able to recover with certainty the site of any one public
building. But so far as we are authorised to judge from discoveries made at various
times in almost all parts, we may safely conclude that the streets and buildings of
the Roman city, if not quite so dense and continuous as those of the modern city,
left but little space throughout the entire area unoccupied, except a portion of the
district between Lothbury and Princes Street and London Wall, and the ground
adjoining the wall from Moorgate Street towards Bishopsgate. We find also, as
might have been expected, that generally towards the northern wall the vestiges of
buildings are by no means so numerous nor so densely packed as towards the south
and in the centre.

---

[1] In the Archæologia, vol. xxix, I have given a more detailed account of the circumstances under which these coins were found ; and I have combated the notions that their presence in this peculiar situation can be explained by the supposition of their having been dropped into the water by accident.

INSCRIPTIONS AND SCULPTURES.

THREE of the following inscriptions were discovered in the neighbourhood of Ludgate. They doubtless belonged to a cemetery which stood immediately beyond the gate of the city, upon the sides of the highway, which was the chief road to the west of Britain.

1.

D.M.
VIVIO MARCI
ANO M LEG.II
AUG.IANVARIA
MARINA CONIVNX
PIENTISSIMA POSV
IT MEMORIAM.

Diis Manibus. Vivio Marciano militi legionis secundæ Augustæ Januaria Matrina conjunx pientissima posuit memoriam.

This inscription, upon a large stone of a coarse grit, was discovered by Sir Christopher Wren in digging the foundation of St. Martin's church, at Ludgate; and is now preserved among the Arundelian marbles at Oxford. It has been repeatedly published, but usually very incorrectly as regards the figure. The annexed cut is a faithful representation of the stone, shewing its peculiarities and the incisions made to accommodate it to building purposes at some remote time. The stone was set up by Januaria Matrina, the most dutiful (*pientissima*) wife (as she styles herself) of Vivius Marcianus, a soldier of the second legion, called Augusta; the word *memoriam* being used, as similar examples shew, as synonymous with *monumentum.*[1] *Conjunx*, for *conjux*, is not unusual in lapidary inscriptions of a somewhat late date. The *Legio Secunda Augusta* came into Britain under the command of Vespasian, in the reign of Claudius; and remained in it until the total abandonment of the

---

[1] Non ob aliud vel *memoriæ* vel *monumenta* dicuntur ea, quæ insignita fiunt sepulcra mortuorum, nisi quia eos, qui viventium oculis subtracti sunt, ne oblivione etiam cordibus subtrahantur in memoriam revocant. St. Augustine, "De cura pro mort." c. iv.

province by the Romans. Its head quarters were Isca Silurum (Caerleon), whence it was removed, at a late period, to Rutupiæ, to form part of the coast guard against the Franks and Saxons. In intermediate times it was repeatedly moved to the north of Britain to assist in constructing the two great lines of defences against the northern barbarians.

2.

D.M.
CL MARTI
NAE AN XIX
ANENCLE
TVS
PROVINC
CONIVGI
PIENTISSIMAE
H.S.E.

Diis Manibus. Claudiæ Martinæ annorum novendecim Anencletus Provincialis conjugi pientissimæ hoc sepulchrum erexit.

This inscribed pedestal (about four feet high) was dug up in 1806, at Ludgate, behind the London Coffee House, together with a female head in stone (the size of life), and the trunk and thighs of a statue of Hercules, which, like many other antiquities found in London, have long since been lost or destroyed. It is probable that the head in stone was that of a figure of Claudia Martina, which may have stood upon the pedestal, evidently intended to be surmounted by some heavy object. Anencletus Provincialis erected this memorial to his "most dutiful" or "most pious" wife, who died at the early age of nineteen years, and was buried where the monument was erected. The dedicator, as his name indicates, was probably of provincial origin, and a civilian. (Plate ii, fig. 3.)

3.

· D.M.
IVL.VALIVS
MIL.LEG.XX.V.V.
AN.XL.H.S.E.
CA.FLAVIO
ATTIO.HER.

Diis Manibus. Julius Valius miles legionis vicesimæ Valerianæ victricis annorum quadraginta, hic situs est, Ca. Flavio Attio herede.

This was discovered upwards of seventy years ago, in Church-street, Whitechapel, and was published soon after in the *Gentleman's Magazine;* but what has become of it, it is impossible to say.[1] Church-street is part of the site of a very extensive Roman cemetery, where immense quantities of sepulchral remains have been disinterred. This memorial was erected to the memory of Julius Valius, a soldier of the twentieth legion, called *Valeriana Victrix*, who died at the age of forty years, by his heir, Caius Flavius Attius. The twentieth legion constituted part of the forces under Claudius in his invasion of Britain, and it was permanently established in Britain apparently throughout its annexation to the Roman empire, or nearly so. Its head-quarters were Deva (Chester): numerous inscriptions show its presence in various parts of the island at particular times; and often in the north, in conjunction with the second legion. A plate of brass, incised with representations of these two legions and their emblems,[2] from the character of the designs and lettering, may be assigned to the fourth century, and probably towards its close. It is particularly interesting as a record of the association of these two British legions at a period when the power of the Roman empire was declining. (Plate ii, fig. 2.)

4.

Diis Manibus. Flavius Agricola miles legionis sextæ victricis vixit annos quadraginta duos dies decem Albia Faustina conjugi incomparabili faciundum curavit.

This was discovered in the Tenter Ground, in Goodman's Fields, near the Minories, in 1787, and is now in the possession of the Society of Antiquaries of London. The slab is of native green marble, about 15 inches by 12, and 3 inches thick. It is inscribed by Albia Faustina to her *incomparable* husband, Flavius Agricola, of the

---

[1] In 1784 it was deposited at Mr. King's, undertaker, in the Old Bailey, *for the satisfaction of the curious.* "Gent. Mag.," vol. liv, pp. 485, 672.

[2] I have described it in the "Antiquities of Richborough, Reculver, and Lymne," p. 25.

sixth legion, surnamed "the victorious". This legion was also styled *Pia Fidelis*. It appears, from an inscription,[1] to have passed over into Britain from Germany in the reign of Hadrian. Here its permanent quarters were, according to Ptolemy and the *Itinerary* of Antoninus, Eburacum (York), where evidences of its long sojourn are numerous. Its movements, at various times, into different parts of Britain, particularly in the north, can be traced by many inscriptions. At the time of the compilation of the *Notitia* it was still in Britain, and, apparently, at or near its usual station.

5.

Diis Manibus Tito Licinio, Ascanius fecit; or it may be read,—*Diis Manibus Titus Licinius Ascanius fecit.* If in the latter case, it must be considered as a dedication to the Dii Manes of the tomb or ground intended by the inscriber for himself and his family.

This stone (2 ft. 8 in. by 2 feet 4 in.) was found in 1778, in digging for the foundations of the Ordnance Office in the Tower, near an old well, at the depth of about eighteen feet.

[1] This inscription records the erection of a statue in the Forum of Trajan by order of Marcus Aurelius, to Marcus Pontius, who, among numerous public officers in the time of Hadrian, was Questor of the province of Gallia Narbonensis and military tribune of the sixth legion, surnamed Victrix, *cum qua ex Germania in Britanniam transiit.*

E

6.

D.M.
GRATADAGO
BITIFILANXL
SOLINVSCON
IVGIKARFC

Diis Manibus Grata Dagobiti filia annorum quadraginta Solinus conjugi karissimæ fieri curavit.

This was discovered at London Wall, near Finsbury Circus; and, at my suggestion, was deposited in the library of the Guildhall. It is a tribute of affection by Solinus for his "dearest" wife Grata, the daughter of Dagobitus, aged forty years. Its chief interest is centered in the name Dagobitus, which is evidently not that of a Roman, but of a Gaul or German. The word is analogous to those of Dago, Dagodubnus, Dagomarus, etc., which will be found in the list of potters' names discovered in London. Nowhere do we find a stronger trace of the mixed Roman and provincial population than in the inscriptions found in England, France, and Germany. They have a peculiar ethnological interest, forming, as it were, a chain of evidence connecting the classical with the medieval nomenclature. (Plate ii, fig. 1.)

7.

Diis Manibus....R.L.F.C.Celsus...Speculator Legionis Secundæ Augustæ annorum ...natione Dardanus Gu......Valerius Pudens et ..Probus Speculatores Leg. II. fieri curaverunt.

This fragment was found, a few years since, in Playhouse Yard, Blackfriars, where it had served as building stone; it then passed into the possession of Mr. W. Chaffers, who communicated an account of it to the *Collectanea Antiqua* (vol. i, p. 125). It is now preserved in the British Museum.

The monument of which this mutilated fragment formed a part, was erected to the memory of Celsus, a speculator of the second legion, by birth a Dardanian. The names of those who erected the memorial, which contained a full-length figure of the deceased, are Valerius Pudens and .. Probus, who were his comrades, and probably his heirs. The *speculatores*, as the word indicates, were a body of soldiers attached to the legions for the various purposes of exploring, reconnoitering, and watching. They are not unfrequently mentioned by the earlier writers, and in inscriptions; and may be considered as identical with the *exploratores*, whom we find stationed by themselves either upon the limits of a province, or in other sites particularly exposed to the incursions of an enemy. Dardania, included in what is now the southernmost part of Servia, contributed towards the Roman military establishment by enlistments into the regular legions (as we have here an instance); and by troops raised exclusively from the district, as appears in an entry in the *Notitia*, of the third cohort of the Alpine Dardani, under the Duke of Pannonia. It is sufficient, in the imperfect state of this inscription, to mention that a Valerius Pudens occurs in an inscription of the time of Severus, found at Kattwyk, in Holland,[1] without suggesting that there may be any affinity between the two, especially as the one was legate and proprætor, and the other apparently of lower rank.

8.

A.ALFID.POMP
O.IVSSA EX TES
TAMENT..HER
POS.ANNOR LXX
NA AELINI
H.S.EST

A. Alfidio Pompo (Pomponio ?) jussa ex testamento heres posuit, annorum septuaginta (Na Aelini ?), hic situs est.

Discovered at Tower Hill, in 1852, with the fragments represented in plate III. The stone measures 6 ft. 4 in. by 2 ft. 6 in. The inscription is faintly cut upon a rough surface, which either had never been smoothed, or else an earlier inscription had been cut away to make room for a subsequent one. It is a memorial to A. Alfidius Pompus, aged seventy years, set up in compliance with his will by his heir, whose name may possibly have been intended to be expressed in the indistinct lettering

[1] Gruter, vol. i, p. clxix, No. 1: Cod. Ins. Rom. Rheni, No. 955.

E 2

between the fourth and fifth lines, which appears to have been interlined after the others had been cut.

9.

DIS

.ANIBVS

.........ABALPINICLASSICIANI

. . . .

Diis Manibus.........(F)ab(ii) Alpini Classiciani.... Upon a stone 5 ft. 4 in. in length, by about 2 ft. 6 in. in width : found at Tower Hill, with Number 8, in 1852.

It is to be regretted that we have here only one of at least four stones which constituted the inscribed part of a monument of a very superior class ; and which must have commemorated some person of distinction. As the name (F)ab. Alpinus Classicianus is in the genitive case, it must be attributed to the father of the person to whose memory the monument was erected. The name Classicianus is of very uncommon occurrence ; and as Julius Classicianus filled the office of procurator in Britain in the reign of Nero,[1] it is quite within the bounds of probability to suppose that this tomb was that of Julius himself. The space in the third line, it must be noted, could only be filled by some such word and the F. or FIL. which doubtless followed it. The inscription, in its perfect state, originally occupied, at least, four large stones, the position of which must have been similar to those which bear the dedication to the Secundini upon their fine sepulchral column at Igel, near Treves.[2] I know of no other example of a monument of this class discovered in England ; so well has the value of the material been appreciated by masons and contractors for building.

This fine fragment owes its preservation to having been built up in the buttress mentioned in p. 15. With it were not only the other sepulchral inscription and the sculptures delineated in plate iii, but a great number of broken cornices, shafts of columns, and foundation stones of a building or buildings of magnitude. There were also fragments of large millstones of Andernach or Rhenish lava ;[3] and a piece of white wall-painting, upon which, in a dark brown, or rather, a reddish colour, were the letters SVP. One of the fragments of sculpture was that represented in fig. 5, plate iii, measuring five feet in length. It has formed part of the decoration of a tomb such as is indicated in fig. 6, of the same plate.

Figs. 1, 2, and 3, are preserved in the British Museum ; but, I infer, that most, if not all, of the other remains have been again applied to building purposes. (Pl. iii.)

[1] Tacitus, Ann. xiv.

[2] "Collectanea Antiqua," vol. ii, pl. xxv.

[3] For a very fine and perfect example of these mills, see "Collectanea Antiqua," vol. iv, pl. xɪ, which represents a specimen in the museum of Orléans.

10.

. . .
. . . .
VRNI . . . .
LEGXX . . .
GAC . . .
M . . .

A fragment of a sepulchral inscription upon an oolitic stone, to a soldier of the twentieth legion. It was discovered by the late Mr. E. B. Price, at Pentonville, where it served as a paving stone before the door of a cottage.

It is engraved in the *Collectanea Antiqua*, vol. i, pl. xlviii A, with another still more defaced sepulchral inscription in Purbeck marble, found in Cloak Lane.

11.

Discovered, during excavations, in Nicholas Lane, near Cannon Street, in June, 1850. It was found at the depth of between eleven and twelve feet, lying close to a wall, two feet in width. There was every reason to believe that other stones having the remainder of the inscription were not far from the one extricated ; but it was impossible to induce either the contractor for the excavations or the " City Authorities" to countenance the slightest search. With some little difficulty the stone was received into the Guildhall, where it was deposited at the foot of the staircase leading to the library. In the present year, being desirous to compare it with my sketch, I ascertained it was not to be found : after an extended inquiry, it appears that it has been abstracted from the Guildhall ; and nobody knows what has become of it. The stone was between two and three feet in length. The fourth letter in the first line, it should be remarked, appeared to me, when I made the sketch, more like a c (which I considered it to be), than it seems to be in the wood-cut.

From the magnitude of the stone, and from the size and character of the letters, it is clear that the inscription surmounted the entrance of some public edifice, apparently that of a temple. It is probably the commencement of a dedication, which might have occupied either two or four stones. The wider distance of the letters in the uppermost line from the top of the stone than those in the third line from the bottom weighs in favour of the belief that we have only the first quarter of the inscription. Accepting it as such, there can be no doubt that the NVM. should be read *Numini*; and that the PROV. BRITA. should be rendered *Provincia Britannia:* the supposed equal length of the second stone, the number of letters required in the second and third line, and the particular letters to complete the sense, render this reading sufficiently satisfactory and obvious. There may be just room for a question as to whether the words should be in the singular or plural number; but the former seems more congenial to the presumed early period of the inscription.

The restoration of the second word in the first line, commencing with the letter c, cannot be effected with equal confidence.

Poetically, *numen* is synonymous with *divus*, as :

> Præsenti tibi maturos largimur honores,
> Jurandasque tuum per numen ponimus aras :[1]

and

> " —præsens divus habebitur
> Augustus, adjectis Britannis
> Imperio, gravibusque Persis."[2]

But in inscriptions *numen* is usually applied to the living, as *divus* was to the deceased emperor, when deified: for example: *Numini Augusti :—Numinibus Augustorum:—Numini Imperatoris Alexandri Augusti :—Numini Domini Nostri Augusti :—Numen Principis Optimi*, etc. I am not aware of its ever occurring in the sense of *deus*, as *Numini Herculeo, Numinibus Conservatoribus*,[3] instead of *Deo Herculeo, Diis Conservatoribus*. It remains, then, to offer an opinion on what the word in the first line may have been, considering it as applied to an emperor then reigning.

The testimony of Seneca and of Tacitus concur as to the fact of a temple having

---

[1] Horace, Ep. 1, lib. ii.   [2] Ibid. lib. iii, carm. v.   because a friend has suggested it as explanatory
[3] I instance this unusual form of dedication,   of the Nicholas Lane inscription.

been erected in Britain to the Emperor Claudius. The former says : " Parum est, quod templum in Britannia habet, quod hunc barbari colunt et ut Deum orant :"[1] the latter locates the templum at Camulodunum ; and after revealing the causes of the rebellion of the Britons observes : " Ad hæc templum, Divo Claudio constitutum, quasi arx æternæ dominationis aspiciebatur ; delectique sacerdotes, specie religionis, omnes fortunas effundebunt."[2] This temple was probably erected shortly after the subjugation of the Trinobantes. As there is this unquestionable evidence of a temple to Claudius at Camulodunum, it may be readily conceived that Londinium may also have possessed either a similar building or some other edifice dedicated to that emperor ; and although, from the inadequate information which this fragment supplies, it is impossible to decide positively, still we cannot avoid associating the historical evidence with the relics of an inscription which must have been of an early period, which is of a rare class, and almost, if not quite, unique in this country.

12.

EX OFFI
HONORINI

Upon an ingot of silver, found, in 1777, in excavations in the Tower of London. It has been engraved and published in the *Archæologia*, vol. v, where it is read, *Ex Officina Honorii*; but Mr. Waller's engraving, fig. 3, pl. xxii, may be relied upon as the more correct reading ; although the last letters are not so clear as the others. It appears to have been cast in an oblong form, and then hammered into the shape of a double wedge ; and from its weight was in all probability originally a Roman pound of silver. With, or near it, were found gold coins of Arcadius and Honorius. There is every reason to believe the stamp upon this ingot does not denote that it was issued from the workshop of any refiner named Honorius or Honorinus ; but that it was so placed as a warranty of its being imperial property ; and it would, therefore, be more correctly read as *Ex officio Honorinio* or *Honoriano*. Most probably it was a portion of the silver which formed part of the British revenue deposited at Londinium previous to its being transmitted to the mints in Gaul. It is preserved in the British Museum. (Plate xxii.)

13.

PRB. LON.—P. BRI. LON.—P. PR. LON.—PPBR. LON.—P. PR. BR...—.........BR.

Prima (Cohors) Brittonum Londinii.

These are stamps upon tiles which have been found, but not in large numbers,

---

[1] De M. Claudio Cæsare, cap. 8.   [2] Annal. lib. xiv, c. 31.

in various parts of the City, recording the fact of their having been made by the first cohort of the Britons stationed at Londinium. It is the first and only instance of the preservation of the name of the City in an inscription, if we except the coins of the Constantine family.

The first cohort of the Britons, in the reigns of Titus and Domitian, was stationed in Pannonia ;[1] in the reign of Antoninus Pius it appears among the auxiliary troops distributed in Egypt and Cyrenaica ;[2] and it is recorded in several inscriptions found in Germany and other parts of the continent, from which we learn that it was styled successively *Flavia*,[3] from Vespasian; *Ulpia*,[4] from Trajan; and *Ælia*,[5] from Hadrian, in consequence of its services under those princes. Other cohorts of the Britons are mentioned in inscriptions, as well as a first cohort surnamed *Britannica*, which occurs in a military diploma, together with the first cohort of the Britons.[6] A sixth cohort appears to have served under Trajan in the Dacian wars.[7] A fourth cohort, surnamed *Antoniniana*, is mentioned in an inscription found in Northumberland ;[8] and upon a fragment of a tile found in the Roman station at Ebchester, in Durham, are the letters ..HIBR., which probably denote the first cohort.[9] The first British cohort is sometimes styled *miliaria*, from its being composed of full a thousand men, though it appears from the explanation given by Vegetius that such cohorts considerably exceeded that number. The first took precedence of the other cohorts, not only in numerical strength, but also in being composed of picked men, and in possessing the privilege of carrying the chief standards.[10] The *Cohors prima Britannica*, which was in Dacia under Trajan, bore the additional distinction of *Cives Romani*,[11] showing they had obtained the rights of Roman citizenship. The style of the British cohorts is also, sometimes, *equitata*, denoting that, in such cases, they were composed of horse and foot mixed.

Tile-stamps are among the most useful of Roman inscriptions, as they prove the presence of the legions and cohorts at particular places. As the soldiers were brickmakers and masons, the stamped tiles are usually very abundant in towns and stations where legions and cohorts were located permanently; and they frequently

[1] Notizia di alcuni nuovi diplomi imperiali di congedo militare, p. 7; Constantius Gazzera Taurinensis, Torino, 1831.
[2] Arneth's " Militar. Diplom.," pp. 33 and 39.
[3] Gruter, 103-13.   [4] Notizia *ante*.
[5] Gruter, 359-3.
[6] Arneth, " Mil. Dip.," *ante*.
[7] Gruter, 1101-3.
[8] Horsley, " Brit. Rom.," pl. 26.
[9] " The Roman Wall," 2nd edit., p. 317.

[10] " Sciendum est autem in una legione decem cohortes esse debere. Sed *prima cohors* reliquas et numero militum et dignitate præcedit : nam genere atque institutione litterarum viros selectissimos quærit. Hæc enim suscipit Aquilam— hæc imagines imperatorum—veneratur. Habet pedites mille centum quinque, equites loricatos centum triginta duos, et appellatur *cohors miliaria*."— Vegetius, l. c.
[11] Arneth, " Mil. Dipl.," p. 49.

afford a peculiar information to be gained from no other source, as in the case of the London tiles, and those of the British *Classiarii*, discovered at Lymne, in Kent.[1] (Plate viii, figs. 3, 4, 5, 6.)

Fragment of a group of the *Deæ Matres*, discovered, during excavations for a sewer, in Hart Street, Crutched Friars, at a considerable depth, among the ruins of Roman buildings. It measures 2 ft. 8 in. in length, 1 ft. 5 in. in width, and 1 ft. 8 in. in depth. It is at present in the library of the Guildhall.

This sculpture, when entire, must have measured at least three feet in height, exclusive of the base, which, probably, was of equal altitude, and contained the dedicatory inscription. Mutilated as this monument is, its chief characteristic features are sufficiently preserved to enable us to understand its object with certainty, and to affirm something respecting it less speculative than the explanations of fragmentary monuments usually are. Comparison with numerous other similar sculptures discovered in this country and on the continent, leaves no doubt that the three seated figures holding baskets of fruit in their laps, are a representation of the Mother Goddesses, the Deæ Matres, Matronæ, or Mairæ, as they are designated and personified; while from the dimensions of the sculpture, it may be

---

[1] " Report on Excavations made upon the Site of the Roman Castrum at Lymne," p. 24, pl. vi.

F

inferred that a temple, or a *sacellum*, dedicated to those divinities, stood upon the spot where it was discovered. It is the only instance, with the exception of the discovery made in Nicholas Lane, in which the site of a temple can be with reason identified from existing remains. It would therefore have been fortunate had the civic authorities instituted or sanctioned a search for the remaining portions of the monument, which were, probably, close alongside of the line of the sewer where the fragment was found.[1]

The knowledge we possess of the Deæ Matres is almost wholly derived from monumental sources. Vast as is the information bequeathed us by ancient writers on the polytheism of the Greeks and Romans, it does not comprise all the forms into which its flexible principles ramified, especially in the north of Europe. With Roman conquest and civilization came the system of mythology which had taken root in Italy. With military discipline were engrafted religious observances : the gods were supplicated for victory ; altars and temples were erected wherever castra secured the advantages of success, and towns and colonies were planted as the foundation of lasting occupation. By far the greater part of the ancient monumental inscriptions which have been preserved and are still daily discovered, emanated from the religious feeling which pervaded all classes, and especially the military. The legions and cohorts surrounded themselves with a host of imaginary deities, from Jupiter, the greatest and best, down to the genii who were supposed to have special interest over the camps and the military stores and paraphernalia. The peculiar circumstances which surrounded the life of the soldier were calculated to foster and develope in superstitious minds this notion of multiplied divine intervention. Change of country, long and arduous marches through unknown and inhospitable lands, the vicissitudes and dangers of war, tended to induce faith in the manifold powers which were supposed to direct the various operations of nature and hold tutelage over the destinies of man.

The arduous life and mutations of the Roman soldiers contributed towards that extraordinary combination of deities, both great and subordinate, which we constantly find examples of in their dedicatory monuments. A præfect of the fourth cohort of Gaul, a native of Italy, raised an altar at Vindolana, on the Roman Wall, to Jupiter and the rest of the immortal gods associated with the Genius of the Pretorium.[2] At Magna, in the same district, Jupiter was invoked in conjunction with Helius and Rome ;[3] and a further explanation of this constantly occurring plurality

---

[1] The stone lay for some time in the City Stone-yard utterly disregarded, and in daily danger of being broken up. "Col. Ant.," vol. i, p. 138.

[2] "The Roman Wall," by Dr. Bruce, 2nd edit., p. 375.

[3] "Collectanea Antiqua," vol. ii, pl. xlviii.

of gods arises from the very nature of the ancient religious sentiment, which, while it recognized supreme gods, indirectly impeached their supervision by the creation of a multitude of terrestrial and inferior deities for special purposes. The feeling doubtless was, that the tenants of Olympus were remote, and, directing the machinery of the vast universe, could not be relied upon for that partial attention to individual interests, and that direct and immediate intervention in human concerns which, it was so consoling to believe, were the attributes of local deities, who were at hand, watched over persons and property and provided the daily necessaries of life.

The worship of the *Deæ Matres*, or Mother Goddesses, which formed part of the religion of the inhabitants of Londinium, appears to have been chiefly confined, at least in the form indicated by monuments, to the northern parts of Europe ; and, from the number of altars and sculptures discovered, must have been very general and popular. It is from such remains we are made acquainted with their personifications and emblems ; and, inferentially, with their functions and attributes, for ancient writers and classical mythology fail in affording direct and positive information. The mystic number three is ever recurring in the myths of remote antiquity ; and frequently as a female triad: thus, there are the three sisters, Juno, Vesta, and Cerès ; the three Fates ; the three Sirens ; the three Furies or Eumenides,[1] and so forth. The characteristics of many of these triads accord with those of the Deæ Matres ; and these are all, probably, varying forms of an early popular superstition of eastern origin, of which the Mother Goddesses, the Mairæ, and the Matronæ are a phase, taking its character from the amalgamation of Roman divinities with those of the Teutonic nations. Plutarch, however, seems to be the only writer who mentions deities by the same name as that applied most usually to the three females of the northern provinces, namely, Μάτερες, *matres* or mothers. From him it appears they were worshiped at Engyium, in Sicily ; and their temple was considered a foundation of the Cretans.[2]

Most of the inscriptions to the Deæ Matres which have hitherto been discovered belong to Germany. They present this characteristic: they are usually accompanied by the names of the localities under their respective protection, in the same manner as we find many of the gods and goddesses named, as Jupiter Dolichenus, Hercules Deusoniensis, Apollo Maponus, etc. Thus, on the borders of the Rhine, altars have

---

[1] Ovid states that three deities presided over the streets, or suburbs, of Rome :

"Mille Lares, Geniumque ducis qui tradidit illos
Urbs habet ; et vici Numina trina colunt."

Fast., lib. v., v. 145. These, however, may have

been the goddesses who preside over the roads, of whom we have evidence elsewhere. At Metz was found a dedication to the *Mairæ* by the inhabitants of the street or district called *Pax* (*Vicani Vici Pacis*). Montfaucon, Sup., tom. i, pl. lxxxv.

[2] Marcellus, pp. 266, 267, vol. ii, ed. Lon., 1723.

been found inscribed *Matribus Treveris* :—*Matribus Vacallineis* :—*Matronis Gavadiabus* :—*Matronis Rumanehabus* :—*Matronis Hamavehis* ; and numerous others,[1] most of which refer to the localities where they have been found. Those of our own country are almost equally abundant ; we have the forms of *Matribus* :—*Deabus Matribus* :—*Matribus Domesticis* :—*Matribus Alatervis et Matribus Campestribus* : and, significant of their foreign origin, *Matribus Tramarinis.* In three instances they are addressed as beings with a wider range of powers. Upon an altar found at Winchester[2] they are designated Italian, German, Gaulish, and

British Mothers : upon one found at York,[3] they are African, Italian, and Gaulish Mothers; and an inscription from the Roman Wall records the restoration of a temple to the Mothers of All Nations. They are most usually personified as three females seated with baskets of fruits in their laps, though in some well-sculptured representations in the museum of Newcastle-upon-Tyne the emblems are wanting. The subjoined cut is an example of the Rhenish altars in the museum of Cologne.[4] The sides of the altar have figures of youths, one of whom carries a basin of apples; the other, a vase. Upon another highly ornamented altar the attendants carry a pitcher-shaped vessel, and a cup resembling one kind of the footless glasses often found in the Saxon and Frankish graves.

Annexed is an example from France, preserved in the museum of Lyons.[5] Here the goddesses are addressed as the "Augustan Mothers," as we find them occasionally styled elsewhere. In

¹ See " Codex Inscript. Rom. Rheni," by Steiner; and Lersch's " Central Museum Rheinländischer Inschriften."
² "Col. Ant.," vol. iv, pl. xiv.   ³ Idem, p. 43.
⁴ I am indebted to Mr. George Virtue for the loan of this woodcut, which is one of the illustrations of "The Celt, the Roman, and the Saxon."
⁵ "Collectanea Antiqua," vol. v, p. 8.

this group the central figure holds a cornucopia and a patera. In some few instances they are represented as standing and holding, each, a cornucopia. In this position they appear upon a fragment of sculpture (fig. 1, pl. vi) found in London.

In investigating the origin of these deities with reference to Germany, it is to be considered that monumental evidence is supported by historical testimony. A passage in Cæsar[1] shews that among the Germans were certain women, *matres familias*, who were looked upon as qualified to act as prophetesses, and who were consulted as such on important occasions. Cæsar having inquired of some prisoners why Ariovistus had somewhat suddenly withdrawn his army without coming to a general engagement as was expected, was told that it was customary among the Germans for the women to decide, by lots and divination, when it would be fit to risk a battle; and that these women had declared that the army would not be victorious if they fought before the full moon. Tacitus corroborates the statement of Cæsar. He states that the Germans believed that their women possessed innate sanctity and knowledge of futurity; and, therefore, they neither slighted their counsels, nor neglected their responses when consulted.[2] He then mentions Velleda, who, in the time of Vespasian, was esteemed as a divinity; and observes that, in earlier times, Aurinia and many other females were similarly venerated. The same historian tells us that inspired women foretold the approaching destruction of Camulodunum, in Britain.[3] In times long subsequent, women, called *Druidæ* or *Dryades*, were believed in as endowed with the power of seeing into futurity, and were consulted as prophetesses. A Druid woman warned Alexander Severus against his insurgent army;[4] and Aurelian[5] and Diocletian[6] both consulted them.

Although the respect shown to these women did not amount to adoration as divinities, yet it may have contributed towards that general devotion to female goddesses which prevailed in later times, subsequent to the Roman immigration; and it must not be overlooked that Tacitus also informs us that the powerful nations surrounding the Longobardi (among whom were the Angli), worshiped in common the Earth (*Terra Mater*), with forms and ceremonies which shewed they considered she presided over all human affairs and came periodically among them, when war ceased, the sword was sheathed, and peace and quietude were then only known.[7] In speaking of the Estii, he states that they worship the Mother of the Gods, whose emblem was a wild boar; and he describes them as peculiarly an agricultural people,

---

[1] "Bel. Gal.," lib. i, c. xl.
[2] "De Mor. Germ.," cap. 8.
[3] "Annal.," lib. xiv, cap. 32.
[4] Lamprid. "Alex. Sev.," c. 60.
[5] Vopisc. "Aurel.," c. 44.
[6] Vopisc. "Numer.," c. 44, 45.
[7] "De Mor. Germ.," c. xl.

cultivating corn and other fruits of the earth with greater industry than the rest of the Germans.[1]

The reverence paid to inspired women as prophetesses, and to druidesses, combined with the worship of personified nature, which prevailed in Germany, in Gaul, and in Britain, were doubtless influential causes for an amalgamation with that portion of the Roman polytheism which accorded best with the national superstitions; and the worship of the Deæ Matres, of which we find so many memorials, seems to have been one of the chief results of this combination. It would be a pleasing investigation, and one probably productive of success, to ascertain how far towards the south monuments of this class can be traced. So far as I can at present speak from personal inquiry, they are by far more numerous in England and in the north of Germany than in Italy and in France. In the last-mentioned country they are rather abundant in the northern and eastern parts; but, so far as I have been able to ascertain, they are by no means of such frequent occurrence towards the south.

As this cult had taken deep root far and wide, and had spread among the rural populations of the northern provinces of the Roman empire, the early Christian missionaries found it more difficult to grapple with than the altars and temples of the higher deities. After the images of Jupiter, Apollo, Diana, and the rest of the more conspicuous objects of pagan devotion, were overthrown and destroyed, and after their fanes were leveled or converted into Christian churches, the Mother Goddesses continued for a long time to retain a strong hold upon the popular religious affections, in common with a crowd of minor deities, such as the nymphs, the dryads (*druidæ* or *dryades*), the sylphs (*sulevæ*), the tutelary divinities of rivers, fountains, hills, roads, villages, and other localities; against whom were especially directed, in the fifth and subsequent centuries, the anathemas of Christian councils, missionaries and princes. Indicated by the mystic number *three*, they may be recognized enacting an important part in the superstitions of the middle ages and even in those of modern times. In popular traditions three ladies and three sisters continually recur; as in fairy legends the same number is often to be noticed, as well as its multiples.

Mr. Wright has contributed some remarkable historical illustrations of these three goddesses, and of the forms under which they reappear in the middle ages.[2] "When, in the sixth century, Columbanus and St. Gal arrived at Bregens (*Brigantium*), in Switzerland, they found that the people there paid adoration to *three*

---

[1] "De Mor. Germ.," c. xlv. [2] "The Celt, the Roman, and the Saxon," p. 282 *et seq.*

images placed together against the wall of their temple.[1] Probably this was a monument of the *dea matres* in their original country."—" In a story of the Italian Pentamerone, *tre fate* (three fairies) are described as residing at the bottom of a rocky dell, and as conferring gifts upon children who went down into it.—In the collection of superstitions condemned by Burchard, bishop of Worms, who died in 1024, we are told that the German women of his time, had the custom, at certain times of the year, of spreading tables in their houses with meat and drink, and laying *three knives*, that, if the *three sisters* should come, they might partake of their hospitality. When Fridaf went to consult the oracle of the fates, he saw, within the temple, *three seats* occupied by *three nymphs*, each of whom conferred a gift upon his son Olaf, two of them giving good gifts and the third an evil one."[2]

"At the beginning of the eighth century, according to a pious legend, a Worcestershire swine-herd, forcing his way through the dense thickets of the forests which then covered that part of the island, in search of a stray swine, came suddenly to a fair open lawn, in the midst of which he saw *three* beautiful maidens, clad in heavenly garments, and singing sweetly, one being superior to the others (we have here the distinction constantly observed in the traditional legends between two of the goddesses and the third); he told his story to the bishop Egwin, who accompanied him to the spot, and was also favoured with the vision. Egwin *decided* at once that it was the Virgin Mary, accompanied by two angels ; and he built on the spot a monastery, which was afterwards famous by the name of Evesham.[3] The vision is represented on the old abbey seal. In all probability the site of Evesham had been a spot dedicated by the unconverted Saxons to the worship of the three goddesses, and Egwin had seized the popular legend to consecrate it for a Christian establishment."

A Latin poet of Winchester, the monk Wolstan, who lived in the middle of the tenth century, has left us a singular story relating to the three nymphs who presided over that district, and whom, differing in this from Egwin, but agreeing with the generality of ecclesiastical writers when they handled the popular superstitions, he has blackened both in person and character.[4] A citizen of Winchester one day went out to visit his farm, and returning somewhat late towards his home, near the little stream which passes by the city, he was stopped by two dark women in a state of

---

[1] *Tres ergo imagines* æreas et deauratas superstitiosa gentilitas ibi colebat.—*Anon. Vit. S. Gal.* —Repererunt autem in templo *tres imagines* æreas deauratas parieti affixas, quas populus...adorabat. —*Walafrid Strabo, Vit. S. Gal.*

[2] "Saxo Grammaticus," lib. vi, p. 102.
[3] MS. Cotton, Nero E. 1, fol. 26, vo., where the story is told by bishop Egwin himself.
[4] Wolstani Mirac. S. Swithuni, MS. Reg., 15 c. vii, fol. 74, vo.

nudity. The man, instead of paying due respect to the ladies by listening to them, ran away in a fright; and they pursued him, threatening vengeance for the disregard which he had shown to their commands. He now gave himself up for lost; and his terror was increased when a third female, who had lain concealed on the hill, stopped his way. It is not improbable that these nymphs haunted the deserted fortress of the pagans of old and the barrow-covered downs which still overlook this ancient city, from which their worship had been banished by the influence of the gospel. In her angry mood the third nymph struck the inobedient mortal senseless to the ground, and then they disappeared in the waters of the river. The man gradually recovered his senses, but he found himself a cripple, and with difficulty crawled to the eastern gate of the city, which was not far distant."

"Another Anglo-Latin poet, but who lived in the latter half of the twelfth century, Nigellus Wireker,[1] has preserved in his *Speculum Stultorum*, a tale which furnishes a still more remarkable illustration of the character of the three goddesses when they had become mere personages of medieval popular fable. Nigellus still compares them with the Latin *Parcæ*.[2] The three sisters, he says, went out into the world to relieve men from their troubles and misfortunes. As they went along, they found, under a shady bank, a beautiful maiden, of a noble family, and rich in the goods of the world, yet, in spite of all these advantages, she was weeping and lamenting. Two of the sisters proposed to relieve her of her grief; but the third opposed their desires, and gave them a short lecture on the ill uses some people make of prosperity. They left the weeping damsel and proceeded to a shady wood, where lay another maiden on a couch : she, like the former, was beautiful and intellectual, and, as it appears, like her also, rich ; but she was lame of her lower extremities, and, unable to walk, she had been brought thither to enjoy the green shade. She courteously addressed the three nymphs, and shewed them the way to the most beautiful part of the wood, where a pleasant fountain gave rise to a clear stream. The two sisters now proposed to relieve the damsel of her infirmity; but the third again interposed, on the ground that the lady enjoyed advantages sufficient to overbalance this one inconvenience under which she laboured, and which were granted to few of those who are made perfect in their limbs. The nymphs again passed on, and, towards evening, were proceeding towards a town, when, not far outside the gates, they saw a rustic girl, who, unacquainted with the delicacies of

---

[1] MS. Harl., No. 2422.

[2] The *tre fate* of one of the preceding stories are interpreted as being equivalent to the Roman *Parcæ*; and the word fairy may be derived from the latin *fata*; but as inscriptions to the Fates are rare and their monuments uncommon, the *good people*, the *sisters*, the *bonnes dames*, the *fairies*, etc., seem to have sprung more directly from the *deæ matres*.

more refined life, performed an act in public which shocked the two nymphs, who
had shown so much compassion on the two former occasions. The third nymph
drew the others back : she shows them that they have here really an occasion of
bettering the condition of one who enjoyed none of the advantages of fortune; and
they determine to give her all sorts of riches, and to make her the lady of the
town."

A few of the inscriptions relating to the triad of the Deæ Matres, will show the
respective peculiarities of those found in Great Britain and those discovered on the
continent. None of these inscriptions, it may be observed, are accompanied by the
statues or representations of the goddesses, which are usually found in a mutilated
state detached from their dedications :—

1.

MATRIB ALA
TERVIS ET
MATRIB CAM
PESTRIB COHI
TVNGR INS
VERSC ARM
O...I...S XXVV.

Matribus Alatervis et Matribus Cam-
pestribus Cohors prima Tungro-
rum, instante. . . . . . f [1]

2.

CAMPES
TRIBUS ET
BRITANNI
Q PISENTIVS
IVSTVS PREF
COH IIII GAL
VSLLM.

Campestribus et Britannis Q. Pisentius
Justus, Præfectus Cohortis quartæ
Gallorum, votum solvit libentis-
simæ merito. [2]

3.

MATRIBV
S TRAMA
RINIS IVL
VICTOR.V.S L.M.

Matribus Tramarinis Julius Victor
votum solvit lubens merito.

4.

DEABVS MATRIBVS
TRAMAR.VEX.GERMA
NORVM PRO SALUTE
RP.V.S.L.M.

Deabus Matribus Tramarinis Vexilla-
tio Germanorum pro salute Rei-
publicæ votum solvit lubens merito.

[1] Horsley, " Scotland," xxix.

[2] Stuart's " Cal. Rom.," pl. ix, fig. 2.

G

5.

MATRIB ITALIS GER MANIS GAL...BRIT .NTONIVS CRETIANVS .F.COS.REST.	*Matribus Italis Germanis Gallicis Britannicis Antonius Cretianus Beneficiarius Consulis restituit.*

6.

MATRIBVS OMNIVM GENTIVM TEMPLVM OLIM VETVS TATE CONLAB SVM.C.IVL.CVS PITIANVS Ɔ P.P.RESTITVIT.	*Matribus Omnium Gentium templum olim vetustate conlabsum C. Julius Cuspitianus centurio propria pe- cunia restituit.*

The first two of the foregoing, discovered in Scotland, are dedications to the field deities (*Campestres*) and to the Deæ Matres of Britain (*Britannicæ*); and to the Alatervian Mothers in conjunction with the Matres Campestres, the former by the prefect of the fourth cohort of the Gauls ; the latter by a cohort of Tungri. The district which is indicated by the word *Alatervis* has not been satisfactorily identified ; though it may with some probability be supposed to be that of the mouth of the river Almond, where the altar was discovered. The third is inscribed to the Transmarine Mothers by Julius Victor, who, as it appears by another inscription, was a tribune of the first cohort of the Vangiones, a people of Germany ; and a vexillation of Germans dedicated the fourth, found at Brougham, in Westmoreland, to the Transmarine Mothers for the safety of the state. The fifth is an inscription upon the altar lately discovered at Winchester, and engraved in pl. xiv, vol. iv, of the *Collectanea Antiqua*. It is addressed to the Italian, German, Gaulish, and British mothers by Antonius Cretianus, a consular beneficiary. An altar, found at York in the last century, and first published in the *Gentleman's Magazine* for 1752, was devoted "to the African, the Italian, and the Gaulish Mothers." Comprehensive as these last two examples are, they are exceeded by one found in Cumberland (No. 6), which is a dedication by C. Julius Cuspitianus, a centurion, to the Mothers of All Nations, on the occasion of the restoration of a temple. For another, somewhat similar to this, found at Dorchester, in Yorkshire, I must refer those especially interested in the subject to vol. iv, *Collectanea Antiqua*. By far the most common formula is *Deabus Matribus*, or simply *Matribus*. In one instance[1] they are styled MATRIBVS SVIS, a form which may be considered as synonymous with *Matribus Domesticis*, occurring also in this country.

A few examples from Germany will suffice for comparison :—

1.

MATRONIS
AFLIABVS
M.MARIVS
MARCELLVS
PRO SE ET SVIS
EX IMPERIO IPSARUM.

Matronis Afliabus M. Marius Marcellus pro se et suis ex imperio ipsarum.

2.

MATRONIS
RVMANEHABVS
SACR
L.VITELLIVS
CONSORS EXPLO
LEG.VI.VICT.

Matronis Rumanehabus sacrum Lucius Vitellius Consors Exploratorum Legionis sextæ Victricis.

3.

MATRIBVS
TREVERIS
T.PATERNIVS
PERPETVVS
CORNICVLAR
LEG.LEG.
XXX.V.V.L.M.

Matribus Treveris T. Paternius Perpetuus Cornicularius legatus Legionis trigesimæ Ulpiæ Victricis lubens merito.

4.

MATRIBVS
SVIS
SIMILIO MIL
ES EH CASSE GE
RMANICA PED
PLER.CRESIMI
V.S.LL.M.

Matribus Suis Similio Miles ex C(l)asse Germanica peditum Pleromariorum Cresimi, votum solvit lætus lubens merito.

[1] Hodgson's " Roman Wall," p. 227.

5.

MATRIBVS
MOPATIBVS
SVIS
M.LIBERIVS
VICTOR
CIVES
NERVIVS
NEG.FRV.
V.S.L.M.

Matribus Mopatibus Suis M. Liberius Victor civis Nervius negociator frumentarius votum solvit libenter merito.

6.

IN
HONOREM
DOMVS DIVI
NAE DIS MAIRABVS
VICANI VICI PACIS.

In honorem domus divinæ Dis Maira-bus vicani Vici Pacis.

With the exception of Nos. 4 and 6 in the above selection from numerous similar inscriptions found in Germany,[1] the three goddesses are surnamed from localities most of which may be recognized. They are here almost as frequently styled *Matrones* as *Matres*, which is not the case in inscriptions found in Great Britain. Nos. 4 and 6 assist in explaining the fragment referred to above (*Matribus Suis*). It is not unreasonable to suggest that the formula *Proxumis Suis*, occurring in some incriptions found in the south of France, such as ATILIA PRIMA PROXVMIS SVIS, at Arles, may refer to the Deæ Matres as domestic divinities, the guardians of families in their dwellings. No. 6, in which the goddesses are styled *Mairæ*, is a dedication to the imperial family by the inhabitants of a street or quarter of Mediomatrica (Metz) called *Vicus Pacis.* The word *Mairæ*, through apparently derived from the Greek Μοῖραι, *Parcæ*, or Fates, may be considered as synonymous with *Matres ;* and which may yet be traced in the German *mahr*, and in our night-*mare.* At the same time the representation of the goddesses upon this monument, the only one, so far as I am aware of, which bears their effigies and name, is somewhat different from those of the Matres and Matrones. They are standing. The middle one and the one on her right hold what appears to be the blossom of a rose ; but the position of the hands and arms is not similar. The figure on the left of the middle one has her left hand under her robes, and her right hand pointing and against her breast. There are peculiarities in the head dresses. The figure in the middle has a small

---

[1] See Dr. Steiner's "Codex Inscriptionum Romanarum Rheni ;" and Dr. Lersch's "Central-museum Rheinländischer Inschriften."

disc upon her forehead : her companion on her right has the ornament usually bound on the head of Isis.[1] One or two bas-reliefs without inscriptions have been discovered in France of the three goddesses, standing. In one instance, at the least, they carry cornucopias, emblems which seem incontestibly to identify them with the Deæ Matres, and prove that the standing posture may be merely the result of the caprice of the sculptor or of local fashion. Fig. 1, pl. vi, which was found in London, is the only example I have yet seen, discovered in the country, in which these deities are sculptured as standing. It is of the rudest workmanship.

PLATE IV. This sarcophagus was dug up, a few years since, at the north-west corner of Haydon Square, about fifteen feet from Sheppy Yard. It lay east and west, at the entire depth of about fifteen feet. Immediately above it were two skeletons embedded in lime, but without urns or other usual accompaniments of Roman sepulture. Above these skeletons some indications of other interments had been noticed ; and still nearer the surface were two encaustic tiles, probably part of the flooring of the religious house of the Sisters of the order of St. Clare, commonly called *Sorores Minores*, from whom the neighbouring street derived its name. The sarcophagus is formed out of a rather soft oolitic stone, apparently Barnack rag; and measures in length nearly five feet, in width about two feet, and in height, including the cover, twenty-two inches. The entire front and the sides are ornamented ; the back is quite plain. The cover, which is roofed or saddle-backed, is ornamented on its face with a foliated pattern, which, together with the striated decoration on the lower portion, may be frequently seen on Roman sarcophagi. In the centre is a sunken circular compartment, containing, in bas relief, the bust of a youthful male figure, clad in a tunic, the head turned to the left, and the countenance marked with an individuality of expression, which suggests the notion of its having been intended for a portrait of the person whose body was deposited within the sarcophagus. The age of the tenant of the tomb, as inferred from the skeleton, supports this opinion. The hair of the head is by no means so well executed as the features of the face, on which some care and skill have been bestowed. Each of the extremities of the sarcophagus is sculptured with a basket of fruit resembling apples.

The sarcophagus contained a leaden coffin, within which were the skull and the disjointed and partly decomposed bones of a boy of about ten or twelve years of age, embedded in lime. The coffin was well preserved, and ornamented with leaden patterns and escalop shells[2] upon the lid, which is slightly turned over along the

[1] Gruter, vol. i, p. 92.
[2] See "Collectanea Antiqua," vol. iii, pl. xiv, in which also are other examples of Roman leaden coffins found in this country.

edge, the corners being cut to admit of the folding necessary to make a cover lapping about an inch over the coffin.

Sarcophagi ornamented with bas-reliefs are of very uncommon occurrence in this country. They are usually either almost quite plain, or worked in a simple pattern, like those found at Keston[1] and York,[2] some of the latter being inscribed in plain labels on the side. But on the continent they abound in great numbers, and are frequently most elaborately sculptured with festoons, genii, mythological designs, hunting subjects, and occasionally portraits of the deceased. One, in marble, published by M. Arneth,[3] bears a bust in the centre, evidently intended for a likeness of the defunct, supported by winged genii, with various accessory ornaments. In the cathedral of Rheims is preserved a marble sarcophagus, the sides of which are covered with scenes of the chase in high relief, and of the most intricate and careful workmanship. Advancing further south, similar marble sarcophagi covered with sculpture are among the most common of the antiquities preserved in the museums and churches. Those of the early Christian epoch are not the least interesting, as they are usually richly sculptured with scenes from sacred writ, blended with mythological and profane subjects. On most of these sarcophagi the designs and ornaments were dictated by popular taste, and not at all selected with any reference to the profession, calling, or history of the persons buried in them. The utter inapplicability of the sculptures, and the constant repetition of the same scenes and myths, show that the sarcophagi were often kept ready made by the manufacturers, to be used as required. In the *Life of St. Frobert*, abbot of Troyes in Champagne, in the seventh century, we read that at her death the abbess of Saint-Quintin asked if they had prepared a coffin? They replied, that they had purchased of an illustrious man, named Walbert, a coffin of stone; but that it would not suit on account of the great stature of the deceased. They then demanded another of the merchant, who ceded that which he had prepared for himself.[4]

There is a story in Bede[5] about the burial of St. Etheldreda, abbess of Ely (seventh century): "She (her sister Sexberga) ordered some of the brethren to provide a stone to make a coffin of: they accordingly went on board a vessel, because the county of Ely is on every side encompassed with the sea or marshes and has no large stones, and came to a small abandoned city, not far from thence, which in the language of the English is called Grantchester; and presently, near the city

[1] "Archæologia," vol. xxii, pl. xxxii.
[2] Wellbeloved's "Eburacum."
[3] "Archæologische Analecten," taf. 1, Wien, 1853.
[4] Mabillon, "Acta SS. Beneditt.," tom. ii, p. 607.
[5] "Hist.," lib. iv, c. 19.

walls, they found a white marble coffin, most beautifully wrought, and neatly covered with a lid of the same sort of stone. Concluding, therefore, that God had prospered their journey, they returned thanks to Him, and carried it to the monastery."

In most of the sarcophagi, the body was placed entire and covered with slacked lime. In other cases, when the body was burnt, the vessels used at the funereal ceremony, the personal ornaments and other objects, were not unfrequently placed in massive rectangular stone cists with covers, such as have been found at Avisford,[1] in Sussex, at Harpendon, in Hertfordshire,[2] and at Southfleet, in Kent.[3] Sometimes these cists are of small dimensions: one, found at Cirencester, had been formed apparently out of part of a shaft of a column, made hollow to receive the cinerary urn. It is remarkable that most, if not all, sepulchral deposits such as these referred to are without inscriptions. It is probable that the epitaphs were cut upon separate stones, which, in the course of time, were destroyed or converted to other purposes. A recent discovery at Densworth, in Sussex,[4] favours this supposition, for, near the cist, were fragments of an inscription upon a slab of Purbeck marble, in well-cut letters, two inches in length.

PLATE V. This figure, in a coarse oolitic limestone, is broken at the knees and at the elbow of the left arm: it is twenty-six inches in height. It represents a youthful personage with long and curling hair, dressed in the Phrygian cap, and a *pallium*, or cloak, fastened by a fibula, or, rather, a button, upon the right shoulder over a tunic and waistband. In the left hand is a bow. The design and treatment of this figure are good; and the drapery is graceful: the right arm, however, is disproportionately thick. It is probably of provincial workmanship; and is of a better style of art than many of the sculptured figures which, from the nature of the material and from other circumstances, may be considered of native manufacture. It may be classed, as of equal merit, with the statues in the Duke of Bedford's collection, discovered, a few years since, by the late Mr. Artis, in Bedford Purlieus, where they had unquestionably been sculptured out of the compact oolite of the locality. In the same class of works of art, may also be placed the Sphinx discovered at Colchester, and a few of the sculptures exhumed upon the line of the Roman Wall.

It was found in Bevis Marks; and having been carried away, by persons in the employ of the Commissioners of Sewers, beyond the precincts of the City, was about

[1] "Collectanea Antiqua," vol. i, pl. xliv.
[2] "Archæological Journal," vol ii, p. 250.
[3] "Archæologia," vol. xiv, p. 28. The last
two examples are now in the British Museum.
[4] Sussex Archæological Collections, vol. x, p. 175.

to be sent to a remote part of the country; but, fortunately, I heard of the discovery, and, with some difficulty, succeeded in recovering it.

Fig. 4, pl. ii, is a small altar, dug up in making excavations for Goldsmiths' Hall, in which building it is preserved, owing to the exertions of Mr. E. Spencer and the late Mr. Saull. The former of these gentlemen accidentally noticing it among the rubbish about to be carted away, interfered to save it; and with the aid of Mr. Saull, ultimately succeeded in securing it. It bears in bas-relief a figure of Diana, with bow and quiver, and a hound at her feet : on the side is a tree ; and upon the back is rudely sculptured a tripod and sacrificial implements.

Sir Christopher Wren imagined that a temple of Diana stood upon the site of St. Paul's cathedral. But he had no better reasons to support his hypothesis than the large quantities of bones of animals found there, such as have since been found in various parts of the City. It is not improbable that there may have been temples to Diana and other divinities in Londinium ; but foundations and inscriptions, or ponderous sculptures, would be requisite to justify us in indicating their sites.

Figs. 3 and 4, pl. iii, the former 2 ft. 4 in., the latter 2 ft. 7 in. in length, were found at Tower Hill, in 1852. With them were numerous other architectural fragments, which had formed parts of cornices, pilasters, and foundations of some large building or buildings; the fragments of a mill-stone, in Rhenish lava, 2¼ ft. in diameter, and pieces of wall-painting, one of which bore traces of an inscription in large letters. Figs. 2 to 8, pl. vi, are also architectural fragments, all of which were embedded in walls as building materials. To these may be added the fragment, in green sandstone, with a trellis and floriated pattern, and the portions of marble pilasters (*Col. Ant.*, vol. i, pl. xlviii B), which were found in the great Roman wall in Thames Street.

Domestic altar, in coloured marble : from the
Thames, near old London Bridge.
Three inches square.

TESSELLATED PAVEMENTS.

Of all the grander works of Roman art which have come down to our times, none are more numerous and remarkable than the tessellated pavements which formed the floorings of domestic dwellings, of temples, and of other public buildings. Viewed simply as part of the construction of habitations, they were admirably contrived for durability as well as for warmth and dryness, essentials towards the comfort and health of life. Even where houses were not furnished with hypocausts, the thick mass of calcareous concrete in which the pavements were laid repelled damp from the moisture of the earth ; but it was seldom a house was not partially warmed by means of heated air ; and in those of the larger kinds, as well as in the extensive villas of which so many remains are yet preserved, the winter and summer rooms are easily to be recognised by the direct communications with the heating apparatus, and by the rooms which are isolated from it. These pavements were designed solely, as may be supposed, for indoors apartments, and not for exposure to the inclemencies of the weather, particularly to frost in damp climates. Of this, practical evidence was given, a few years since, in the attempt made to pave the area of the new Royal Exchange with tessellated work, somewhat in imitation of the Roman, when the first frost disintegrated the tessellæ and compelled the adoption of a more suitable pavement.

But apart from their adaptation to the material purposes of life, the Roman tessellated pavements were pictorial embellishments, wrought with infinite skill, to gratify the eye by the representation in colours of various subjects, which, by their character and execution, served to relieve the dwelling apartments of that gloom with which we of the present day, at least, associate rooms deprived of visual connexion with the life of the external world. Like other works of art they possessed their grades of goodness : some were rough enough ; many of mediocre design ; but many of the highest excellence. In the last of these degrees may be placed the Bellerophon killing the Chimera, discovered at Autun, and exhibited in London a few years ago. It is a masterpiece of art, whether the drawing of the group be criticised, or the wonderful care displayed in selecting and disposing the coloured tessellæ so as to give the effect of light, shade, and relief, such as is produced in the finest oil paintings ; and grand as is this particular specimen, many others, almost or

H

quite equal to it, could be readily appealed to. Our own country abounds in fine examples, such as those so well known in the west and south of England ; and, in short, they are still plentiful throughout what constituted the Roman empire.

It is the universality of the evidence of this art, and the perfection to which it was carried in all countries, that place it among those striking emanations of the genius of the ancients which excite our wonder and admiration. It was an art which, like others, flourished under particular circumstances, and waned and decayed when those circumstances ceased to exist, never again to appear in its pristine perfection. Towards the south it may be traced to the eleventh and twelfth centuries in Christian cathedrals and churches ;[1] and the Italians are still celebrated for compositions in mosaic ; but the Roman tessellated pavements belonged to the genius of a nation and declined with it, like sculpture, coin engraving, and fresco painting. In all these arts it is possible to produce meritorious works ; but in comparison with their archetypes, they are the exception and not the rule. With the ancients they were the result of the peculiar education of the national mind : with the moderns the national mind is not, and cannot be, trained to revive and maintain what it is not adapted for. The sculptor who devotes a life to attain perfection in his profession, finds, too late, that his best historical and ideal achievements are but sparingly appreciated ; and the best engravers of the mint are mortified and discouraged in being restricted to the trite and uninstructive demands of modern taste. With the ancients, artists, as is testified by their works, were so numerous that it would seem almost every man possessed an innate gift, a peculiar organisation framed by nature for accomplishing readily what is now only to be attained by individuals, here and there, with pain and labour. Witness the countless works yet remaining of the genius of the ancients ; consider alone the endless variety and number of Greek and Roman coins, the architectural remains, the statues which their towns and cities counted by hundreds and by thousands ; their gems and ornaments : view these and other works only as a small fragment of what has survived a general destruction; and we may form a faint notion of the diffusion of artistic genius in the mind of the ancients. The persons employed for the common purposes of a house, such as wall-painting and the laying down of the pavements, were artists whose equals in the present day would be accounted eminent; and yet they were probably often exercising at the same time two or three occupations, in a subordinate social position.

The Greeks were the inventors of this art, which originally appears to have been

---

[1] In the north of France, at St. Omer and Arras, are preserved some fine examples ; but that of the church of St. Rémy at Rheims, executed at the latter part of the eleventh century, is perhaps the finest and most elaborate in the north of Europe.

somewhat analogous to fresco painting ;[1] but there are evidences of its introduction in Rome at a very early period. The term tessellated, which we apply to the particular kind of pavement under consideration, is not strictly correct ; for the word would imply that *tesseræ* or squares were used, such as were employed by the ancients in a different description of pavements (*pavimenta tessellata*), formed exclusively either of large squared stone, or of small squared dies of coloured marble and stone, which only admitted of arrangement into certain geometrical figures on account of their regular forms. It belonged to the same class as the *pavimentum sectile*, which was made up of pieces cut into squares, triangles, hexagons, etc., which admitted of a greater variety of designs. It is probable these kinds, on account of their being adapted for easier combination, preceded the more laborious and intricate pavements, in which were represented the figures of men and animals. Suetonius states that Julius Cæsar carried the materials for making these pavements as part of the military baggage.[2] The term *vermiculata* correctly expresses the character of those with which we are familiar under the name of tessellated pavements. Instead of being constructed as the above-mentioned varieties, they are formed chiefly of irregularly shaped pieces of marble, stone, and other materials, often, indeed, approaching to squares, but by no means wholly so. These pieces are arranged to make up pictures in undulating lines, which somewhat resemble the twisting together of worms, and hence the term *vermiculated* : in such pictures it is obvious that square pieces would be utterly unmanagable, and we find they are only used in certain geometrical figures and in the borders to wavy compositions, which are made of straight parallel lines. A reference to the plates viii to xii will explain this distinction readily. The vermiculated pavement was also called *opus musivum* or *musiacum* (whence our word *mosaic*), though, from a passage in Pliny (*H. N.*, xxxvi, 21), it would seem that *musivum* was originally used for walls and ceilings : in later times, however, it seems to have been a general term for the better kinds of vermiculated pavements. Spartian speaks of a representation of Pescennius Niger (*pictum de musivo*), in a portico in the gardens of Commodus,[3] at Rome, in a composition of portraits of the friends of that prince, he, Pescennius, carrying the sacred insignia of Isis. Trebellius Pollio also uses the term (*picturatam de museo*) in describing a pavement at Rome which represented the Emperor Aurelian con-

---

[1] Pavimenta originem apud Græcos habent, elaborata arte, picturæ ratione, donec lithostrata expulere eam. Plin. "Nat. Hist.," lib. xxxvi, cap. 25.

[2] In expeditionibus tessellata et sectilia pavi-menta circum tulisse.—"Jul. Cæs.," cap. xlvii.

[3] Hunc in Commodianis hortis, in porticu curva, pictum de musivo inter Commodi amicis-simos videmus sacra Isidis ferentem.—"Pesc. Nig.," c. 6.

ferring the senatorial garb upon the Tetrici, and receiving from them the sceptre and civic crown.[1]

Procopius[2] also records a pavement in giving a curious anecdote relating to Theodoric, king of the Goths. He states that the head of his effigies (executed in *opus musivum*), in the Forum at Naples, came away from the body, the stones separating of their own accord; and that the death of the king followed shortly after.

These passages are also interesting as preserving some subjects of tessellated pavements, which the Romans themselves considered remarkable, both historically and pictorially. The *opus musivum*, therefore, whenever we find it mentioned in ancient writers, indicates the finer kinds of coloured pavements for the interior of habitations : the *opus tessellatum* designated the coarser descriptions of pavements, formed of squared stones, such as were used in courts, in passages, and sometimes in the walls of towns and buildings, being calculated to withstand the action of the winter atmosphere, to which the delicate *opus musivum* was altogether unsuited.

As before observed, these pavements include a great variety of subjects and several grades of design and workmanship, some being of comparatively rude execution, while many are finished works of the highest art, exhibiting the finest conception of arrangement and of light and shadow, correct drawing, and that broad and free treatment which mark the best Greek and Roman schools. The Bellerophon of Autun has already been appealed to. Nothing can be more successful than the workmanship of this difficult subject, which is equal to the grandeur and spirit of the design : the noble bearing and graceful pose of the rider, the fire of the horse, and the wounded monster beneath, are all drawn by a master hand, and so well has the workman copied the design, that the composition has all the effect of a highly finished painting. Many of the continental museums possess examples quite equal in merit; and it must always be remembered, that the nature of the materials demanded the nicest care in arrangement to produce the gradations of colour and shade so necessary to produce a pleasing and harmonious picture.

The finest discovered in this country are those at Woodchester and Cirencester, in Gloucestershire ; at Horkstow, in Lincolnshire ; at Frampton, in Dorsetshire ; at Littlecote Park, in Wiltshire ; at Thruxton and at Bramdean, in Hampshire ; in Somersetshire ; at Bignor, in Sussex ; in Northamptonshire ; and in Yorkshire.[3]

---

[1] Tetricorum domus hodieque extat in monte Cælio inter duos lucos contra Isium Metellinum, pulcherrima, in qua Aurelianus pictus est, utrique pretextam tribuens senatoriam dignitatem, acci-piens ab his sceptrum, coronam civicam pictura-tam de museo.—"Trigint. Tyran.," xxiii.

[2] "De Bello Gothico," lib. i, c. 24.

[3] Examples will be found in the following

I am not aware that many have been found north of Yorkshire : in Northumberland, in the great stations, they give place to floorings of very large flagstones resting upon square columns of stone : unlike the middle and south of Britain, the antiquities of the north are more exclusively military. The county of Kent, the most fertile and most civilized part of Britain, can boast of none of these beautiful works of ancient art, and none of a very high class have ever been recorded as discovered in it. The absence of these peculiar evidences of civilization and luxury, is to be attributed to the populous and cultivated state of Kent being far less favourable to the preservation of such remains than districts which were but partially tenanted and tilled, perhaps, for centuries after the Romans left Britain.

The subjects are sometimes historical, as the well-known battle of Issus, between Alexander and Darius ; and portraits of eminent men : more frequently they are mythological; sports of the circus and amphitheatre; hunting scenes; animals, flowers, and rural pursuits; while a great many are chiefly confined to geometrical patterns, relieved by the introduction of flowers, vases, and scrolls. Sometimes they are accompanied by inscriptions relating to the subjects of the work. In one of the Frampton pavements, beneath a head of Neptune, in the beard of which are two dolphins, is a metrical description ; and there are the remains of another, beneath a figure of Cupid, in the same pavement. Below two Cupids holding a basket of fruit, in one of the floorings of the Woodchester villa, is inscribed BONVM EVENTVM, and in another compartment BIINII colite (*Bonum Eventum bene colite*), an admonition to pay proper regard to Bonus Eventus, the god of good luck. A square compartment of a pavement discovered at Mienne, near Marboué (Eure-et-Loire), has two cupids, bearing between them a circular shield, inscribed EX OFICINA FERONI FELIX VT ISTE LEGO, denoting that Feronus was the artist, and wishing him prosperity.[1] In one of the pavements discovered upon the site of the ancient Italica in Spain, are busts of the nine muses and their emblems, each superscribed with her name. In the later times of the Roman empire the pavements begin to reflect the influence of Christianity : first by the introduction of the cross, or the monogram of Christ, among profane subjects ; next by scriptural personages and scenes intermixed with mythological subjects ; and lastly, in the general substitution of scriptural

works : "Reliquiæ Britànnico-Romanæ," of S. Lysons ; "Illustrations of the Remains of Roman Art in Cirencester," by Messrs. Buckman and Newmarch ; "Collectanea Antiqua," for pavements found at Bramdean, Basildon, Daventry, and Carthage ; "Durobrivæ Illustrated," by E. T. Artis; "Reliquiæ Isurianæ, the remains of the Roman Isurium (now Aldborough), illustrated;" by H. Ecroyd Smith.

[1] The latter portion is somewhat equivocal. It has been suggested that the last word may be *Leco*, the nominative to the sentence, and not the verb *Lego;* but it looks more like the latter. "Mem. de la Soc. des Ant. de France," tom. xii, p. 153.

for pagan representations, but still treated in the classical style. In the later works inscriptions are more frequently introduced. A pavement excavated at Salona, in 1848, exhibits two stags, among trees and flowers, drinking out of a large classic vase ; and, above, is an application from the Psalms : SIC *Cervvs* DESIDERAT AD FONTES AQVARVM ITA DESIDERAT ANIMA MEA AD TE DEVS. Others, at Rome, and in several of the continental cities, are remarkable for the confusion of sacred and profane matters, such as Theseus with David and Goliah, or Orpheus with other sacred personages, the inscriptions clearly deciding the characters and subjects.

The London tessellated pavements which I am about to describe are, so far as I am aware of, all that have been preserved, either wholly or in part ; but they cannot be considered as constituting, upon the most moderate calculation, the tenth part of the number destroyed during the present century, or, perhaps, during the last twenty or thirty years.

PLATE VII represents a view taken of a pavement, *in situ*, discovered, in 1854, between Bishopsgate Street and Broad Street, when the Excise Office was pulled down. It lay beneath the vaults of the south-eastern area, at the depth of from thirteen to fourteen feet below the level of the present street. It had formed the floor of an apartment twenty-eight feet square, of which the walls had been removed, and also the contiguous parts of the villa of which it formed part, probably one of the summer rooms. This pavement is a good example of the pleasing effect produced by the judicious arrangement of numerous and complex patterns, which can only be fully understood by seeing the pavements themselves or by engravings. If the work is not of the first excellence, it is quite equal to the generality of the pavements of this peculiar class, examples of which are afforded in plates ix, x, and xi ; but inferior to that of plate xii, which is altogether of a higher order. In the square central compartment, are the remains of a female figure seated upon an animal. This has been conjectured to represent Ariadne upon the Panther ; but the treatment of the sitting figure, and the action of the animal, seem to favour the supposition that the artist intended to portray Europa upon the Bull. This portion of the pavement is badly preserved, but Mr. Fairholt has succeeded in giving the outlines of what remained. It is stated in the *Archæologia*, vol. xxxvi, p. 211 (where a coloured engraving is given), that the pavement was removed carefully, with a view to its being exhibited at the Crystal Palace.

With this discovery may be mentioned that which took place, a few years previous in Bishopsgate Street, at an adjacent spot, from which it will be seen that the site of another room of this villa may be considered as ascertained. In sinking a square drain, to the depth of thirteen feet from the street level, in the cellar of Mr.

Volkman, No. 101, a portion of a pavement, plate viii, fig. 1, was laid open. It lies fifty-three feet from Bishopsgate Street, from what was the yard of the old Excise Office, and therefore contiguous to the pavement found in 1854. It was in good preservation, and was saved from all immediate casualties by a layer of bricks placed upon it. In the same cellar, and close to the street, I was informed, stood an arch formed of square flat tiles, laid in mortar of such extreme hardness that it was with difficulty the structure was pulled down.[1]

The two pavements represented in plates ix and x were discovered in the spring of 1841, in excavating the foundation of the French Protestant church, in Thread-needle Street, to prepare the site for the Hall of Commerce. The area of the church was excavated to the depth of about fourteen feet. It was intersected with chalk walls, apparently belonging to some part of the Hospital of St. Antony, which formerly occupied the site. One of the walls had been built into the first of these pavements (pl. ix), which had evidently been further injured at the same time, when adjacent pavements, of which only traces remained, were destroyed. This, indeed, can only be considered as a fragment, apparently of a passage. It measures about six feet by five, and is composed of rows of red tesserae an inch square, which enclose squares and lozenges, the latter arranged lengthways and transversely, the spandrils being the halves of lozenges similarly disposed. The squares are filled alternately with rosettes of eight and four leaves, frets, and wheels or whorles; the lozenges with a labyrinthine pattern. The tesserae are white, black, slate colour, and a dull green, formed from natural stones; and red and yellow from artificial: the green, apparently from a native marble, is much worn by time and weather.

The pavement (plate x) was discovered on the north side of the former, and at about six feet and a half from it. The extreme length of it is thirteen feet and a half: it was impossible to ascertain how far the outer border originally extended, but it was probably much deeper. Within the white border next to the red, is a kind of embattled fret in red and yellow, within which is a smaller white border, and one of two rows of blueish tesserae of Petworth marble. The central figure is of an elaborate and elegant kind. It may be described as a flower or rosette of eight leaves, from behind which the points of eight others are visible.

[1] A note appended to my communication of this discovery to the Society of Antiquaries is as follows: "It is so seldom that I have witnessed, during my researches in London, either in public bodies or in private individuals, any disposition to encourage or tolerate antiquarian investigation, that an instance of an enlightened and conservative spirit deserves especial notice. I therefore make honourable mention of Mr. John Shelton, who very promptly gave notice of the discovery of the pavement, and was thus instrumental in saving it."

Each of the eight upper leaves has in its centre a trefoil, and these are connected by a band of two rows of red tesseræ. In this the artist has given a representation of three surfaces, and although it would perplex the naturalist to determine the class and order of the flower, the pictorial effect produced by the ingenuity of the design is striking and pleasing.

The extent of the villa to which these pavements belonged could not be ascertained; but it must have been spacious. The vestiges of other floorings and of passages were noticed, but the walls had entirely disappeared. From the remains of wall-paintings, the rooms had been decorated in a superior style: the ground of some of the paintings was red, bordered with green, blue, black, and yellow; other fragments were painted with flowers and foliage in red, yellow, white, and green, upon a black ground. A considerable quantity of charcoal and some charred barley was found upon the same level as the pavements, suggesting fire to have been the agent of destruction of this villa. The earliest of the coins found among the ruins was of Claudius, the latest of Constantine.[1] It appears by one of the journals of the day that in 1792, while digging for a sewer from St. Peter-le-Poor to Threadneedle Street, a tessellated pavement was laid open in this locality. It is described as having been circular, and of great extent. Upon it was a quantity of burnt corn and charcoal, pottery, and coins, some of which are spoken of as copper, plated with silver.

As the villas to which these remains belonged were partly situated beneath Threadneedle Street, they exclude it, as a street, from any claims to a remote antiquity; and wherever excavations were made between this part of Threadneedle Street and Cornhill, the foundations of buildings and pavements were intersected. Some of the pavements were evidently of a superior description. Among the fragments was a female head, of the size of life, formed of coloured stones and glass.

In 1805 the pavement represented in plate xi was discovered under the south-west angle of the Bank of England, about twenty feet west of the westernmost gate of the Bank, opening into Lothbury, and at the depth of twelve feet below the street level. The entire floor is stated to have been eleven feet square. The ornamental portion is a foliated cross, the limbs of which terminate in flowers and tendrils, surrounded by a square guilloche pattern, with flowers in the angles. The white ground is studded with dark stones. This pavement is preserved in the British Museum. During the late excavations for sewerage I noticed the remains of a

---

[1] The late Mr. Moxhay, the proprietor of the premises, afforded me every assistance in my researches. He allowed the pavements to remain *in situ* for some time, allowing the public free ingress to inspect them; and subsequently, at my suggestion, deposited them in the British Museum.

tessellated pavement in Lothbury, opposite Founders' Court. It was upon the same level as the above.

A very superior description of tessellated pavements was found in Leadenhall Street, in 1803. It was discovered by workmen digging for a drain, about nine feet below the pavement in front of the East India House, opposite to the easternmost columns of the portico. The centre portion, about four feet square, was taken up complete, the remainder in separate portions, and it was deposited in good condition in the library of the East India House. After some years it was unfortunately placed in the open air, when the action of the atmosphere loosened the tesseræ ; and destroyed all but the central portion, which, a few years since, was recovered from among the débris, and by order of Professor Wilson securely fastened upon a slab of slate and restored to the library. Fortunately a good engraving was made, soon after its discovery, by Mr. T. Fisher, from which plate xii has been carefully prepared by Mr. Basire, giving a faithful representation of its elaborate and elegant design, of which no written description could convey a correct notion.

The central design exhibits Bacchus reclining upon the Panther. In his right hand he holds an empty drinking-cup, and in his left hand the thyrsus ; a mantle falls from the right shoulder, which is gathered over the left leg and the right thigh; and he wears the *cothurnus*, or high boot, laced in front. His head is decorated with vine leaves, fastened by fillets which hang down on each side of the neck. The blue or purple and green colours in this composition are formed of glass ; the others, of natural stones and coloured argillaceous earths. Mr. Fisher reckoned no less than twenty distinct tints used in the entire design of this pavement.

The treatment of Bacchus and the Panther very closely resembles that of a similar subject in one of the pavements of the Roman villa at Thruxton, near Weyhill, in Hampshire,[1] except that in the latter the figure of the god is more erect, that of the panther more crouching, and the right arm, holding a wine cup, is extended : the position of the thyrsus, the arrangement of the drapery, the vine leaves upon the head, as well as other details, are very similar.

The depth at which this pavement lay was only nine and a half feet, while that of the others was from twelve to thirteen feet, which was the depth of a tessellated pavement discovered in Crosby Square, Bishopsgate; and of one in Paternoster Row, which I thus described at the period of its discovery.[2] "An extensive and superb tessellated pavement, discovered at the depth of twelve feet six inches, was cut through and destroyed during my unavoidable absence from the works. I gathered

---

[1] Drawn on stone by J. Lickman : printed by J. Holloway, Salisbury, 1823.   [2] "Archeologia," vol. xxvi, p. 396; *Idem*, vol. xxix, p. 155.

the following particulars from a person who was present at its destruction. It extended at least forty feet. The border of the pavement, so far as I can decide from the description, was composed of the rich guilloche pattern, enclosing rosettes. Towards the centre were compartments, in which were depicted birds and beasts. In one division was an object resembling a star-fish. This meagre account, calculated only to excite curiosity and regret, is all I am able to supply : nor can I give more satisfactory information on a portion of another fine pavement, discovered under similar circumstances in Bartholomew Lane, near the Bank. Of this a large piece was preserved by the City authorities, but where it has been deposited I cannot learn." In Paternoster Row, at a depth somewhat greater than that of the pavement, was a skeleton in a tile-tomb, similar to an interment found in Bow Lane, and deposited, of course, long anterior to the construction of the pavement.

In July last a portion of a coloured tessellated pavement was laid open in Fenchurch Street, in digging the foundation of the house numbered 37, opposite Cullum Street.[1] The annexed wood-cut shews the fragment *in situ*, as it was

sketched by Mr. Fairholt. Its dimensions are 3 ft. 4 in. by 2 ft. 6 in. The predominant colours of the peacock and vase are a dull brown, red, yellow, black, white, and blue, upon a white ground. Of these the blue is composed of glass. The guilloche border is red, white, and black ; this is enclosed by borders of white, black, red, and black, in coarser tesseræ. This fragment was found at the depth of eleven feet and a half. The locality which afforded this fragment of what would seem to have been an extensive pavement, is full of foundations of Roman houses, as I noted during the excavations made there some years since.

The depths at which these tessellated pavements are discovered give a good notion of the increase of the soil since the period of their construction. This must have been, in most of those described and referred to, nearly a foot a century ; but

[1] I am indebted to Mr. W. W. King, of King Street, Cheapside, for early information of this discovery.

local circumstances would have some influence. The Fenchurch Street pavement, the last discovered, was not at so great a depth as the others; while in College Street, on the site of Dyers' Hall, one was found at the depth of from fifteen to sixteen feet. In Lombard Street, on the contrary, I have noted that, in 1839, a tessellated pavement was observed at the depth of eight feet only, running under the present street. This pavement must have been made at a very late period, as earth, impregnated with Roman remains, extended to a very considerable depth immediately under it.

The substruction or bed in which the tessellated work was laid is, invariably, a thick concrete, composed of lime with gravel or pounded tile, and sand. In the summer rooms this rested upon the native ground. In the winter apartments it was placed upon pillars or square columns, formed of tiles and mortar, arranged in rows at equal distances from each other, to the full extent of the floor. Upon the top of these pillars were larger tiles, mortared together, forming an even surface. Upon this was laid the concrete into which the tesseræ were worked. From a furnace, situated on the outside, heated air flowed beneath the rooms, and passed up the walls through hollow tiles, examples of which may be found in a further part of this volume. In the villa at Bramdean the arrangement of the hypocaust can be seen by remains yet extant, together with the tessellated pavement of one of the rooms heated by it.

Another kind of flooring, very frequently brought to light during the late excavations, remains to be noticed. It is of the kind called by Vitruvius, vii, 1, and Pliny, *H. N.*, xxxvi, 25, *spicata testacea;* and was so named from the resemblance which the small oblong red bricks composing it have, in the manner in which they are disposed, to the natural arrangement of the grains in an ear of corn (*spica*). This pattern answers to our popular architectural expression *herring-boned.* The bricks or tiles are from four to six inches in length, or even smaller, about three inches wide, and about one and a half inch thick. They were laid edgeways in a thick bed of concrete. Examples of this description of flooring are preserved in the British Museum.

WALL PAINTINGS.

DECORATING the walls of domestic apartments with paintings laid upon the plaster, is another ancient art which has, long since, decayed and given place to a substitute which, at the best, can hardly be said to equal the ancient mode of decoration in richness and chastity of effect, while for durability it is very far inferior. The walls of the houses of Pompeii and Herculaneum have vastly contributed towards our knowledge of the effect produced, of the skill of the artists, their favourite subjects, and the composition of the colours employed. Chemistry has enabled us to understand perfectly well the various pigments, and the composition of the strata of mortar and plaster upon which they were laid; but the utmost efforts of royal commissioners and academies will never restore to vitality an art which is not fostered by the wants and taste of the moderns. It can only be practised, here and there, with great cost and labour, and without a chance of that public support which would ensure a continuity of competent artists and reestablish its popularity. With the Romans, workers in fresco and distemper-painting were so common, as to be regarded merely among the artizans, whose business it was to supply the requirements of everyday life. Among the remains of the humblest cottages, wall-paintings are always found, executed, apparently, with the same skill, and certainly upon the same principle, as those of the villa and town houses, the latter differing only in their more elaborate designs.

The pigments used in the paintings of Herculaneum and Pompeii, and those from the walls of villas and houses discovered in France and England, are found by analysis to have been mostly identical. The reds are composed of the oxides of lead and iron, of vermillion and ochres; the yellows are ochres with or without oxide of lead; the blue, oxide of copper; the greens, various combinations of copper; the blacks and browns are mostly ochres; the white, refined chalk or lime, or marble finely powdered. The stratum of lime, sand, and very small gravel which was laid upon the wall, varied from three or four to seven or eight inches in thickness. Upon this was laid a very fine cement, made of marble or quicklime, which coating, while still wet, received the colours, *udo tectorio*, as termed by Vitruvius (lib. vii, c. 6), and *fresco buono* by the modern Italians. The colours, in drying, became of one substance with the wall.

A recent visit to Sens, in France, has enabled me to introduce here an appropriate and interesting illustration of the process of wall-painting, from the sepulchral monument of a Roman painter, who exercised his profession in that once important city. The sculpture, unfortunately, has received rough usage in former times ; and the figures, in high relief, have been intentionally mutilated; but enough remains to indicate the details, particularly as I have had the benefit of the assistance of the practical knowledge of my friend

Dimensions, three feet six inches by three feet.

Mr. Waller, who accompanied me on the occasion referred to.

The subject represents the decoration of a corridor in fresco painting. A low scaffold is constructed, partly on tressels, and partly resting upon the basement of the corridor. Upon this scaffold are the painter and his plasterer. The latter is on the right side of the relief, and is exhibited in the act of laying on the thin finishing coat of plaster (*intonaco*) for the painter, who is following him. He has his *float* in his left hand, and is passing it over the wall, while his right hand is thrust downward into a pail of water, most likely to reach a brush to sprinkle the rough coat or ground so as to render it sufficiently moist to receive the *intonaco* or thin cement of lime, which, in general, would not be thicker than a crown piece. The painter is following the plasterer, to lay on his colours while the plaster is still wet. He appears as if resting one foot upon a stool, which, perhaps, has also a tablet of mixed colours upon it. Behind him is a cylindrical box, in which, it may be imagined, he has his rolls of paper or parchment with designs of the work he is engaged upon. There is a short ladder to mount the scaffold, by the side of which is a stool, with a tablet of colour upon it ; and close by this the painter's assistant is mixing tints ; and his action is energetic, no doubt to indicate haste. This is quite in accord with the modern practice of fresco-painting, which requires every department to be conducted with rapidity as well as with skill. The assistant must always have the tints ready mixed, and in sufficient quantity for the work. Under the arch of the corridor, at the left side of the relief, is the director or master designer. He is seated with an open book or tablet before him, and appears to be studying or reviewing the design.

The fragments of wall paintings discovered throughout London have been exceedingly numerous. In some localities I have seen them carried away by cart loads. Enough has been preserved of them to decide that the rooms of the houses were usually painted in square panels or compartments, the prevailing colours of which were bright red, dark grey, and black, with borders of various colours. The centres of these compartments were frequently designs in arabesque work, birds, or

One-third the actual size.

other animals, flowers, stars, and fanciful objects. From the fractured condition in which these paintings were excavated, and the total want of any provision for extricating them with care, the entire designs could seldom be recovered. An example, however, from Great St. Helen's, here given, affords a complete subject of an entire compartment, if not of the whole wall, if we may judge from the large quantity of fragments similar to that shown in the woodcut.

The ground is red; the figure of the youth and the trellis pattern are yellow; the stars and circles are white; and the ornament towards the top, on the left side, is purple or dark blue: the borders are white and dark blue or purple.

PLATE XIV exhibits imitations of porphyry and verde antique (fig. 1); and a fluted column. (fig. 2.)[1] The head of a Mercury upon a red ground (pl. xiv, fig. 3) is full of spirit, and free in its execution. The fragment of a goat (pl. xiii, fig. 1) is very spirited, and, as well as the others, is executed in a bold and vigorous manner, shewing great readiness of hand and a thorough knowledge on the part of the painter of the necessities as well as the capabilities of the material. The fragment containing the lower portion of a female head and bust issuing from leaves (pl. xiii, fig. 8), seems to belong to a class of decorations resembling those dis-

[1] This has been accidentally reversed in the engraving.

covered in the baths of Titus at Rome, studied by Raphael for the decoration of the Vatican.

A further example is shewn in the annexed cut. The foliage and flower are of a fawn colour, and light green, upon a dark red ground.

In the *Antiquities of Richborough, Reculver, and Lymne*, are examples of Roman wall-painting discovered at Richborough, and at Chesterford, in Essex. In Lyson's *Roman Antiquities Discovered at Woodchester*, plate xxxi is devoted to fragments of wall-paintings, which are precisely similar to some of the London specimens. Among them are portions of an inscription in white letters upon a dark ground. Further examples, found at Aldborough, in Yorkshire, are given in Mr. Ecroyd Smith's *Reliquiæ Isurianæ*; and others, found at Cirencester, in Messrs. Buckman and Newmarch's *Illustrations of the Remains of Roman Art*. These are all inferior as works of art to the better class of those discovered in London. Some fragments from the villa at Chesterford, in the museum of Lord Braybrooke at Audley End, approach nearest to the London specimens as regards design and variety. One of these, the lower part of a female figure, bears in treatment a remarkable resemblance, as regards the drapery flowing round the

Half the actual size.

ankle, to that of the well-known bacchante, or dancing nymph, in one of the tessellated floors of the Roman villa at Bignor. Monsieur B. Fillon has published, in a report of discoveries made at Saint-Médard-des-Prés (Vendée), a description of the wall-paintings found among the ruins of a villa, which, from the nature of the contents of a tomb adjoining, seemed to have belonged to a female artist.[1] One of them represents the bust of a female, holding up her hair in the right hand; the gesture and expression of countenance would seem to indicate that the figure had formed part of a composition of a serious, if not of a tragic, kind. On other fragments were depicted portions of a young female figure in a sitting posture; a pleasing head of a child; numerous limbs of human figures; a female foot sandeled; a large fish, and a basket of mushrooms : others, of smaller dimensions, include a Cupid with blue wings carrying a vase; the torso of a man holding the reins of a courser; a basket of fish; marine horses, of which the nostrils, breast, and legs are

[1] Description de la villa et du tombeau d'une femme artiste Gallo-Romaine, découverts à Saint-Médard-des-Prés (Vendée), 4to., 1849.

rose-coloured; there were also fragments of a landscape; a part of a panther; a vase containing an aquatic plant; two swans; and a blue sky. Other pieces were ornamented with Tritons, of a greenish hue, bound with sea-weed. The paintings were bordered with rays and fillets, in black, yellow, green, and red colours; a garland of laurel with golden pendants; and strings of pearls, from which vases are suspended; and birds of rich plumage playing among the foliage. Such descriptions, and the remains daily brought to light, prove that the mural paintings of the houses of the provinces were always elegantly, often sumptuously, decorated, in a style and taste in perfect harmony with those of Italy, and probably, often quite equal in design and execution.

The subject of a fresco-painting at Treves, in the time of Ausonius, has been handed down by the poet, who tells us that the beauty of the composition, and the poetic character of the subject, suggested to him the theme of his poem entitled *Cupido cruci affixus.* It ornamented the wall of the *triclinium,* or dining-room, of Æolus, or Zoilus, and represented Cupid fastened to a cross by women who had been disappointed in their loves. The paintings upon the walls of the house of Trimalchio at Rome, are minutely described by Petronius Arbiter. Among them were represented, subjects from the *Iliad* and *Odyssy;* and Trimalchio himself and scenes in his own life, in which were incorporated Minerva, Mercury, Fortune, and the Fates weaving a golden thread. Of course this description, as regards individuality, is quite imaginary; but the whole of this writer's satirical romance gives, no doubt, a faithful picture of life at Rome in the time of Nero, and the decorations of Trimalchio's house were probably such as he himself had often seen in the villas of the wealthy and luxurious.

BRONZES.

WHILE the remains of several of the ancient cities of France and Germany excel those of Londinium in many respects, in some they are inferior. In architecture, in sculpture, and in tessellated pavements, we can produce no such examples as abound on the continent; but in works of bronze, there are but few of the continental museums which can exhibit specimens of a higher class of art than those which are here given in plates xv to xxii, and in the frontispiece. But it must ever be borne in mind that the comparative absence, at the present day, of materials for forming a correct judgment on the public buildings and on the sculptures which may have belonged to them, in no way can be admitted as proving their non-existence in former times. Those who start such an hypothesis might, a few years ago, with equal plausibility have denied to Londinium the extraordinary works in bronze now before us, had not mere accident saved them from the melting-pot, or from wandering into collection after collection, separated from every testimony that could fix their discovery to London rather than to Rome, or to any other place; and it would be absurd to suppose that such objects had never before been discovered in London because such as had been found are not extant at the present day.

The head of the emperor Hadrian, which forms the frontispiece to this volume, was dredged up from the bed of the Thames, a little below the site of old London Bridge, on the Southwark side of the river, and passed immediately into the possession of Mr. John Newman of the Bridge House; and subsequently into the British Museum. It belonged to a colossal statue, two of which, it is probable, we

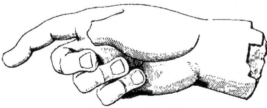

Hand, in bronze, thirteen inches in length.

K

may reckon among the public embellishments of Londinium ; for excavations in
Thames Street, near the Tower, brought to light a colossal bronze hand (shewn at
the foot of the preceding page), thirteen inches in length, which had been broken
from a statue of about the same magnitude as that from which the head was
severed ; and apparently, judging from the attitude, from a statue of Hadrian also.
The posture is precisely similar to that of the marble statue of this emperor in
the British Museum, and in other sculptured representations of Hadrian.

With the neck this head measures sixteen inches and a half in height.
The features, the hair, and the beard, exhibit those unmistakable characteristics
with which we are familiar in the portraits of Hadrian. The neck bears marks of
reparation, such as are not unfrequently found in metal statues, from defects in the
casting. The head is not laureated, but quite bare, as it often appears upon
coins, and usually in sculptures. The nude head is generally indicative of cæsars
or sons of emperors, real or adopted ; and though it is not exclusively confined
to them, it occurs in representations of Hadrian so commonly as to suggest
in it a special meaning, significant of the simplicity which Hadrian studied in his
costume as well as austerity in living. Spartian says he was accustomed to endure
both cold and hunger with the head unprotected ; and the better to maintain the
discipline of his army, which he rigidly enforced, he himself set an example by
marching at the head of his legions, twenty miles a-day, exposed to the inclemencies
of the elements; and subsisting on the coarsest fare, such as fell to the lot of the
common soldier.

The modelling and execution of the portrait exhibit great artistic skill, as well
as perfection in the difficult art of casting in metal. The reign of Hadrian was
peculiarly favourable to the fine arts, as numerous busts and statues of that epoch
which have come down to us sufficiently testify. Some of these rival the finest
productions of the early Greek school. The coins of Hadrian are of peculiarly
finished workmanship, and are not surpassed in beauty and variety of design, or in
poetical imagery, by any in the whole imperial series. From Pliny[1] (who wrote
not long anterior to the ascension of Hadrian) we learn many interesting particulars
of the eminent workmen in brass in his own and in earlier times ; and these artists
were not confined to Rome or Italy, but flourished in the provinces also. "There is
not," observes this writer, "a good town within our provinces in which they have
not begun already to adorn their market-places with many such ornaments of
brazen statues and images, together with titles, honours, and dignities engraven at
the bases, for the better continuance of men's memorials, that posterity might be

[1] "Nat. Hist.," lib. xxxiv, c. vii-viii.

informed by such inscriptions as well as by their tombs and sepulchres." Among the workers in metal of this epoch was Zenodorus in Gaul, who fabricated in that province many works of great merit; and among them a colossal statue of Mercury, for the capital city of the Arverni; and at Rome a statue of Nero, one hundred and ten feet in height. The bronze statue of Antinous, of heroic size, found at Lillebonne, between Rouen and Havre, figured in the third volume of the *Collectanea Antiqua*, and now preserved in the Louvre, may be appealed to as an example of the style of the school to which this head of Hadrian belongs. In our own country may be instanced the head of Apollo found at Bath; and a fragment of a leg and hoof of a horse, found at Lincoln, and preserved in the collection of the Society of Antiquaries at Somerset House.

The personal inspection which Hadrian made of the provinces, to correct abuses, to quell discontent, and to review and readjust the boundaries of the Roman empire, is one of those conceptions and achievements which stamp the character of a great statesman. His visit to Britain is recorded by coins, and by that wonderful monument of engineering skill and of labour, the wall which extended from the Tyne to the Eden. This vast line of separation between the Romano-Britons and the Caledonians has received important illustrations from the inscriptions to Hadrian erected there by the second, the sixth, and the twentieth legions, who were employed in this stupendous undertaking.[1] During his inspection of the various provinces he also built temples and other public edifices in the chief cities, remitted arrears of taxes, and gave largesses to the poor, acquiring by his munificence the proud title of *Locupletator orbis terrarum*. None of the Roman princes gained such popularity in the provinces by well-timed liberality and by the correction of abuses. The historian Spartian has recorded many of the benefits he conferred upon remote cities, in restorations and in the erection of public buildings and monuments. To this he was excited, not merely for the public good, but also from his passionate love for architecture. Among the works he constructed is mentioned a basilica at Nismes, in honour of Plotina the wife of Trajan, which is said to have been of wonderful workmanship (*opere mirabili*). The heroic bronze statue of Antinous,

[1] These inscriptions have been found in or near the walled stations upon the line of the Wall; but most of these stations have never been even partially excavated. Our Governments busy themselves in detaching all kinds of foreign ancient monuments from their localities and placing them in the British Museum; but they carelessly neglect those at home, which so strikingly illustrate the history of our own country. The feeling which induces this inconsistency seems, unfortunately, to spring from national indifference and want of patriotism. The Duke of Northumberland, a few years since, tried, in vain, to institute a Committee of research on the line of the Wall, at the head of which he offered to place the Society of Antiquaries, and to pay the entire expenses!

before referred to, was probably erected at Juliobona, in compliment to him, about the same time as the bronze statue or statues, of which we possess these fine fragments, were set up in Londinium.

The subjects of plates xv to xix were discovered during an excavation of the bed of the Thames, in 1837, near London Bridge, for the purpose of rendering the river more navigable. They are of the very highest class of art, and in every respect merit the engravings furnished by the Society of Antiquaries of London, at the recommendation and under the direction of the late lamented Mr. Gage Rokewode.

The youthful Apollo (pl. xv), is a masterpiece of ideal grace and beauty. The countenance is pensive and full of gentle expression with earnest thought, such as Raphael has so admirably bestowed upon the fine personification of this god in his charming painting of Apollo and Marsyas, in the possession of Mr. Morris Moore. The hair, parted at the forehead, is gathered in undulating tresses on either side of the head, and, tied at the neck, flows luxuriantly down the back :

> Intonsi crines longa cervice fluebant,
> Stillabat Syrio myrtea rore coma.[1]

Two ringlets straying over the shoulders complete the elegant and somewhat unique coiffure. The entire figure is beautifully moulded to pourtray early youth, unlike the muscular development and manly fire of the slayer of Python as exhibited in the Apollo Belvidere. In the repose of the body and the placidity of the countenance, the artist apparently intended to represent the god as Ovid[2] makes him describe himself to the flying Daphne :

> "—— Nescis, temeraria, nescis
> Quem fugias, ideoque fugis : mihi Delphica tellus,
> Et Claros, et Tenedos, Patareaque regia servit ;
> Jupiter est genitor. Per me quod eritque, fuitque,
> Estque, patet. Per me concordant carmina nervis.
> Certa quidem nostra est ; nostra tamen una sagitta
> Certior, in vacuo quæ vulnera pectore fecit.
> Inventum medicina meum est, opiferque per orbem
> Dicor ; et herbarum est subjecta potentia nobis."

The attributes are, unfortunately, wanting ; but it is probable the right hand held a laurel branch, and the left a lyre, as *Apollo Salutaris* is represented upon coins.

The Mercury (pl. xvi) is quite worthy of companionship with the Apollo. It is of the best and chastest design and of the most finished workmanship : the proportions of the figure are correct, the attitude graceful and easy, the countenance

---

[1] Tibullus III, iv, 27.   [2] Metam., lib. i, l. 514.

full of animated beauty ; and we may imagine him charged with a mission from Olympus, and, in the words of Shakspeare,—

"New-lighted on a heaven-kissing hill."

The statuette in plate xvii I had considered as intended to represent a priest of Cybele ; and under that view had conjectured the object in the right hand to be cymbals, held in that peculiar position to admit of the left hand being at liberty to adjust the veil or fillet upon the head, which, it might be inferred, had become loosened in dancing. Supposing cymbals are intended, they would seem to have been used with hinges, as a clapper, or in the manner of our modern castanets. But it may, with equal probability, be meant for a mirror, by the aid of which the head-dress is being arranged. The figure is hermaphroditic.

The fragment of a larger male figure upon a pedestal (pl. xviii) was assigned to Jupiter, chiefly from its muscular development ; but the *pose* is remarkably like that of the Mercury. In the absence of any attributes to guide us it is difficult to decide satisfactorily. The anatomical outline and proportions of this figure are admirably correct and life-like.

The Atys (pl. xix), though inferior as a work of art to the preceding statuettes, is well executed, and particularly interesting as affording a representation of a mythological personage whose effigies are somewhat uncommon. He wears the Phrygian cap, indicative of his origin ; and in either arm he carries boughs heavily laden with fruit, symbolical of his prolific power. His dress is composed of a short tunic and trousers *(bracca* or *anaxyrides)*, thrown open in front, at the waist, and buttoned from the knee to the ankle over a sandal. This arrangement of the costume is as obviously designed as the fruits, to leave beyond doubt, so far as symbolism could express, the attributes and functions of this deity. The costume may be compared with that of a sculptured figure upon a column found at Wroxeter, and engraved in the *Collectanea Antiqua*, vol. iii, pl. vii, which, in other respects, resembles Bacchus.

The popular mythological history of Atys, or Attis, describes him as a beautiful Phrygian or Lydian shepherd, of whom Cybele became enamoured, and made him her high priest ; but failing to keep his vows, the goddess displaced him from his sacred office, maimed and disgraced. He then adopted the dress and manners of the female sex :

"Quod enim genus figuræ est, ego non quod habuerim ?
Ego mulier, ego adolescens, ego ephebus, ego puer."[1]

As high priest of Cybele, Atys instituted religious ceremonies in honour of the Great

[1] Catullus Car., lxi, l. 63.

Mother, or Mother of the Gods, as Cybele is usually styled ; and he travelled through the world teaching the nature and worship of the gods. But, as is usual with most of the ancient mythological personages, his fabled history is full of discrepancies and of varied versions, possessing, with some peculiar features, others which are common to other deities. Montfaucon gives several representations of him. In one of these he holds the pastoral flute of unequal tubes in one hand, and in the other a pine branch. The dress, in most respects, corresponds with that of the statuette from the Thames. In a second example, the flute or pipe is suspended from the sacred pine : the shepherd's crook is by his side, while he plays on the tympanum before the goddess Cybele. Another variety approximates closely to our example, except that Atys carries the fruit in his lap. The pipe and branch are the attributes which Macrobius[1] assigns to him, explaining that Adonis, Attis, Osiris, and Horus, were all different personifications of the Sun. To this definition all the

accounts of Atys from ancient writers converge, and also that his worship, associated with Cybele, was introduced from Phrygia. It is also equally clear that there was a similar affinity between Atys and Mithras of the Persians, whose worship was very extended in the western provinces of the Roman empire. In inscriptions Atys is always connected with Cybele, as Mother of the Gods, and he is styled *Sanctus* and *Invictus*, titles of Mithras and the Sun, and also *Menotyrannus*, or King of the Months.

From the same site in the Thames, but long subsequently, was obtained the disjointed and decapitated figure of which a wood-cut is here given.

It appears to have represented a captive, seated, with the arms bound behind the body; and possibly it may have formed one of two figures, with a trophy between them.

It is very apparent that these bronze figures have been intentionally mutilated. This is

Actual size.

[1] Solem vero sub nomine Attinis ornant fistula et virga : fistula ordinem spiritus inæqualis ostendit. Lib. i, c. 21.

particularly palpable in the present instance. The image of Apollo bears on both sides of the legs, just above the point where they are sundered, marks of some sharp instrument, such as a hatchet would leave if struck with force: this could not possibly have happened after they were thrown into the Thames, but must have been perpetrated by the early converts to Christianity, who, unable to appreciate fine works of art, looked upon them as demons or emanations of the devil. Before such fanatical ignorance every tangible representation, whether of gods or of human beings, fell indiscriminately; and the effigies of the soldier, or of the peaceful civilian upon his tomb, were as systematically cut and hammered to pieces as the statues and images of gods and goddesses.

Plate xx represents the figure of an archer, discovered in Queen Street, in 1842, by Mr. W. Chaffers, who, in the same year, communicated an account of it to the Society of Antiquaries of London.[1]

Mr. Chaffers observes: " While watching the progress of the excavations recently made in Queen Street, Cheapside (for the formation of a sewer), I was fortunately enabled to obtain possession of several rare and curious specimens of Roman art. A short distance from Watling Street, a fine piece of Roman wall, running directly across the street, was exposed to view in a remarkably perfect condition, built of flat red tiles, embedded in solid and compact mortar. Several others, lower down the street, were also discovered. Within a few yards of the wall, one of the bricklayers, removing some earth, struck his trowel against something which he conjectured to be a brass tap ; but, on clearing further, he found it was the right heel of his figure, which lay upon its face.—The height of the figure, if standing erect, would be fifteen inches ; but in its stooping posture, the perpendicular height from the base to the crown of the head is only eleven inches. It is evidently intended to represent a person in the attitude of shooting an arrow from a bow. The bow and arrow were probably of richer metal than the figure itself ; but no vestiges of them were discovered. The aperture for the bow is seen in the closed left hand which held it, and the bent fingers of the right appear in the act of drawing the arrow to its full extent previous to its evolation. The eyes are of silver, with the pupils open ; the hair disposed in graceful curls on the head, as well as on the chin and upper lip. The left hand, which grasped the bow and sustained the arrow, is so placed as to bring the latter to a level with the eye ; and the stedfast look and determined expression of the whole face are much heightened by the silver eyes.—It was found at about the depth of between twelve and thirteen feet."

It is difficult to identify the subject of this fine work of art. It is possible it was

[1] " Archæologia," vol. xx, p. 543.

intended to represent Hercules shooting the centaur Nessus ; but as it has none of
the attributes which usually accompany the figures of this god, and as the portrait
does not accord with his accepted marked features, it may, with greater probability,
be considered to be intended for an ideal personage.

It is now in the collection of Lord Londesborough.

Plate xxi exhibits, in actual dimensions, a bronze forceps, found in the bed of
the Thames, near the site of old London Bridge. It consists of two shanks, which,
although they are now separated, were evidently joined by a hinge at the upper
extremity ; and connected, probably by a bolt and screw, at the lower end. The
inner sides are denticulated, doubtless for the purpose of squeezing or crushing.
The lower extremities are narrowed, and, at first sight, would seem to have been
intended for handles ; but the hand could not fully grasp them so as to bring upon
the instrument the power that would seem to be required to put it into operation ;
and the two longitudinal perforations indicate a connecting bar, which would seem
to have been worked by a screw, particularly as there are manifest signs of considerable force having been used, and one of the shanks has been broken and ingeniously
repaired. If worked by a screw it would, apparently, be required that the upper
extremity be fastened to some solid body, or provided with a handle like that of
a tongs: if, however, there were originally a spring or clasping bar, it might have
been held in the hand for cracking or crushing ; but then this mode of using the
instrument would not explain the fracture. In either case, the manner in which
the forceps was used is not very clearly seen ; nor is it obvious for what object
such an elaborately ornamented and complicated instrument was fabricated ;
but the heads of the divinities which adorn it seem to stamp its sacred
character, and indicate that it was employed in some religious rites or ceremonies.

The deities represented upon the forceps are : on the right, Cybele, crowned with
towers ; Mercury, wearing the emblematic wings ; Jupiter, crowned with olive ;
Venus ; and Ceres, wearing the *modius :* on the left are Juno, Mars, Diana, Apollo,
and Saturn, all clearly indicated by their attributes. Upon the top, below the busts
of Juno and Cybele, are heads of horses ; below the other busts are heads of bulls;
and heads of lions terminate the handles.

The busts upon the shanks of the forceps are those of the deities who presided
over the days of the week ; and they have been arranged, as it will be seen, with
an intention to exhibit them in this character and in regular order. Commencing
from the bottom, on the left side is Saturn, to whom was dedicated the *Dies
Saturnii,* Saturday ; Sol, representing *Dies Solis,* or Sunday ; Luna, *Dies Lunæ,*

Monday ; and Mars, *Dies Martis*, Tuesday : on the right side, proceding downwards is Mercury, for *Dies Mercurii*, Wednesday ; Jupiter, *Dies Jovis*, Thursday ; Venus, *Dies Veneris*, Friday : the remaining one, Ceres, making the number eight, equalizes the number on each side, and, at the same time, represents the old Roman week of eight days, from which is derived the French form of *huit jours*, and the German *acht tage*. A group of these deities, in eight compartments, to complete the division prescribed by the ancient calendar, appears upon one of the tessellated pavements in the Roman villa at Bramdean,[1] in Hampshire ; and upon a votive altar in the museum at Mayence.[2] These planetary groups are aptly illustrated by the eclogue of Ausonius, entitled *De nominibus septem dierum :*

> " Primum, supremumque diem radiatus habet Sol.
> Proxima fraternæ succedit Luna coronæ.
> Tertius assequitur Titania lumina Mavors.
> Mercurius quarti sibi vindicat astra diei.
> Inlustrant quintam Jovis aurea sidera Zonam.
> Sexta salutigeram sequitur Venus alma parentem.
> Cuncta supergrediens Saturni septima lux est,
> Octavum instaurat revolubilis orbita Solem."

In all the above examples, as well as in others, Saturn stands first, contrary to the order in which Ausonius places the days of the week, commencing with Sol, the planet which ruled the *dies Dominica*, the first day of the Christian week. The busts of Juno and Cybele, which surmount the whole, were, apparently, selected from their prominence in the mythological system, Juno presiding, also, over the calends of the months ; and Cybele, the Great Mother, directing the regular return of the seasons and guiding the revolution of the year. The symbols of the horse, the bull, and the lion have, all of them, a connexion with the history and worship of this goddess.

In 1825, a small silver figure of Harpocrates was found in the Thames, and passed, shortly afterwards, into the British Museum. It is shewn, of the actual size, in two views in plate xxii. The attitude of this little figure is natural and full of grace, and the modelling well expresses the fleshy rotundity of early youth. A delicately wrought gold chain crosses the figure in front and passes through a strong loop at the back, together with a gold ring. This mechanism is a part of the original design, and indicates that the image was intended to be secured to some more solid and weighty object, probably to stand among the tutelary divinities in the house

---

[1] "Collectanea Antiqua," vol. ii, pl. xxi.   [2] *Ibid.*, p. 61.

of some person of opulence. The representations of Harpocrates which have come down to us are by no means uniform, except the position of the finger towards the mouth, advising silence. In this instance he is winged, but chained, to restrain his flight : upon his head he wears a crescent ; and at his feet are two dogs and a tortoise, emblems of watchfulness and of taciturnity. The tortoise was also symbolical of a good housewife who kept within her own doors ; and some such symbolism was probably here intended.

It is not, however, improbable, that this elegant statuette may have been meant for Cupid, with attributes of Harpocrates ; and if so, the unexplained object behind the left leg may be either a quiver or a torch.

The bronzes which remain to be noticed are mostly from the Thames, obtained by the workmen employed in dredging ballast, or in clearing out the drifted sand and gravel along the line of old London Bridge.

The first of these appears to have been seated across a stand, which has also supported the circular convex object held in front by means of a rivet of lead, which is still remaining. The head is well designed and executed, and is remarkable for the peculiar style of the hair and beard, which resembles that of the portrait of Juba, king of Mauritania, upon his coins. The eyes are of silver. The body is dressed in a tunic, over which is a garment arranged to give play to the right arm, which is raised, while the left hand supports the circular adjunct upon which the attention of the personage seems bestowed. The feet are covered with shoes (*calcei*) : the left one, being intended to be seen, is open on the instep : the other the artist has not been so patient with. It cannot fail to be noticed in ancient works of art, and even in those of great merit, that parts which do not directly meet the eye, are not only carelessly designed, but often left rough and unfinished. It is the case with the left hand of this figure, which is also very disproportionate. It is difficult to understand the original condition of this figure in relation to accessory objects now wanting. It seems to have been intended to represent an artisan of some kind, at work : possibly an armourer making a shield ; or, quite as likely, a baker with a large moulded pie or loaf ; and, as one or the other, it may have been designed to represent a character in some popular drama.

Actual size.

The goat (fig. 1) is in iron, plated with silver, the workmanship remarkably fine; and the figure affords a good example of the neat and workmanlike manner in which the ancients coated the baser, with the precious metals.

Fig. 1.   Actual size.   Fig. 2.

The peacock (fig. 2) has probably stood at the foot of a statuette of Juno; and at the back is a loop for fastening it. It is of inferior work. The tail, found separated, was in my possession at least a year before the body was discovered;

and I was puzzled what to make of it, until, being in the dredging-barge one day watching the operations, I saw the body of the peacock brought up among the gravel from the bed of the river, and immediately identified it and its tail: I soon confirmed my belief that they had been severed from each other.

Head of a Wolf or Dog, from a mass of ferruginous conglomerate, in which was also a coin of Carausius.

It has served as a steelyard weight, and the chain which suspended it from the beam was fixed to the loop between the ears; but it was broken off and lost before the head came into my possession. It is of good and highly characteristic workmanship. The same praise may be awarded to the Prow of a Galley, which may probably have been an *ex voto*, or votive offering, suspended in a temple by

Actual size.

L 2

some person who had made a prosperous voyage. The ornamental head was called *cheniscus* (a Greek word), from its resemblance to the head and neck of a goose. At the bottom, just above the keel, projects the *rostrum*, terminating in an animal's head.

The very elegant Handle of a Vase (fig. 1), is studded with small silver knobs, and the eyes of the heads of birds, which were fixed to the rim of the vessel, are also of silver.

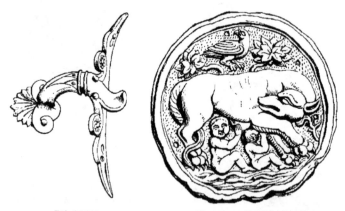

Fig. 1. Actual size.   Fig. 2. Actual size.

The circular plate (fig. 2), which is formed of thin metal, in which copper largely predominates, was shaped by stamping, and afterwards finished by rude chasing and frosting with a punch. It appears to have been fixed to wood. The design is an illustration of the popular story of Romulus and Remus suckled by the Wolf, a favourite subject with the ancient Roman artists. In this instance it is treated more than usually in detail, by the introduction of the Fig-tree and the Woodpecker.

This design is illustrated by a passage in Ovid's *Fasti* :[1]

> " Arbor erat: remanent vestigia : quæque vocatur
>   Rumina nunc ficus, Romula ficus erat.
> Venit ad expositis (mirum) lupa fœta gemellos.
>
> .   .   .   .   .
>
> Constitit, et cauda teneris blanditur alumnis,
>   Et fingit lingua corpora bina sua."

[1] Lib. ii, l. 411.

The Woodpecker shared with the Wolf the honour of feeding the infant heroes :

" Lacte quis infantes nescit crevisse ferino,
Et picum expositis sæpe tulisse cibos ?"[1]

This plate was found in Moorfields, between Finsbury Circus and Liverpool Street, with a thin star-shaped piece of similar metal, perforated in the centre.

Plate xxiii contains a few examples of minor objects in bronze. Fig. 1, is a steelyard weight ; fig. 2, the bust of a statuette of Minerva ; and fig. 5, a boss which has, apparently, served as an ornament to a small coffer. Fig. 4, a serpent twisted round a column, is in silver ; and fig. 3, a gladiator, given in two views, is in terra-cotta. They are all etched of the actual size.

It may suffice to refer to a few other objects enumerated in the *Catalogue* of my Museum of London Antiquities, such as the Branch of a Shrub or Tree (No. 27), probably the fir or pine, which has perhaps been either held in the arm of a figure of Silvanus, or fixed to the pedestal of an image of Cybele, or, possibly, of Pan : a columnar ornament (No. 30) ; and a diminutive piece of art, representing a seated captive : it has been perforated through the side and head, as if it had been attached to some object.

[1] " Fasti," lib. iii, l. 53.

Actual size.

POTTERY.

It is not surprising, when the durability of the material and the purposes for which it was wrought, are considered, that such an infinite number of ancient works in clay have descended to our times. Among the most accessible and abundant components of the earth, its applicability towards supplying many of the daily necessities of man was palpable to all, from the savages who used it for their rude huts and their drinking-cups baked in the sun, to civilised nations who converted it into bricks for buildings, and a variety of objects for luxury as well as need. Accordingly works of clay are among the most curious and important which engage the attention of the ethnologist and the antiquary, as they afford very frequently considerable assistance towards the correct appropriation of ancient remains, the types of urns and fictile vessels being among the clearest and most accepted evidences of different races and peoples. It is not uninteresting to look back upon some remarkable inventions in clay ; such as, for example, the earthenware coffins of the Babylonians and other eastern nations ; and the use of burnt clay for various sepulchral purposes by the Etruscans, the Greeks, and the Romans. If durability be the chief object in the solicitude evinced in all ages for depositories and monuments for the dead, baked clay is certainly far more lasting than lead, and almost or quite as cheap as wood, which perishes in a few years ; at the same time it is not so adaptable, as stone and marble, for other uses, when the original purpose is no longer regarded or respected. The ancient invention, valuable in its way, was never developed to its full capability; it became obsolete, to be revived, perhaps successfully, some day not far remote. The stamps upon the Babylonian and Assyrian bricks, and upon the Greek and Roman pottery, show another invention which, never matured, died in its infancy. In it was the crude idea of modern printing, its very principle, discovered ; but the germ of this divine art of perpetuating thought was never vivified, though, it has been proved, an ordinary mind might have caused it to spring and fructify.

The perfection which the ancient Etruscans, Greeks, and Romans attained in the manufacturing of fictile vessels can only be understood by those who have studied, or, at least, taken some pains to examine the numerous varieties which are preserved in our private and public collections and in those of the continent. They are all marked by a strong nationality in design and in ornament ; and a like distinctive

character is attached to those of other nations, so that the archæologist, in no branch
of his researches, walks on firmer or surer ground than that trodden by the labours
of the ancient potters. The elegant painted vases from the tombs of Etruria and
Greece, covered with representations of scenes in popular traditions and fables,
bespeak the refinement of the people to whom such exquisite works were as familiar
as the old willow-pattern service to the English eye. The Roman fictile vases,
totally distinct in character, were not less historically and artistically interesting;
and are, perhaps, even more so, because connected with, and forming part of, the
antiquities of our own land; for from such prototypes the potters in Britain found
an almost endless variety of vessels for domestic uses, which have survived to this
day, and give us excellent means of knowing the very kinds of cups and dishes
which, sixteen hundred years ago, stood upon the tables of our predecessors in the
country in which we dwell.

Researches made during the last twenty or thirty years have thrown much light
upon the origin of several varieties of the fictile ware discovered so abundantly
throughout this country. From these researches we have been enabled with certainty
to refer particular classes to the localities in which they were largely, though
probably not exclusively, fabricated. As Londinium was the great centre of the
commerce of Britain, it might be expected that upon its site would be found traces
of the products of most of these factories, especially of those from which intercourse
was direct and frequent. There, also, we should naturally look for examples of the
pottery made in neighbouring foreign countries. Accordingly nowhere in England
has such an immense quantity of various kinds been discovered as in London.
Examples of most of these will be given in this volume.

From a manuscript of John Conyers, a collector of antiquities,[1] it is clear that
the remains of Roman kilns were brought to light, in 1677, in digging foundations
at the north-west of St. Paul's. He states the depth to have been twenty-six feet;
but it is much more probable that it was only fifteen or sixteen. He gives a very
rough sketch of one of the kilns, and states there were four of them made in the
sandy loam, in the fashion of a cross foundation, of which only the one sketched was
left standing. It was five feet from top to bottom and of the same width, and
"had no other matter for its form and building but the outward loam, naturally
crusted hardish by the heat burning the loam red, like brick; the floor in the
middle supported by, and cut out of, loam, and helped with old fashioned Roman
tyles' shards, but very few, and such as I have seen used for repositories for urns, in

---

[1] In the British Museum, Sloane MSS. 958, fol. 105. I am indebted to Mr. Franks for the
loan of a copy, and for a tracing of the sketches.

the fashion of and like ovens.—The kiln was full of the coarser sort of pots, so that few were saved whole, viz., lamps, bottles, urns, and dishes." The sketch shows two mouths to the kiln. What, however, is of more importance, is a drawing he made of the vessels found in the kiln, which are identical with those we are most familiar with in the collections made from discoveries in London in more recent times.

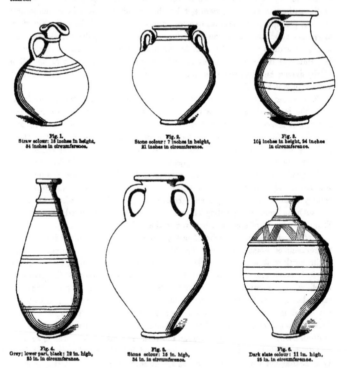

Fig. 1.
Straw colour: 12 inches in height,
34 inches in circumference.

Fig. 2.
Stone colour: 7 inches in height,
21 inches in circumference.

Fig. 3.
10½ inches in height, 34 inches
in circumference.

Fig. 4.
Grey; lower part, black: 19 in. high,
25 in. in circumference.

Fig. 5.
Stone colour: 15 in. high,
34 in. in circumference.

Fig. 6.
Dark slate colour: 11 in. high,
25 in. in circumference.

Some of these are similar to the types introduced upon this page, particularly figures 1, 2, and 3. There are also two of the small drinking-cups with slender stems, of which a variety, in pale red clay, is shewn on the right of this page; and a broad, shallow vessel, termed *mortarium*, in every particular resembling the specimen appended below, which is of a pale clay, with a mixture of pounded red tile and white silicious particles worked into the inner surface to counteract the wearing effects of trituration, these vessels having been intended for pounding or rubbing vegetable substances as well as cooking them over a fire. They are exceedingly numerous, not only among the remains found in London, but also in all parts of the country, on the sites of Roman buildings. At Headington, near Oxford,

Height, six inches.

among the ruins of a villa, Mr. Ll. Jewitt found the fragments of at least two hundred of these vessels, which, from peculiar indications, appeared to have been fabricated in or near the locality; and the same remark would hold good with respect to other kinds of the pottery found at Headingham. The mortaria vary in dimensions from seven or eight inches to nearly two feet in diameter; and from three to about five inches in depth. Those found in London are often inscribed with the makers' names across the rims, as shewn in the lower cut upon this page; but those found in other parts of the country do not seem so frequently inscribed: it does not appear that any of those discovered by Mr. Ll. Jewitt were.

Upon the bank of the Medway, opposite the village of Upchurch, and extending for a considerable distance towards the mouth of the river, was a settlement of Roman potters, who manufactured the excellent clay which abounds in the district into various descriptions of ware. Traces of the kilns themselves have not been noticed; but the evidences of the potteries are so decided as to admit of no doubt as to their establishment over a long period of time.[1] Although our investigations have led us to ascertain that these potteries produced many kinds of vessels, chiefly for common domestic purposes, yet we could but be struck by the prevalence of those which are of a peculiar dark colour, approaching nearest to what may be called a blue-black, all of which, though of a great variety of form and ornamentation, were clearly the result of some particular process in baking, which was explained by the discoveries of my friend the late Mr. Artis, made in the

[1] Those who are particularly interested in this branch of British archæology, are referred for full information on the subject to my papers in the "Archæologia," vol. xxiv; and in the "Journal of the British Archæological Association," vol. ii; and to Mr. Wright's "Wanderings of an Antiquary."

M

neighbourhood of Castor. He was led to the conclusion that these and similar
vessels of blue and slate-colour were coloured by suffocating the fire of the kiln, at
the time when its contents had acquired a degree of heat sufficient to insure
uniformity of colour; and he had so firmly made up his mind as to the process of
making and firing this peculiar kind of earthenware, that long before he was able to
demonstrate the fact from existing proofs, he termed the kilns in which it had
been fired "smother kilns." At length he discovered a kiln, and his opinions were
fully confirmed. The clay of which the bricks, or tiles, of the kiln were composed,
had been mixed with about one third of rye in the chaff, which, being consumed in
the fire, left cavities in the room of the grains. This might have been intended to
modify expansion and contraction, as well as to assist the gradual distribution of the
colouring vapour. The mouth of the furnace and the top of the kiln were, no
doubt, stopped, for every part of the kiln, from the inside wall to the earth on the
outside, as well as every part of the clay wrappers of the dome, was penetrated and
saturated with the colouring vegetable exhalation. As further proof that the colour
of the ware was thus produced, Mr. Artis collected the clays of the neighbourhood,
including specimens from the immediate neighbourhood of the smother-kilns; and
having submitted them to a series of experiments, became further convinced of
the correctness of his theory, that this colour could not be attributed to any
metallic oxide, either in the clay or applied externally; but solely to impregna-
tion from the confined smoke. It may be added that this colour is so volatile

as to be entirely expelled by
a second firing in an open
kiln.

Examples of three varie-
ties of this class of vessels are
here given. We may conclude
that the numerous specimens
found in London were manufactured on the banks of the
Medway.

Height, 5¼ inches.   Height, 5 inches.

It is probable that the vessels representing another singular kind of ware, of
which examples are given in the next page, are of native manufacture; but they
are not of very frequent occurrence. One of this class (in the possession of
Mr. Peacock) has recently been found at Chester, in a tomb formed of tiles, with a
coin of Domitian.

Mr. Artis published a valuable set of plates, entitled *The Durobrivæ of*

Antoninus Identified and Illustrated,[1] in which some of the kilns are engraved, together with examples of pottery found in them. The subject receives much additional light from information which this intelligent and zealous antiquary

Dark blueish clay: diam., 5¼ in., height, 8 in.

Ash colour clay: dimensions, 7 in.; height, 6 inches.

Dark red clay: diameter, 4 in ; height, 2¼ in.

Light red clay.

communicated to me. "I have now traced," he observes, "these potteries to an extent of upwards of twenty miles. They are principally confined to the gravel beds on the banks of the Nen and its tributary streams : the clay used at some of them appears to have been collected at some little distance from the works. The kilns are all constructed on the same principle. A circular hole was dug, from three to four feet deep, and four in diameter ; and walled round to the height of two feet. A furnace, one-third of the diameter of the kiln in length, communicated with the side. In the centre of the circle so formed was an oval pedestal, the height of the sides, with the end pointing to the mouth of the furnace. Upon this pedestal and side wall the floor of the kiln rests. It is formed of perforated angular bricks,

[1] Mr. Artis, in a circular to his subscribers in reference to the plates, says : "If they had been accompanied by letter press, the publication would have come within the operation of an Act of Parliament which requires that eleven copies of each work shall be given up to as many public libraries: this would have subjected the author to a tax (nearly £100) which he would not have been able to bear." At my instigation Mr. Artis resolved on giving an illustrated volume which should supply this deficiency: but the support promised was not encouraging; and, before any step, beyond preliminary measures, could be taken, his death justified the prognostication that he would probably be prevented from ever laying before the public "any further information than what the plates themselves could convey." There remain in my possession some notes made, at my request, by himself, and memoranda which I was accustomed to make during conversations on the subject while he was staying with me in London.

M 2

meeting at one point in the centre. The furnace is arched with bricks moulded for
the purpose. The side of the kiln is constructed with curved bricks set edgeways
in a thick *slip* (the same material made into a thin mortar), to the height of two
feet. The process of packing the vessels and securing uniform heat in firing the ware
was the same in the two different kinds of kilns, namely, that before described, called
'smother-kiln'; and that for various other kinds of pottery. They were first
carefully loose-packed with the articles to be fired, up to the height of the side
walls. The circumference of the bulk was then gradually diminished, and finished
in the shape of a dome. As this arrangement progressed, an attendant seems to
have followed the packer, and thinly covered a layer of pots with coarse hay or
grass. He then took some thin clay, the size of his hand, and laid it flat over the
grass upon the vessels : he then placed more grass on the edge of the clay just laid
on ; and then more clay ; and so on until he had completed the circle. By this
time the packer would have raised another tier of pots, the plasterer following as
before, hanging the grass over the top edge of the last layer of plasters, until he had
reached the top, in which a small aperture was left, and the clay nipped round
the edge : another coating would be then laid on as before described. Directly
afterwards gravel or loam was thrown up against the side wall where the clay
wrappers were commenced, probably to secure the bricks and the clay coating. The
kiln was then fired with wood. In consequence of the care taken to place grass
between the edges of the wrappers, they could be unpacked in the same size pieces
as when laid on in a plastic state ; and thus the danger in breaking the coat to
obtain the contents of the kiln would be obviated. In the course of my excavations
I discovered a curiously constructed furnace, of which I have never before or since
met an example. Over it had been placed two circular vessels : that next above
the furnace was a third less than the other, which would hold about eight gallons.
The fire passed partly under both of them, the smoke escaping by a smoothly
plastered flue from seven to eight inches wide. The vessels were suspended by the
rims fitting into a circular groove or rabbet formed for the purpose. They contained
pottery both perfect and fragmentary. It is probable they had covers ; and I am
inclined to think were used for glazing peculiar kinds of the immense quantities of
ornamented ware made in this district. Its contiguity to one of the workshops in
which the glaze (oxide of iron) and other pigments were found, confirms this
opinion."

Mr. Artis thus describes the manner in which he considered most of the
ornamented kinds of pottery made in the Castor district were decorated.

"The vessels upon which are displayed a variety of hunting subjects, representations of fishes, scrolls, foliage, and human figures, were all glazed after the figures were laid on : where, however, the decorations are white, the vessels were glazed before the ornaments were added. Ornamenting with figures of men and animals was effected by means of sharp and of blunt skewer implements and a slip of suitable consistency. These implements seem to have been of two kinds : one thick enough to carry sufficient slip for the nose, neck, body, and front thigh ; the other, of a more delicate kind, for a thinner slip for the tongue, lower jaws, eye, fore and hind legs, and tail. There seems to have been no retouching after the slip trailed from the implement."[1]

The two leading classes of the Castor ware, thus briefly described, may be illustrated by the annexed specimens, discovered in London :

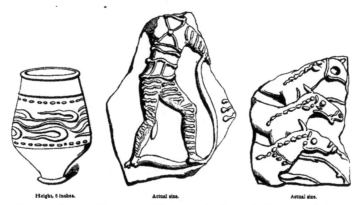

Height, 6 inches.   Actual size.   Actual size.

The examples upon this page are such as were glazed after the figures were laid on : those on p. 86 were glazed first ; and ornamented with designs in white, afterwards.

The manufactory of the first class to which these examples belong, seems to have been more exclusively confined to Northamptonshire than the other, many varieties of which have been found on the site of Roman potteries in the western district of the New Forest in Hampshire, an account of which is published in the *Archæologia*, vol. xxxv. The ornaments upon many of the vessels, which more

---

[1] Those to whom Mr. Artis's plates are not accessible may find some excellent illustrations in Mr. Wright's " Celt, Roman, and Saxon."

strictly belong to what, for the sake of distinction, we may term the Castor ware, are scrolls and foliage, dolphins; and dogs chasing rabbits, hares, and stags. In the fourth volume of the *Collecta-nea Antiqua* are some remarkable examples, one of which has a gla-diatorial combat, a group repre-senting the train-ing of a bear, and a hunting scene: others represent mythological sub-jects. In almost all, the designs are executed with skill and spirit,

Black pottery with white painted pattern : 6 in. in diameter, 7 in. in height.

Dark reddish brown with white ornaments; 6 in. high, 2½ in. diameter in centre.

especially when the very simple and off-handed process, as described by Mr. Artis, is taken into consideration. This kind of pottery has been discovered in Holland, Flanders, and Belgium, and, I believe, more sparingly, in some parts of the north-east of France ; but I did not notice any specimens in the public collections of the towns of the south and west of that country ; neither can I refer to any in the French archæological publications with which I am acquainted.

Vessels in a fine red clay have been found in London which were probably

Height, 3½ inches.

Height, 7 in.: circum., 7 in.

Height, 3½ inches.

imported into Britain. They are usually of the shape of the perfect example on the preceding page, and are ornamented at the mouth with masks, such as are there introduced. Further examples are given in the *Antiquities of Richborough, Reculver, and Lymne*, p. 74, which, with a perfect vessel found at Canterbury, are now in the museum of Mr. Mayer, of Liverpool. They seem to have served as patterns for some in a light yellow or straw-coloured clay with masks, the hair and eyelashes of which are painted of a chocolate colour : of these examples are given in plate xlix of *Durobrivæ Illustrated*.

The cup in the annexed cut is one of a very common form, ornamented with circular rows of indentations, which upon some of the varieties are of a very complex form, such as may be best described by reference to the patterns upon watch-cases, called "engine-turned". A basin-shaped vessel with over-lapping cover, both entirely covered with this pattern, found at Castor, is figured in No. xlix of Mr. Artis's plates.

Height, 6 inches.

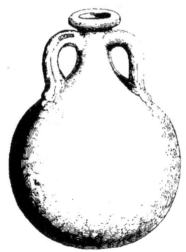

Height, 28 inches; diameter, 21 inches.

Of the larger kinds of earth-enware vessels, the amphora has been met with so frequently in London among the remains of dwelling-houses, that in some localities it might almost have been supposed that manufac-tories of them had been esta-blished there. They had, how-ever, been mostly broken to pieces before discovered ; and the quantity of fragments merely indicated the general use of the vessels for domestic purposes, such as storing of wine, oil, and vinegar. A perfect example is here shewn; but many, as could be judged from the fragments, were of still larger dimensions. They seem to have usually ranged from the capacity of four or five to that of ten or twelve gallons. Caylus, in his *Recueil d'Antiquités*, has figured an amphora, found in Italy, which was four inches thick, five feet six inches in height, fifteen feet in circumference, and capable of containing nearly six hogsheads of liquor; and many continental museums contain examples both of the amphora and of the *dolium* (a wide-mouthed globular vessel), both of huge dimensions. It was a very common practice with the Romans to use the amphora, after separating the upper part, as a cist or coffin for the cinerary urn. One found near Lothbury seemed to have been used for that purpose; and in the Charles Museum, at Maidstone, is preserved one from a family walled cemetery in Lockham Wood, near that town, in which was deposited a large glass urn filled with burnt human bones. Whether, in such cases, the selection of a wine-jar for the remains of the owner was dictated by respect for his habits and taste, is more than I can say: probably the solidity of the amphora insuring the protection of the more fragile urn was the cause. The dolium, from its large dimensions and wide mouth, was also used as a depository for the cinerary urn.

The other kind of amphora, such as is commonly represented on ancient monuments, is long and slender, but frequently of enormous dimensions. Examples will be found in the *Collectanea Antiqua*, vol. ii, p. 26, 27, discovered with various other vessels of domestic use and implements of cooking apparatus, in a Roman burial-place near Colchester.

There is every reason to believe that many of the amphoræ found in London are of local manufactory; but others were doubtless continually imported with the produce of Italy, such as wine, oil, and fruits.

The marks and names of the potters, impressed usually upon the handles of the London examples, are:

A.A.F	CRADOS	L. C. F. P. C. O.	Q. S. P.	SCALENS
ÁERI	CARTVNIT. M.?	MVN(?)MELISSAE	CAT. QVIE	L. SER. SENC
C. F. AL	CORI	MELISSE	CANTON. QV	C. SEMPOL
AXII	F. C. CVFIA	L. IVNI(?)	CANTON. QV. ET	L. S. SEX
BELLVCI	L.F.CRESCIV.FE?	MELISSE	CANT. QVESI(?)	L. C. SOL
L. VI. BR	E1PC	M. P. R.	ROMANI	SVENNR
C.	EROV. IF	MCC	L. V. ROPI. M	C. MARI. STIL
C. IV. R	FAVSTI.MANIB	MIM	QIMFN	S. YENNR
C. V. H	L. A. GE	NYMPH	RVFSANI	VALERI
L. CES	GMT	P. S. A.	SAENVS	VENVSTI
C. AP. F.	HILARI	POR. L. AN	OF. SANI	VIBIOR

There are many more, so very indistinctly stamped as not to be intelligible.

The potters' names on the mortaria (see p. 81) are :

ALBINVS	DOINV	MARINVS. FECIT	RIDANVS.	SECVNDVS
ALBINUS. FECIT	DO...	MARTINVS. F	RIDANVS. M.	SOLLVS. F.
APRILIS	ESVNERT	MARTVCENVS	RIPANI	TANIO
ANDID. FECIT	Q. VALERI }	MARTVSENS. F	A. TEREN }	SEX. VAL
AMMIVS	LICINILVS	MAXI	RIPANI }	Q. VALC. F }
BRIXSA	LITVCENTI	PRASSO. OF	RVCCVS	VERANI. F }
CAS...	LVGVDI. F	PRIMVS. F	SAVRANVS	Q. VALERIVS }
CATVLVS. F	F. LVGVDV	L.LVRIVS.PRISCVS	SATVRNINVS. FEC	VERANIVS }
DEVA...	LVGVDV. FACTV	P. P. R.	Q. VA. SE.	T .. S: VALEN
DVBITATVS	L. E. ECIT	P. R. B.	L. CAN. SEC.	VIALLA

Some of these names occur in the more copious list of the makers of the red glazed pottery. Those reading *Lugudi F.*; *F. Lugudi*, and *Lugudu Factu*, would, from the more complete form, LVGVDVni FACTVs, appear to have been fabricated at Lugudunum, or Lugdunum, Lyons. This supposition is supported, not merely by the spelling in inscriptions being often Lugudunum, but by the name of the potter, Ripanus Tiber, being associated with the name of this city, upon a mortarium found at Ewell, in Surrey.

THE RED GLAZED POTTERY.

A class of Roman pottery of a very peculiar kind has been found in great abundance in and around London. From the great interest attached to it on account of variety and beauty of form, superior material, and the classic designs with which it is frequently decorated, plates xxiv to xxix, as well as many wood-cuts, are here introduced with the object of making it more fully understood and appreciated. This is the more desirable because the pottery is found, not only in our towns of Roman origin and almost wherever a villa has stood; but also upon the continent ; and in almost all antiquarian works it is described or referred to, most usually under the appellation of "Samian" pottery. But it has been nowhere found more plentifully than in London, as will be best shewn by these illustrations and by the potters' stamps, which present upwards of three hundred varieties.

N

The characteristics of this pottery are a fine red clay, of a very compact texture, covered with a brighter or coral-colour glaze; slightly porous, and sonorous when struck. Its forms are those of the dish or patera, the cup, and the bowl; and so seldom was it used for the narrow-mouthed vessels, that among many hundred examples I can only call to mind one specimen of a fragment which appeared to have belonged to a bottle-shaped vessel, and that is ornamented with a white raised beaded pattern. In the museum at York there is also a fragment of a patera with foliage in white.

The most usual varieties are shewn in the accompanying cuts. Of these figures 1 to 5 are the most uncommon; and figures 10 and 14 are remarkable for their large size. Figures 6, 8, 12, 13, and 14 have usually the makers' names stamped across the bottom on the inside, as in the annexed examples.

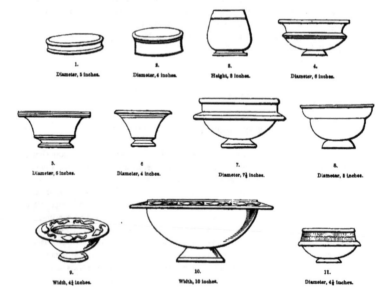

1.
Diameter, 5 inches.

2.
Diameter, 4 inches.

3.
Height, 8 inches.

4.
Diameter, 6 inches.

5.
Diameter, 6 inches.

6.
Diameter, 4 inches.

7.
Diameter, 7½ inches.

8.
Diameter, 8 inches.

9.
Width, 4½ inches.

10.
Width, 10 inches.

11.
Diameter, 4½ inches.

12.

Diameter, 7 in.; depth, 1¼ in.

13.

Width, 10 in.; depth, 2 in.

14.

Diameter, 4 in.

Besides these there is another class, which, from the overlapping edge, the spout,
and the mixture in the inner
surface of minute pieces of
silex or quartz, may be called
mortaria. The spout of the
smaller of the two examples
here given is the mouth of a
lion's head. It is probable they
were used for table dishes,
in which slight trituration
only was necessary, which the
rougher surface would accelerate.

Diameter, 14 inches.

The other divisions of the red glazed pottery, so far as regards the body of the
ware, and the shining red colour of the
glaze, is precisely similar to that exemplified by the foregoing examples. But
it differs in form, and in being, more or
less, richly embossed, of which numerous
varieties are exhibited in plates xxiv to
xxix, and in the wood-cuts upon the following pages. This embossing was partly
executed by means of moulds, and partly

Diameter, 8 inches

by separate stamps, as may be perceived by a close examination of the designs,
which occasionally shew marks of a double impress where the first has not been
sufficiently distinct, or was stamped irregularly. Of this pottery with raised
ornamented designs there are two distinct kinds, that just described, and a
much rarer description, the figures upon which were moulded separately and
then affixed to the vessels. Only a few of the latter kind have been discovered;
but they are quite sufficient to assist us in coming to a conclusion as to their
origin and the origin of the more numerous class, that commonly known as

N 2

"Samian." There is, moreover, a third variety, also very rare, with incuse ornaments.

The term "Samian," though generally applied to this peculiar ware, does not appear to be warranted by any ancient authority. The clay of Samos, and the pottery made from it, are spoken of as being of a peculiar fine kind ; but it nowhere appears that its colour was red, nor is the ware so described as to admit of its being identified in the pottery under consideration. Pliny enumerates several places eminent for pottery; but he does not point out the characteristic qualities of the vessels so that we can recognise them ; and although passages may be found in other ancient writers which may seem to refer to this very elegant red ware, yet it is doubtful if we are warranted in so applying them. The most simple and decisive way to understand what were the various kinds of fictile vessels mentioned by ancient authors as manufactured at particular places, would be to ascertain what peculiar kinds are most abundantly discovered in the several localities ; and until this is done, it is better, as in the case of the assumed Samian, to designate them from some distinctive qualities rather than from a questionable locality.

The prevailing forms of the ornamented vessels are bowl-shaped and upright, of which the two cuts subjoined may serve as examples. The sides of some of the

Diameter, 8¼ inches; height, 5¼ inches.   Diameter, 6¼ inches: height, 4½ inches.

latter are sometimes not quite perpendicular, but slightly expanding towards the top, as in examples given in plate xxvii. A very few have been found with imitative handles, of which a fine bowl is represented at the top of the opposite page.

The vessels before referred to with incuse patterns are so exceedingly rare, that no perfect example has been met with during the London excavations. The

Diameter, 9 inches; height, 5¼ inches.

fragments, which have belonged to at least five varieties, are here brought together in one view. The material and glaze are precisely similar to those of the other descriptions; but the ornaments, instead of being raised, are incised with great sharpness and skill.

Half the actual size.

The designs with which the red glazed pottery is ornamented include a great variety of subjects, most of which are treated with freedom and taste; and many are arranged with much elegance, particularly some of those with scrolls and foliated patterns. The figures of men and deities are usually well drawn, as are those of animals ; and some of the former are evidently copies of statues, such as a representation of Venus, which closely resembles the well-known statue of Venus de' Medici. While many of the designs are merely fantastical, others are not uninstructive as affording representations illustrative of social and religious habits and customs. Mythology is a fertile source of the designs ; and the London examples afford us scenes from the labours of Hercules, and from the story of Actæon and Diana ; Apollo and Daphne ; Bacchus ; the Pygmies and Cranes ; Luna Lucifera in the Biga ; Fortune holding the rudder and cornucopia ; Victory ; Anubis ; Cupids ; Bacchanalian orgies and processions, as in the annexed cut, a

group of Silenus, with Satyrs and Fauns. The central figure is drinking from a horn supplied from a wine-skin held in his left hand. Musicians are often introduced, playing upon the harp and the double flute ; and upon others are sphynges, hippocampi, griffins, tritons,

Two-thirds the actual size.

harpies, and other creations of the imagination.

A very numerous series is composed of representations of flowers, fruits, and foliage, arranged either in scrolls or among other ornaments, or interspersed with cupids and birds. Some have trees from which hang masks, the *oscilla* offered to Bacchus to procure fertility to the vines, as mentioned by Virgil :[1]

> " Et te, Bacche, vocant per carmina læta, tibique
> Oscilla ex alta suspendunt mollia pinu :
> Hinc omnis largo pubescit vinea fetu."

Of the plants introduced upon these vessels, the vine, the ivy, the strawberry, the fern, and the seed-vessels of the thorn or the myrtle, are the most easily recognized ; but probably the botanist may identify others.

Field sports constitute the subject of another numerous series ; and almost equally common are scenes from the sports of the amphitheatre. The first of the subjoined cuts represents the close of a bull-fight : the bestiarius, armed with a shield and a hatchet, is about to despatch the wounded animal. Gladiatorial combats were as favourite a subject with the potter as with the worker in mosaic. The costume and equipments of the combatants are usually well defined, and accord with similar representations in other works of ancient art, and with the descriptions given by classical writers. In the groups here given are shewn a Retiarius and a

Secutor (fig. 2) : the former of these was usually armed with a net as well as a trident, as depicted in the wall-paintings at Pompeii and upon the Bignor pavement. Others, as fig. 3, appear to be Thraces, so called from being armed with the curved swords and small shields used by the Thracians. The legs are protected by greaves and the arms by metal or bands of leather. Others exhibit the crested helmet, the gauntlets, the broad belt or girdle, and the armour upon the left leg only, as described by Juvenal[1] in satirising the debased taste of the Roman ladies :

> "Quale decus rerum, si conjugis auctio fiat,
> Balteus, et manicæ, et cristæ, crurisque sinistri
> Dimidium tegmen."

The retreating gladiator in fig. 4 is armed with a short strait Roman sword ; the pursuer carries a small round shield, and, with the exception of the legs, is without armour. Figs. 5 and 6 represent the close of combats. In the one the gladiator with the oblong shield appears to be wounded and prepared to receive the fatal

[1] Sat., vi, l. 254.

stroke from his antagonist ; in the other the vanquished fighter is imploring the protection of the spectators.

It will be sufficient merely to allude to another class of subjects, which, strange to say, did not seem to be too indelicate to be displayed in the daily service of the domestic board. Such fictile works Pliny[1] mentions and censures : " in poculis libidines cœlare juvit, ac per obscenitates bibere" ; and " vasa adulteriis cœlata".

As before observed, there is a doubt as to whether glazed red pottery was manufactured at Samos : there is no doubt of its having been made abundantly at Arretium, in Italy, one of the towns mentioned by Pliny as celebrated for the finer kind of earthenware. He does not mention the colour ; but Dr. Fabroni, an Italian antiquary, has published engravings[2] of specimens of a beautiful kind of red embossed pottery discovered at Arezzo, the ancient Arretium, the material, colour, and glaze of which are identical with those of the ware discovered at London. The only material difference consists in the superior design and execution of the ornaments, which are usually of the highest school of art. I have found in this country fragments with designs which have been obviously copied from some of those which appear in Dr. Fabroni's plates ; copied and recopied, so that the original designs had been lost sight of, and the copies become degraded ; but their primitive source was easily to be recognized. The potters' stamps of the Arezzo ware are also of a peculiar type ; and one of these, in the form of a human foot, was in Mr. Chaffers's collection of antiquities discovered in London.

The examples which I introduce on the opposite page are of much higher art than any of the other vessels selected for illustration in this volume. They are of great rarity ; these comprising, I believe, almost if not all the specimens which have been found in London ; and I can only refer to one more fragment found in this country ; and that is in the York Museum. Neither is this description of the red glazed pottery common in France or in Germany. The only instance in which I have met with it is in the public museum at Evreux, where I noticed the fragments of a vase so closely resembling that on the opposite page that they appeared to be from the same mould. In all the examples here given the figures, instead of forming part of the body of the ware, as cast in moulds or as stamped by separate matrices upon the vessels, were luted to the surface while the clay was soft by a very delicate process, and retained in this position by the tenacity of the clay and by the glaze. In the fragments, fig. 1, this mode of affixing the figures will be apparent, as the body of the vases, being thinner, has broken away from the stronger masses of clay

[1] "Nat. Hist.," lib. xxxiii, and lib. xiv.
[2] Storia degli antichi vasi fittili Aretini, del. Dott. A. Fabroni, Arezzo, 1840.

1.
Actual size.

2.
Actual size.

3.
Height, 11 inches.

which formed the figures. These figures are in high relief, and are cut with great skill and effect. The lower fragment in fig. 1 has belonged to a distinct vase from that to which the upper fragment was an ornament; and fig. 2 was appended to a third. Further examples will be found in figs. 5, 11, 13, and 15, pl. xxix; and in the beautiful figure of Cupid, engraved in the *Catalogue of the Museum of London Antiquities,* fig. 2, pl. vii.

It appears, then, that there are two very distinct kinds of red glazed pottery. The superior description we are warranted in referring, if not wholly to Arretium as the place of manufactory, at least to some part of Italy. There will be now no doubt of our being equally justified in assigning the more abundant varieties, such, in fact, as have been erroneously called "Samian," to Gaul and Germany. Long since, before I had access to any evidence beyond the nomenclature of the potters' stamps, I concluded that this pottery was manufactured in the north of Europe; and discoveries in France and Germany have fully justified that opinion and confirmed its correctness. In the first volume of the *Collectanea Antiqua* I have discussed the question somewhat fully; but on the present occasion it may be desirable to go partly over the ground again, recapitulating the main arguments with a few additional observations.

In no instance have we ever found any vessel of the red glazed pottery in the kilns discovered in this country or among the unquestionable products of those kilns. In the neighbourhood of Colchester have been dug up, among other Roman remains, paterae which in form resemble some of the common kinds of the red glazed ware; but in form alone: the material is imperfectly tempered, and has a whitish hue, with a thin coating of black carbonaceous matter. The potters who made these paterae had evidently taken the red glazed as models for form and for stamping their names across the centre; but they either did not attempt to imitate the body and the colour, or they failed in the effort.[1]

The vessels found in England, in France, and in Germany, are identical in every respect; not only in the material of which they are made, and in the colour, but also in the forms, and even in the designs with which they are ornamented. Moreover, the potters' names upon the vessels discovered in England, in so many instances agree with those upon the continental ware, even in the most minute details of the stamps, that it is evident the vessels so marked, though found so far apart, were made by the same persons. A complete London list of potters' names will be given in the following pages, and also a list of those collected at Douai, in France, which will suffice to prove the common origin.

---

[1] Some of the paterae are figured in the "Collectanea Antiqua,", vol. ii, p. 35.

At Rheinzabern,[1] situated between Spire and Lauterbourg, towards the French frontier, upon the site of the *Tabernæ* of the Roman itineraries, several hundreds of fragments of the red glazed pottery, as well as entire vessels, have been exhumed; and with them were their moulds, proving that at this locality an extensive manufactory was established. In every respect, most of the engraved specimens are identical with those found in London. The author of the illustrated description of the pottery, M. Schweighæuser, has also published[2] a plan of a kiln found near the village of Heiligenberg, in the valley of the Bruche, about three miles from Mutzig, where, he states, several kilns had been formerly disinterred. Near the furnace were a large quantity of fragments of the red pottery; and a small lump of clay prepared for making the ware, but not yet subjected to the fire: its colour was not of so deep a red as that of the baked vases. Upwards of sixteen moulds for the vessels, ornamented with bas-reliefs, were discovered. With a single exception, they were adapted for casting the vessels in one piece, the contraction of the clay during desiccation sufficing to disengage them from the moulds. The construction of these kilns, as well as of those at Rheinzabern, is described in M. Brongniart's *Treatise on Pottery*,[3] in which are also recorded discoveries of the remains of kilns at Lezoux, in Auvergne, which supplied one of the dies for impres-

sing the name of the potter, Auster, upon the soft clay. It is shewn in the annexed cut, together with a die for stamping the peculiar patterns which may be noticed upon so many of the vessels forming a frieze above the other ornaments. The name of this potter occurs in the London List, and also that of Cobnertus, one of whose dies, found in France, is preserved in the Sevres museum. Mr. Birch has published[4] a mould of a vase found near Mayence, in the museum of which town, as well as in that of Wiesbaden, are several varieties procured from the neighbouring districts.

It seems, then, to be fully established, that the red glazed pottery was manufactured in Gaul and in Germany, and thence imported into Britain; and that the Arretine vases, and probably those of some other cities in Italy, supplied the arche-

---

[1] "Antiquités de Rheinzabern:" par. J. G. Schweighæuser: Strasbourg, 15 plates, 4to.

[2] "Mémoires de la Société des Antiquaires de France," tome v, pl. li.

[3] "Traité des Arts Céramiques ou des Poteries," etc., Paris, 8vo., 1844.

[4] "History of Ancient Pottery," vol. ii, p. 352.

Half the actual size.

Height, 8 inches; diameter, 8 inches.

Half the actual size.

types. The copies of the original designs, from being repeated by successive generations of potters, became more and more inferior to the originals ; but still capable of being traced to their source, like the barbarous designs upon the latest Roman coins.

The makers' names are usually stamped across the centre of the plain vases, in a slightly concave label. The embossed vessels are not so frequently impressed ; and when the names do occur, they are chiefly upon the exterior surface, in long narrow labels slightly raised. In a few instances they occur in disjointed parts among the ornaments. In one instance, the potter, Frontinus, has used two different forms, OF.FRONTINI, in the centre, and upon the exterior, in another type and incuse, FRONTINI. In a very few instances the names occur in circular stamps. The formulæ used were O, or OF, or OFFIC, for *officina*; M for *manu*; and F, or FE, or FEC, for *fecit*. In one instance, the potter has used the stamp of an oculist, intended for one of his eye ointments.[1] The letters are frequently ligatured, as in the first two of the annexed examples, PATERNVLI, and MEDETI.M.

The double I (II) is very often used for E, as AIISTIVI for AESTIVI, and SIIXTVS for SEXTVS ; and other peculiarities will be noticed in an examination of the list. To the philological interest which this long array of potters' names excites, is attached considerable ethnological importance. Many of the names are obviously and purely those of Gauls ; while others seem derived from a mixture of races, Among those of a more marked Gaulish origin are, Beliniccus, Bonoxus, Cobnertus, Dago, Dagodubnus, Dagomarus, Divicatus, Durinx, Suobnedo, Tasconus, and Tascillus ; while such names as Aquitanus and Senonus were probably derived from localities in Gaul ; and others will suggest names still in use in France. Occasionally a female would seem to have exercised the trade of a potter, as we may infer from the names Tascilla and Vertecisa.

[1] "Catalogue of the Museum of London Antiquities collected by C. R. S.," p. 47.

Anubis.

Winged genius.

POTTERS' MARKS ON THE RED WARE TERMED SAMIAN DISCOVERED IN LONDON.

A.	ALIVS. F	ATILIAN. OF	BIO. FECIT
ABALANIS	AMABIVS	ATILIANVS. F.	BISENE...
OF. ABALI	AMANDO	ATTICI. M	BLAESI
OF. ABARI	AMARILIS. F.[1]	AVCELIA. F	BOINICCI. M
ABIANI	AMATOR	AVGVSTALIS	BONOXVS. F
ABILI. M	AMATORIS	AVGVSTINVS	BORILLI. M
ACCILINVS. F	AMMIVS. F	AVLIVS. F	BORILLI. OF
A. C. E. R. O	AMONVS.	AVSTRI. M	BORILLI. OFFIC
ACVRIO. F	ANNLOS. F[2]	AVSTRI. OF	BORVSI. FE
ACVTVS	ANVNI. M	AVSTVS. F.	BOVTI. M
ADIVTORI	A. POL. AVSTI	AVENTINI. M	BRACKILLO
ADVOCISI. OF	APOLAVCIR	AVITI. M	BRICCI
AELIANI. M	OF. APRILIS	AVITOS OF	BRICC. M
AEQVIR. F	OF. APRIS	AVITVS	BRITAENII
ÆQVR. F	OF. APRO	B.	BVRDO. F
AESTIVI. M	APRONIS	BALBINVS. F	BVRDONIS. OF
AIISTIVI. M	AQVIINVS	BANOLVCCI	BVTRIV
AISTIVI. M	AQVIT	BASSI	C.
AETERNI. M	AGVIT	OF. BASSI	CABIAN
AGEDILLI.	OF. AGVITA	OF. BASSICO	CACAS. M
AGEEDILLVS. F	OF. AQVITANI	BELINICCI	CACILANTRO
AGILLITO	ARACI MA	BELINICCI. M	CADDIRON
OF. ALBAN	ARDAC	BELINICCVS. F	CAI. M. S.
OF. ALBANI	ARGO. F.	BENNICI. M	CAIVS. F.
ALBANI. M.	ARICI. M	BENNICI. M	CALENVS. F
ALBILLI. M.	ARICI. MA	BIGA. FEC	CALETI. M
ALBINI. MA	ARRO	BILLICI	OF. CAI. IVI.
ALBVCI	ASCILLI. M	BILLIC. OF	CAI. M. S.
ALBVCIANI	ASIATICI. M	OFIC. BILICANI?	T. CALIXA
ALBVS. FE	ATILIANI.M	OFIC. BILICAT.	CALMVA. B.

[1] Probably *Amabilis.*   [2] *Annius F.?*

CALVI. M

OF. CAL

OF. CALVI

CALVINI. M.

CAMBVS. F

CAMPANO

CAMTI. M

CANAI. M

CAN. PATR

CANRVCATI

CAPAS

CAPRASIAS. FE

CAPRASIVS

CARANI

CARANI. F

OF. CARAN

CARANT

CARANTINI. M

CARETI. M

CARBONIS. M

OF. CARI

CARINVS

CARO

CARVSSA

CASSIA. OF

CASSIVS. F

CASTVS

CASTVS. F

CASVRIVS. F

CATASEXTVS. F

CATIANVS

CATVCI

CATVLII

CAVPI...FECI

OF. CE

OF. CEI

CELSIANI. F

L. C. CELSI. O

CELSINVS

CELTAS. FC

CENSORI

CENSORINI

OF. CENSO

OF. CERA

CEREA

CERIALIS

CERIAL. M

CERTVS. F

CETI

CHRESI. M

CIAMAT. F

CINNAMI

CINTIRIO. M

CINTVAGENI

CINT. VGENT

CIN. T. VSSA

CINTVSMI. M

CINTVSMIX

CINTVSMV.

CINTVSMVS. F

CIRRI. M

CIRRVS. FEC

CIVPPI. M

CLEMENS

COBNERTI.M

COBNERTVS

COCCII. M

COCCILLI. M

COCVRNV. F

COCVRO

COCVRO. F

COLLO. F

COLON

COMITIALIS

COMPRIN. F

COMPRINNI. M

CONGI. M[1]

CONSTANS. F

CONSTAS. F

COSAXTIS. F

COSIA. F

COSI. R...

COSIRVFIN

F. L. COS. V.

COSMI. M

COTTO. F

OF. COTTO

CRACIS. M

CRACIS. S. M

CRACISA. F

CRACVNA. F

CRANI

CRASSIACVS. F

CRECIRO. OFI

OF. CREM

OF. CRES

OF. CRESI

M. CRESTI

M. CRESTI. O

OF. CRESTIC

CRIMVS. FE

CROBRO. F

CRVCVRO

CVCALI. M

CVCCILLI. M

CVNI. IA. F

D.

DAGO

DAGODVBNVS. F

DAGOMARVS

DAGOMARVS. F

DAGOMARVS. FE

DACOIMNVS. F

DAMINI. M

DAMONVS

DAVICI. M.

DECMI. M

DECVMINI. M

DIGNVS.

DIOGNATO

DIVICATI. M

DIVICATVS

DIVICI. M

DIVIX

DIVIXI

DIVIXTVL

DOCALI. M

DOCCIVS. F

DOIICCI

DOLIC?

DOMETOS. F

DOMINCI

DOMINICI

DOMITIANVS. F

DOMITVS

DONATVS

DONNA. M

DONNAVC

DONTIONI

DOVIICCVS

DOVIIICCVS

DRAVCVS. F

DVRINX

[1] CONDI. M ?

E.
ELVILLI
EPPA
ERICI. M
EROR
ERRIMI
ETVS. F

F.
OF. FAGE
FALENDI. O
FELIX. F
FELIXS. F
FELICIO. O
OF FELICIS
FELICIONIS
O. FELMA
FESTVS. F
FIR. .
O. FIRMONIS
FIVI. M
FRONTINVS
FRONTINI
O. FRONTI
OF. FRONTINI

G.
GABRVS. F
GAIVS. F
GALRINVS. F
GEMINI. M
GENIALIS. FECI
GENITOR. F
G.E.N.I.T.O.R.F
GENIV.
GERMANI. OF

GERMANVS
OFF. GER
GLVPEL M
GONDI. M
GRACCHVS
GRANANI
GRANI
GRANIANI

H.
HABILIS. F
HELI...VS.FI.FE
HELL...S. FEC
HIBI ..

I.
IABI
IABVS FE
IANVARI. OP
IASSO. F
ICMCRIMO. F
IGINI. MA
ILLIANI. M
ILLIOMRIN
IMANN.
INPRINTV. F
IOENALIS
IOVANTI
ISABINI. F
OF. IVCVN
IVENALIS. MA
IVSTI. MA
OF. IVSTI

K.
KALENDI. O[1]

L.
OF. LABIONIS
LALLI. MA
LANCIV...
LATINIAN. F
LATINIANVS
LATINVS
LIBERIVS
LIBERTVS
LIBERTI. M
OF. LICINI
LICINILVS
LICINVS. F
OF. LICINI
OF. LICINIAN
LICNVS
LILTANI. M ?
LINIVSMIX[2]
LOCCO. F
LOGIRN. M
LOLLIVS. F
LOSSA
LVCANVS
LVCANVS. F
LVCANTVS. F
OF. LVCCEI
LVPEL. M
LVPI. M
LVPINI. M

LVPPA
LVTAEVS
LVTAEVS. FEC.
LVTAFVS

M.
MACCAIVS. F
MACCIVS. F
MACILLI. M
MACIRVS
MACRI. M
MACRINVI
MACRINVS
MACRIANI. M
MAGNVS. F.
MAIANVS
M. AIORI. M
MAIORIS
MALLI. M
MALLIACI
MALLIACI. M
MALLICI. M
MALLVRO. F
MANDVIL. M
OF. MANNA
Q. MAR. F
MARCELLI. M
MARCIILLI. M
MARCELLINI. M
MARCI
MARCI. F
MARCI. MA
MARCI. O
MARINI. M
MARITVS. M

[1] This may be FALENDI.O.

[2] CINTVSMIX?

MAROILLI. M

MARSVS. FECI

MARTANI. M

MARTIALIS. FEC

MARTINI. M

MARTINV

MARTINVS. F

MARTII. O

MARTIVS

MASCVLVS. F

MATERNINVS

MATERNNI. M

OF. MATE

MATRIANI

MATVCENVS

MATVRN

MAXIMI

MAXMII. M

MAXMINI

MEMORIS. M

MERCA

MERCAO

MERCATOR

MERCATOR. M

MEDETI. M

METHILLVS

METTL. M

MICCIO

MICCIONIS. M

MIDL M

OF. MINI

MINVLL M

MINVS. FE

MINVS. O

MINVTIVS. F

OF. MO

OF. MODESTI

OF. MOE

O. MOM

OF. MONTANI

OF. MONTI

OF. MONTO

MOSSI. M

MOXIVS

OF. MVRRA

OF. MVBRANI

MVXTVLI. M

MVX. TVLLI. M.

MVXIVIII. M¹

N.

NAMILI

NAMILIANI

NATALIS

O. NATIVI

OF. NEM

NEPOTIS

NERT. M

NERTVS

OF. NERI

NEQVREC

NICEPHOR

NICEPHOR. F

OF. NI

OF. NIGRI

OF. NIGRIAN

NIGRINI

OF. NITORI

NOBILIANI. M

NVMIDI. M

IVL. NVMIDI

O.

ONATIVI (?)

OPPRIN (?)

OPTATI. M

OSBI. MA

P.

PASSENI

PASSI. F

OF. PASSIENI

OF. PASSIENVS

O. PAS. F (?)

PAZZENI

PAVLIVS. F

PAVLI. M

PAVLIANI. M

PAVLLI. M

PAVLLVS. F

PATER. F

PATERATI. OF

PATERCLINI. OF

PATRCILINI

PATRCIINI

PATERCLOS. FEC

PATERCLVS. F

PATERIRANVS. FIT

PP. PATERMI

PATERNI

PATERNI. OF

PATERNVLI

PATIIRNV

PATNA. FEC

PATNI. FEC

PATRICI. M

C. AN. PATR

OF. PATRC

OF. PATRICI

OF. PATRVCI

PECVLIAR. F

PECVLIARIS. F

PERE...²

PERPET

PERRVS. F

PERVS

PERVS. FE

PITVRICI. M

OF. POLIO

OF. POLLIO

OF. PONTEI

OF. PONTHEI

PONTI. OFFIC

POTIACI

POTITINI. M

POTITIANI. M

PRID. FEC

PRI.IMO

PRIMANI

PRIMVLI

PRIMVL. PATER

OFIC. PRIM

OF. PRIMVL

PRISCINI. M

OF. PRM

PRIVATI. M

PROBI. OF

PROBVS. F

OF. PVDEN

PVRINX

PVTRI. M

Q.

QVADRATI

QVADRATVS

¹ Probably *Mustulli M.*, as those preceding.   ² *Peregrinus* most probably.

P

QVARTVS	OF. RVFIN	SENO. M	**T.**
QVARTVS. F	RVFVS. FE	SENONI	TASCONVS. F
QVIETVS. F		SENTRVS. FE	TASCILLA
QVINNO	**S.**	SERRVS	TASCIL. M
QVINTINI. M	SABELLVS	SERVILIS	TAVRI
QVINTINIANI[1]	SABELVI	SEVERI. OF	TAVRIANVS
QV. C	SABIANI	SEVERI. M	TAVRICVS. F
	SABINVS	OF. SEVERI	TEBBIL
R.	OFF. SAB	SEVERINVS. FE	TERRVS
RACVNA. F	SACERVASIII	OF. SEVERPVD	TERCII. M
RAMVLVS	SACERVASIFF	OF. SEVIEMI	TERTI. M
REBVRRI. OF	SACER. VASI. OF	SEXTI. O	TERTIVS
REBVRRIS	SACIANT	SIIXTI. MA	TETTVR
REBVRRVS. F	SABINIANVS. F	SILDATIANI. M	TITTICI
RECMVS	SACIRAPO.	SILVANI	TITTILI
REDITI. M	SACREM	SILVIIRI. M	TITTIVS
REGALIS	SACROTI. M	SILVINI	TITVRI. M
REGIŅI. M	SACROT. M. S	SILVINI. F	TITVRONIS
REGINVS. F	SALV. F	SILVINVS. F	TVLLVS. FE
REGVILL	SANTINVOV. O	SILVI. OF	TVRTVNN
REGVLI. M	SANVCIVS. F	C. SILVII	
RIIOGENI. M	SANVILLI. M	SILVI PATRI. O	
RI. IOGENI	SANVITTI. MA	SILVIPATRICI	**V.**
OF. RICIMI	SARENTIV	SINTVRNV...	VALERI
RIPANI	SATERNVS ·	SITVSIRI. M	VASSALI
RIIGNVS	SATERNINI. O	SOLLVS	VECETI. M
RIVICA	SATVRNNI. OF	SOLLVS. F	VEGETI. M
ROFFVS. FEC	SATTO. F	MA. SVETI	VENERAND
ROFFVS. FE	SECANDI. M	SVLPICI	VENICARVS. F
ROIPVS. F	SECVNDINI	SVLPICIANI	VERECVNDI
ROLOGENI. M	SECVNDVS	SVOBNED. OF	VEREDV. M
ROPPVS. FE	SEDATVS. F	SVOBNI. O	VERTECISA. F
ROPVSI. FE	SEDETI. M	SVRIVS	VESPO. F
ROPPIRVI. M	SENI. A. M	SYMPHO	VESPONI
RVFFI. MA	SENICI. O		VEST. M
RVFINI	SENNIVS. F		VESTRI. OF

[1] J. Conyers, Sloane MSS. 958, fol. 105.

OF. VIA	OF. VIRILLI	OF. VITA	Q. VOVO
VICARVS. F	OF. L. C. VIRIL	VITALIS. FE	VNICVS. F
VICTORINVS	VIRONI. OF	VITALIS. M. S. F.	VRNINI
VIDVCOS. F	VIRTHV	VITALIS. M. S. FECIT	
VIIRI. M	VIRTHVS	VITALIS. PP	
VIMPVS	VIRTHVS. FECIT	VITINVS. F	X.
VIRIL	OF. VIRTVTIS	VOSIICVNNVS	XIVI
VIRILIS. F	VITA	Q. VO	XVNX

In the *Collectanea Antiqua* I have given several collections of potters' names from France and Germany, for comparison with those of our own country. I here append, with the same object, those preserved in the museum of Douai.[1]

ACERN.	BOVDOI.	CRESTI OF.	LICACI.
ACOMN	BRARIA M.	CRICVRO.	LOLLI M.
ACVRIO. F	BVRD. OF.	CRICVRO F.	LOTII.
ADVOCISI. O	CAII M (?)	CRISPVS	MACER F.
ALBVCI	CAIAVA. F.	DAC...	MACIIR.
ALBVC. F.	CARATI. M.	DAGOM	MACRINVS.
ANISATVS. F.	CASSI. M.	DEMODES.	MANL.
ANTIANI. OF. C.	CAVINTIO.	DEMOI	MARCELLIN.
ARDACI	CERIALI MA.	DOCRISI	MAR.
ASIATICI	CER. AL. M.	EBVRV	MARINVS M.
ATILIAN. O	CERMNI[2]	EMIN.	MASCI. ILLIO[3]
AVCELI. M.	CIMVO	EXOMN.	MATVRIN.
AVENNIN. M.	CINTIS. M	FELIX.	MEMMNN.
AVILI	C. IN. T. VSSA	FELIX. FE.	MENA.
AVITL. M.	C. IRO. OFF.	FELIXS. FEC.	MERCATO.[4]
OF. BVSSI	COCVRO. F.	IAVENVS.	MIITTI M.
BELINICCI. M.	COMPRINNI.	ILLIXO	MISC. F.
BELSA. ARVI.	COSRV. F	IVLLIINL	MLLIA.
BORIO MA	CRACVNAT.	IVNCIIO.	MMORI[5]
			NAMANI

---

[1] Collected by M. Cahier, and published by M. De Caumont in the "Bulletin Monumental," vol. xxv, p. 11-12.

[2] GERMANI?   [3] MASCELLI.O.?   [4] MERCATOR.   [5] MEMORIS?

.. .S) SE.		PRIMI. M.	SENNIVS F.
	.SEVERPVD	PRISCI M.	SENTRVS. F
	- SILVNL I	PRIS.	SEXTI MA.
	—- VITALIS.	QVARTI M.	SILVANI.
	— VITAL.	REGINI OF.	SILVI.
.IN.I	— VIT.	REDITI M.	SIIVIIR.
.ANIA.L[1]	— VRS.	RENTI	SMMA.
.I.IN.	PATERNVS.	RES.	SVOBN. D. OF.
MO.	PATNA. F.	RVFFI M.	SVRBVR. O.
PATRIC.	PATRICIVS F.	RVFIN.	.SYMPHORI M.
PRIM.	PATRICI	SACIBOM.	TIBERI M.
OFIC. PRI.	PAVLLI M.	SACRILLI.	TITTILI M.
- - PONTI.	PAVI.	SANCI.	TITVRONIS.
OF. PONT	PIINTII. AAM.	SATVRNINI.	TOCCIVS.
OF. SATOR.	PRIMANI.	SDATI M.[2]	VEGETI.
— SECVNDI.	PRIMVS.	SENITA F.	VELOX.

Nearly three-fourths of these names from Douai are to be found in the London list; and among the remaining fourth are some which have been found in other parts of this country. When it is considered that other continental collections contain additional names to be met with in Great Britain, it is conclusive that the importation of the red glazed pottery must have been very great and continuous, probably ceasing only at the breaking up of the Western Empire, when the ceramic shared the general decadence of the arts; the red glazed pottery ceased to be made, and modern attempts to imitate it have resulted in failure.

This record of the red glazed pottery found in London would be incomplete without mention of four or five stamps upon the lower parts of the external surface of embossed vessels in characters which have not been satisfactorily explained.

One of these is here given as closely as possible in fac-simile. There is another in the British Museum, found at Exeter, which Captain Shortt informed me had been interpreted by Mr. Foster, "Daoud, made me"; but I am not in possession of a knowledge of the medium through which the explanation has been made.

Names scratched upon the London pottery, probably by the owners, may also be mentioned. They are: ATTVI—COR. F.—FELICVLA—GEE—IALLV—MOMVVL—PAVLIS—SINX. N.—VIARRA; and IN PAX, possibly used for a funereal purpose and intended for the formula *in pace*.

[1] LICINI MA?   [2] SEDATI M.

CLAY STATUETTES.

Fragments only of small figures, chiefly from six to nine inches in height, in a fine white clay, have hitherto been found in London ; but on the continent they are very abundant ; and scarcely a public museum in France is without a variety of specimens. They were cast in two moulds longitudinally, and then fixed upon a circular pedestal. They served for domestic ornaments, for votive offerings, and as lares and penates in the dwellings of the humbler classes. A very common image in the collections in France represents a female seated suckling an infant, and sometimes two, a personification of Fecundity. Venus Anadyomene is another favourite figure ; but this branch of the Roman potter's art comprised a wide range of mythological subjects, imperial and other personages, and animals. Among a vast number of votive offerings discovered among the ruins of the temple of the Dea Sequana, at the source of the Seine, were busts of infants.[1] The sites of some of the manufactories of these images have been ascertained ; and one has recently been discovered near Moulins which has afforded a variety of objects of

One-third the actual size.
London.

One-third the actual size.
Near Moulins.

[1] " Rapport sur les découvertes faites aux sources de la Seine," par M. H. Baudot,
Paris, 1845.

... the potters' names. Among the figures of deities are
... Venus, Abundance, and Fecundity. In one instance
... decorated shrine.[1] There are also imperial busts, and
... ...ds, some of very superior design and workmanship. The
... this kind of pottery are a novel feature, which adds to the
... ...ntry. By the kindness of M. Tudot, of Moulins, I am enabled
... ...t of some of the London fragments, a perfect analogous figure of
... design, from the collection alluded to.

LAMPS.

All the lamps discovered in London, with a single exception, are of terra-cotta ; and chiefly of small size, three or four inches in length. The greater number are of a reddish clay, quite plain, furnished with a handle, and a single nose for the wick.

Others have two or more noses. When used they were often placed in circular earthen stands with an upright rim and a projection for the nose. A considerable number of the small plain kind were found toge- ther in Southwark ; and as they

Lucerna Mlychnis. Length, 7¼ inches.

resemble others which have been abundantly met with in all parts of London, and also one sketched by Conyers, which was taken from the kiln discovered in St. Paul's churchyard, we may consider them of home manufacture. These are almost invariably without the potters' names. Those of better workmanship and ornamented are probably of continental origin.

Plate xxx represents lamps with six different designs. Fig. 1, is the apotheosis of an emperor: fig. 2, a tragic mask: fig. 3, the fable of the fox and the crow, resembling one which, Mr. Birch states, was found at Naples, and is now in the British Museum.[2] The object which the fox holds in his fore paws in our specimen is indistinct ; but upon that in the British Museum it appears to be a pair of pipes.

[1] An illustrated account of this interesting discovery, supplied by M. Tudot, will appear in current volume of the "Collectanea Antiqua."

[2] "History of Ancient Pottery," vol. ii, p. 286.

Fig. 4 is a mule turning a mill, such as I have given an etching of in the *Collectanea Antiqua*, vol. iv, plate xi, from an example in the museum of Orleans. The same subject occurs upon lamps found at Pompeii. Fig. 5 is a gladiatorial scene ; and fig. 6, Cupid playing with a dog. Other designs are, a lion seizing a stag : a bear and an alligator : a slave kneeling : two masks or heads upon a stand : wreaths of flowers : a negro's head, in the form of which the lamp is made ; and a juggler (*circulator*), showing tricks with an ape, a couple of hoops, and a dog mounting a ladder.[1] The lamps found at Colchester[2] in peculiarity of form closely resemble most of these. They bear, among others, designs representing a caduceus between two cornucopias, as upon consular, early imperial, and British coins : a centaur carrying an amphora : a fuller at work ; and a Victory upon a globe : the upper part of one has a helmet in high relief.

The subjects which exercised the skill and the fancy of the designers for lamps are of great variety, and embrace the wide field of mythology, scenes in private and public life, the animal and vegetable kingdoms, and the regions of imagination. Towards the decline of the Roman empire, the pagan influence is partly supplanted by that of Christianity ; and the monogram of Christ, the Good Shepherd, and other religious symbols, are of frequent occurrence ; but it is remarkable that very rarely, if ever, such allusions appear upon the lamps or upon other descriptions of pottery found so far north as Britain. Among some interesting examples recently published by Mr. Birch,[3] are a group, of Mercury, Fortune, and Hercules ; and an exhibition, crowding the entire surface of the lamp, of the games of the circus, wherein are four quadrigæ at full gallop, the stalls, the turning posts, and other arrangements of the course, with tiers of seats filled with spectators. One found at Nismes has the busts of the twelve greater gods and goddesses ; and a sacrificing scene upon a flat circular handle.

Lamps are frequently found among the vessels consecrated to funereal purposes : many have been thus found in the ancient cemetery at Colchester which lay by the sides of the highway to Londinium. Among the miscellaneous contents of the stone coffin found at Avisford, in Sussex,[4] were three lamps ; and there was at each angle of the cist a bracket, upon which was a lamp-stand. It was a very universal custom to use lamps in the services of the dead ; and from this custom must have originated the absurd stories about finding in sepulchres lamps still burning. One of the

[1] Mr. Rich has used a similar design, from a terra-cotta lamp, to illustrate the word *circulator*, in his "Illustrated Companion to the Latin Dictionary and Greek Lexicon."
[2] "Collectanea Antiqua," vol. ii, pl. xv.
[3] "History of Ancient Pottery," vol. ii, pp. 282, 288, 290.
[4] "Collectanea Antiqua," vol. i, pl. xliv.

tendencies of ignorance and credulity is to magnify, distort, and mystify ; and to support irrational solutions of what is not easily understood ; of this the excavations of tumuli and graves have afforded curious instances. Sepulchral inscriptions occasionally allude to the custom of offering lighted lamps at the tombs of the departed ; as the following taken from Gruter :[1] " Havc Septima : sit tibi terra levis. Quisque huic tumulo posuit ardente[2] lucernam illius cineres aurea terra tegat." *Adieu, Septima : may the earth lie lightly upon you. Whoever places a burning lamp in this tomb, may a golden soil cover his ashes;* and in another mention is made of—" Cupidines ii cum suis lychnuchis et lucerna Larum :" *two Cupids with their lamp-stands, and the lamp of the Lares.* The burning of lights for the dead is, no doubt, derived from this ancient pagan custom ; and as such was often objected to in the ordinances of the early Christian church.

The use of lamps was not entirely superseded by candles in the middle ages ; and may be found occasionally at the present day towards the south. At Treves I noticed a large quantity, of the classical type, just brought from a manu-factory.

The potters' names upon the lamps found in London are but few : indeed only the following have come within my own observation :—ANTIMETI—ATTIIM. F.—EVCA. EVCARIS—FORTIS—STROBILI.

TILES.

Although the word *tile* (tegula), strictly applied, signifies a *roofing-tile*, yet the term is commonly used as a general term, in contradistinction from *brick*, because bricks, such as our houses are built of, were not made by the Romans : at all events we find nothing resembling them, unless it be those of a small kind before mentioned as used for the herring-bone pavement. Thus, we speak of roof-tiles, bonding-tiles, hypocaust-tiles, flue-tiles, draining-tiles, etc. They are all made of well-tempered clay, usually of a red colour, are extremely hard, and break with an almost vitreous fracture. The durability of the material is solely to be ascribed to the great pains taken to prepare the clay, which, before it was baked, was seasoned by long exposure to the atmosphere ; and the spring and autumn were the seasons selected for baking the tiles.[3] The modern brickmakers do not regard the durability of their bricks so long as they hold together through the present generation : they

---

[1] Tom. ii, p. mcxlviii, No. 17.   [2] For *ardentem.*   [3] Vitruvius, lib. ii, c. 3.

prefer a sandy loam to good clay, as requiring less skill and time to prepare for a
cheap market ; and hence the reason why, while the Roman tiles of fifteen hundred
or of two thousand years are as good as when drawn from the kiln, the modern
bricks will scarcely endure a century ; and many not half that comparatively brief
period. Of the various kinds of Roman tiles an enormous quantity have been found
in London, both perfect and in fragments. Not unfrequently they are met with
in the masonry of early medieval houses, having been taken from Roman buildings
which occupied their sites. In the walls of churches of an early date they are often
to be found ; and in some they are so plentiful as to constitute a striking feature in
the masonry, especially when they are arranged, as is not unfrequently the case, in
the Roman manner. In some of the Colchester churches they are very plentiful, as
well as tiles which resemble the Roman, and which were there manufactured in
the Roman fashion for centuries after the Romans had left Britain.

The roofing-tiles vary in dimensions from fifteen inches by eleven to eighteen
by fourteen inches. They have raised longitudinal edges, and were adapted by
being curved slightly inwards, and by the raised edges being notched at the extremities, to be joined one to another, the narrower end of one tile overlapping the end
of that next to it. The lateral junctions were covered with semi-cylindrical tiles
(*imbrices*). This arrangement will be clearly understood by the engravings which
show a roofing tile detached, and others connected with the imbrices. These tiles
were used for various other pur-
poses. They are often to be found
in the bonding courses of walls ;
and they were used occasionally for carrying off water from
the courts and sides of houses.
Very frequently they formed
the cist for the cinerary urn, the
lining of the grave for the body,
and a roof-shaped covering for
both. In excavating a Roman
tumulus at Rougham, called
Eastlow Hill, Professor Henslow

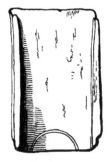

discovered a leaden coffin protected by a chamber of masonry of a most substantial construction, which was roofed with twelve rows of the flanged tiles on
each side, each row composed of four, arranged as shown in the smaller cut above,
but without the semi-cylindrical tiles : the junction lines were covered with mortar,

Q

which embedded the elevated edges.[1] The Roman houses, however, were by no means always roofed with clay tiles. Frequently in the ruins of villas in this country hexagonal tiles of slate and of stone have been found which had been used in the roofings. They were fastened with nails and over-lapped each other in the manner in which they are used in Treves, and probably in other places, at the present day.

The tiles (*lateres*) used chiefly in the walls of the houses in Londinium are about seventeen inches in length by eleven in width, and from an inch to an inch and a half in thickness: this kind appears to be the *Lydion* of Vitruvius and Pliny. The pillars of the hypocaust are formed of tiles varying from seven to nine inches square, which seem to correspond with the *tetradora*; and the larger square tiles which form

the base and the crown of these piles, as well as the flooring of the rooms, we may consider the *bipedales tegulæ*, and the *sesquipedales*; and they also may represent the *pentadora*; but it is very clear from the constantly varying measurements of the Roman tiles that the terms used by the ancient writers when applied to those we discover must be accepted with some latitude, and with allowance for the fluctuation of habits and fashions in different ages.

The flue tiles are also of very various dimensions. The most prevailing patterns are shown in the subjoined cuts :

1.
Length, 16½ inches, width, 4½ inches.

2.
18 inches by 12 inches.

3.
Length, about 18 inches.

[1] The "Bury Post," July 1844.

They are usually of a single channel with lateral apertures for the heated air to pass through; but fig. 2 has a double channel without the side openings. They were
arranged one upon the other and carried up the inner sides of the walls of the rooms to which artificial heat was to be given from the hypocaust; by which means it was easy to regulate the temperature. As in many other matters of antiquity, it is only from a correct knowledge of the objects themselves that passages in ancient writers can be fully understood, as in the younger Pliny's[1] description of a bed chamber in his villa warmed by the hypocaust and the tiles with narrow openings : " Applicitum est cubiculo hypocaustum perexiguum, quod angusta fenestra

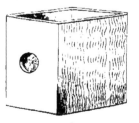

9¾ inches, by 6¾ inches.

suppositum calorem, ut ratio exigit, aut effundit aut retinet."   They were also used for the purposes of the baths, one of which, in the villa at Hartlip, in Kent, was supplied with a seat, the entire length of the bath, formed of these hollow tiles coated with plaister.[2]   A chamber in the castrum at Jublains is yet in part standing with one side of it entirely coated with the tiles.   A portion of the flooring is also

remaining, with indications where the piles of flat tiles stood which gave it the main support. This is, perhaps, one of the most perfect illustrations of the kind that has been preserved.[3]

The flue tiles are often elaborately ornamented, as in the examples from London here introduced. Others, found in Essex and Surrey, have dogs and stags with foliage, and letters which are probably the initials of the maker; and upon some found at Plaxtol, in Kent, the word CAMBRIABANTVS is repeated over the entire side. Although so much pains were bestowed in ornamenting these tiles, the decorative

---

[1] " Epist.," lib. ii, 17.   [2] " Collectanea Antiqua," vol. ii, p. 8.
[3] Ibid., vol. iii, pl. xxvi, and p. 115.

work must have been wholly concealed from view, and seems to have been

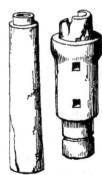

Length, 25 in.   Length, 23 in.

·intended chiefly to attach the mortar more firmly. Occasionally the hollow tiles were used in the place of pillars of stone and of flat tiles, by being set one upon another and filled up with mortar. The substructure of a house thus formed was discovered in Bush Lane, near Cannon Street, from which the example at the top of the preceding page was taken.

A considerable number of draining-tiles have been discovered in various parts of London. In length they range from twelve inches to twenty-five, and are from four to eight inches in diameter. They are usually made to fit into each other, as will be explained by the examples on the side of this page.

To the antiquary the Roman tiles are particularly interesting, and even important, from their being often stamped with the names of the legions and cohorts quartered in the particular localities where they were made, as in the case of those found in London and already noticed (pp. 33-33).

The three legions stationed in Britain are recorded upon the tiles they made ; and even their movements may, to a certain extent, be traced by the same evidence. At Slack, in Yorkshire, supposed to be the Cambodunum of the Itinerary of Antoninus, tiles are found stamped COH. IIII BRE., *Cohors quarta Breucorum,* " the fourth cohort of the Breuci." The Breuci, a people of Pannonia, are not

Fragment of roof-tile.

mentioned in lapidary inscriptions ; but it is probable they may have been the Pannonii who, it appears from rescripts of the time of Trajan, were among the Roman forces in Britain. The British Classiarii are also only recorded upon tiles found on the site of the Portus Lemanis in Kent. At Rodmarton in Gloucestershire, tiles have been found stamped TPFA, TPFC, and TPFP, which apparently are merely the initials of the maker : the last letter of each probably refers to some regulation of the manufactory. Such may be the initials upon fig. 3 in page 114.

GLASS.

THE disposition to underrate the state of the arts among nations of far remote antiquity is as natural as it is general. The works of our contemporaries being before our eyes we are well able to appreciate them and to judge of their peculiar merits and claims by comparison. But when we look retrospectively the means for forming correct judgments become more and more limited as we recede beyond the boundaries of our own times, until they become undiscernible in the obscurity of long past ages. Where the achievements of the ancients are demonstrated by existing and accessible monuments, such as sculptures and architectural remains, popular judgment formed upon such evidence is more just and truthful, simply because the verdict is formed from evidence which is intelligible ; and it is solely in respect to the more perishable products of certain arts that the more erroneous opinions have been formed and adopted, until slowly overturned by testimony long hidden and unsuspected. Among the arts of the ancients none have been less understood, until recently, than that of glass-making ; and the reason must be sufficiently obvious, when the proverbial brittleness of the material has been the main cause why so few examples, until very recent times, were extant, or, rather, were supposed to be so. Whether it be that popular errors are agreeable and people do not like to give them up, or whatever may be the cause, they do not easily die out of themselves and are not readily surrendered by their advocates. Among popular errors, there is none more remarkable than that which has so long prevailed respecting the antiquity of glass making, and the facts which confute misrepresentations and correct mistakes on the subject. It is rather singular, moreover, that people generally well informed, and even many of antiquarian tastes and learning, have fallen into the common belief ; and while apparently interested in the question, and even while discussing it, have not taken the slightest steps to make themselves acquainted with the discoveries which have been made and the conclusions which have naturally resulted from them. For it is almost solely from discoveries that we are enabled to estimate the proficiency of the ancients in this as in some other arts ; and it is further remarkable that graves and the sites of tombs and sepulchres have contributed some of the best and most perfect examples. The celebrated Portland vase was taken from a tomb ; and to the custom of burying

glass vessels with the dead we owe the preservation of most of those of Greek and
Roman origin which are to be found in public and private collections to a far greater
extent than is generally imagined.   The great natural catastrophe which entombed
Herculaneum and Pompeii has tended to preserve many exquisite works of art
which are never found perfect in the ruins of cities destroyed by the hand of man :
in Pompeii was exhumed the glass amphora now in the Naples museum, which
rivals the Portland vase ;[1] and evinces conception and skill such as have never yet
been attained by the most accomplished modern glass makers.   It is probably
owing to the cessation of the custom of interring glass vessels with the dead, that
for many centuries the history of glass-making is almost unillustrated, except by
window glass and treatises chiefly describing the processes in use for colouring, and
painting upon glass for windows.   The Saxon and Frankish graves have supplied
a copious and unsuspected store of glass drinking cups, which prove that in the
north of Europe the art of glass-making had survived the decline of the Roman
empire ; but it is in the succeeding ages, from about the tenth to the fifteenth
century, that the best collections fail to supply examples ; or, if a few exist, they do
not admit of being classified with certainty.   As the arts generally were further
removed from Roman influence, decadence followed ; but it is questionable if many
which are supposed to have been lost, were ever entirely extinguished.   The
treatises of Eraclius and Theophilus[2] (of the tenth and eleventh centuries), prove
how much had been preserved by the clergy, the sole inheritors of the artistic
mysteries of their Roman predecessors.

   To convey a full insight into the state of glass-making among the Greeks and
Romans would demand a volume of itself, with illustrations to almost every page ;
for various kinds of vessels are not only remarkable for their peculiar and generally
elegant forms, but also for their beautiful and combined colours.   Reference to the
chief antiquarian works of the present day is indispensable ; because, as yet, in no
one publication, has it been proved possible, on account of the expense of coloured
representations, to do perfect justice to the wide range of the subject.   In this
volume it will only be attempted to give a notion of some of the more uncommon
kinds of Roman glass discovered in London.   They are, unfortunately, mostly
fragmentary ; but their rarity will preclude their being likely to be met with in
accessible antiquarian or artistic publications.

   No vestiges of the furnaces of Roman glass-makers have been met with in

[1] It is engraved in colours in Mr. Apsley
Pellatt's " Curiosities of Glass Making."
[2] See the " Translation of Theophilus " by
Mr. Hendrie; and Mrs. Merrifield's " Original
Treatises on the Arts of Painting in Oil, on Glass,
etc."

this country. Pliny[1] states that in his time the art of glass-making had spread throughout the Gaulish provinces and Spain. Among the numerous inscriptions which throw considerable light upon the commercial state of Lugdunum in Gaul (now Lyons), is one to the memory of a glass-maker (*opifex artis vitreæ*),[2] named Julius Alexander, a native of Africa and a citizen of Carthage. From his age, seventy-five years, his numerous children and grandchildren, whose names are also recorded, it may be inferred that he had exercised his profession at Lugdunum for a considerable period of time. The inscription is important as confirming this statement of Pliny; and it will also be noted that this glass-worker came from one of the regions which ancient writers concur in speaking of as distinguished for their trade in glass. The abundance of Roman glass, and its great beauty and variety, must strike every one who visits the museums in France, the greater portion of which may be considered of home manufacture.[3] One of the earliest historical notices of glass subsequent to the Roman period shows that Gaul retained the eminence she had acquired in the manufacture of glass. Bede[4] states that (in the latter half of the seventh century) Benedict Biscop, Abbot of Wearmouth, wishing to glaze the windows of the church he had built, and not being able to get workers of glass in Britain, procured them from France; and that they executed the special work for which they came over, and instructed the English (Saxons) in the art of making glass for windows and for other purposes. The latter half of the seventh century is close upon the limits assigned to the most recent of the Anglo-Saxon and Frankish graves which have yielded such a variety of elegant and curious glass drinking cups; indeed it may be that some may be quite as late or later. The testimony of Bede must therefore be considered of weight on the side of France, as the primary place of manufacture of the glass used by the early Anglo-Saxons.

Window glass, from this statement of Bede, would appear to have been common in France in the seventh century; and, doubtless, long anterior, as it is expressly mentioned by earlier ecclesiastical writers, as used in church windows. Classical authors, although they often speak of glass, its origin, the various purposes to which

[1] "Nat. Hist.," lib. xxxvi, cap. xxvi.
[2] The orthography of this inscription is remarkable for its incorrectness; as, *Alexsadri* for *Alexandri; Carthaginesi* for *Carthaginensi; omini* for *homini; vitriæ* for *vitria; anos* for *annos; sene* for *sine*, etc.
[3] Plates i and ii, vol. i, "Collectanea Antiqua," are devoted to examples in the Boulogne Museum. The table of the Society of Antiquaries of London, a few years since, was covered with very beautiful glass vessels from Nismes, of which, unfortunately, a few examples only are engraved in the "Archæologia," vol. xxxiv, pl. vii, and p. 70. Fig. 2 of this plate is, however, worthy of particular notice, as it affords a perfect example of the form of the rare bowls, of which coloured fragments are given in plates xxxi and xxxii of this volume.
[4] "Opera Historica," 1722, fol., p. 295 *et seq.*

it was applied, and the perfection to which it had attained, do not refer expressly to its use in windows; probably not because it was not so used, but because windows, especially external ones, did not form so important a feature in the architecture of the buildings of the ancients, as in those of the middle ages, and of modern times. Seneca,[1] in saying that in his time a person seemed poor and mean, unless the walls of his house shone with large and precious orbs (mirrors), and unless his chamber was covered with glass, may have intended to include the glass of windows, as well as that which was used as a more costly decoration than marble for the walls of the dwellings of the rich and luxurious. A passage, however, in Lactantius,[2] who lived in the reign of Constantine, is decisive upon this point, for he speaks of windows of *glass*, and of *lapis specularis*, a transparent talc, which was probably more commonly used for this purpose. But what is yet more conclusive on this point is the fact that both glass and transparent talc have been discovered in the window-frames of houses in Pompeii.[3]

Among the Roman glass discovered in London, are several fragments of a flat and semi-transparent kind, with a greenish hue, which have every appearance of having been used as window-glass. At first, I was inclined to think they may have belonged to the large square vessels which must have been commonly used for domestic purposes; but a close examination, and a comparison with the fragments of such vessels, proved them to have been fabricated for some other object, which there is now every reason to believe was that of window glazing. These fragments were procured from among the debris of houses, which strengthens our convictions that there can be but little doubt of their being veritable pieces of window-glass. Similar fragments have been found in the rooms of Roman villas;[4] and Mr. Wright reports that some of a particularly marked character, suggesting their inapplicability to any other purpose, have been recently discovered in the excavations now making at Wroxeter, upon the site of the Roman Uriconium.

The rarer kinds of Roman glass found in London have belonged chiefly to bowls or wide-mouth cups. One of a pale green colour, has been ornamented in relief, with a representation of the sports of the circus. With this should be compared

---

[1] Pauper sibi videtur ac sordidus, nisi parietes magnis et preciosis orbibus refulserunt, nisi vitro absconditur camera. "Epist." 86.

[2] Verius et manifestius est mentem esse, quæ per oculos ea, quæ sunt opposita, transpiciat quasi per fenestras lucente vitro aut speculari lapide obductas. *De Opificio Dei*.

[3] This fact seems perfectly well authenticated.

Mr. Apsley Pellatt cites an authority which seems unquestionable: "Curiosities of Glass-making." p. 6.

[4] One is etched in plate ix, volume ii, "Collectanea Antiqua," from the villa at Hartlip, in Kent. The edges of two sides of it, where unbroken, are rounded, for fitting into a frame.

the embossed cup found in the Roman villa at Hartlip ;[1] and another of the

London specimens with figures
which has formed the lower
part of a cup, apparently
from the same, or a very
similar, mould. It is covered
with figures of gladiators, with
their names, and chariot races.

Equally rare are the ornamental bosses, all the vessels to
which they belong having long
since disappeared ; the bosses

Actual size.

themselves owing their preservation to the extra thickness of the glass. From examples in foreign collections the vessels appear to have been of an oval shape, with

a long neck and a protruding
mouth. They had a single handle
reaching from the centre, either
to the mouth or to the lower part
of the neck : at the lower extremity of the handle was affixed
the boss. Those here introduced
are in transparent green glass.
Caylus, who engraved some in
his *Recueil d'Antiquité*, mistook

them for ornaments of the dress. A still rarer variety, found in Leadenhall Street,
and now in the collection of Lord Londesborough, is engraved in pl. xxxi, fig. 5.
This is in a dark blue glass streaked with opaque white, a near approach to which in
colours is the fragment, fig. 11, pl. xxxii. Another variety, in opaque white, is the
handle of a small vase with a boss representing a lion's head.

The form of the basins, imperfectly shown by the fragments, fig. 2, pl. xxxi,
figs. 1, 2, 3, 4, 5, 6, 8, pl. xxxii, and by the wood-cut at the top of the next page, will
be understood by that of an example discovered at Nismes, on the site of a Roman
cemetery. They have projecting pillars on the outside, the interior being quite smooth.
The pillars, Mr. Apsley Pellatt tells us, " were formed partly by moulding, and partly
by rapid rotation, increasing the projection on the principle of centrifugal force."[2]
Among the " curiosities" of the valuable little work published by Mr. Pellatt, there

[1] "Col. Ant.," vol. ii, p. 17.   [2] " Curiosities of Glass Making," pp. 10 and 105.

R

is nothing more curious or remarkable than the information he gives respecting

Actual size.

Niames.
One quarter the actual size.

the patent taken out by the late Mr. James Green for pillar moulding, which is considered one of the greatest triumphs of modern improvements in glass making, and is now extensively used for a variety of vessels for the table and the toilet, as well as for decorative purposes. The patent had been worked for some years under the full belief that it was entirely a modern invention, until Mr. Pellatt recognised in the fragments represented in this volume evidence of the antiquity of the supposed modern invention. It will be seen by the plates xxxi and xxxii that these bowls were of a variety of colours, simple and compound. To the examples here given are to be added others found in London and on the continent, which increase the variety. Some are of a deep semi-transparent blue, when held to the light; but under other points of view they seem to be of a dark copper colour: others are in an opaque variegated glass of dark iron red, with shades of brown, black, and yellow, and a tinge of green: a further variety is of pink, thickly streaked with yellow and white; and one is of a fine transparent olive.

A few years ago some remarkable glass vessels were found in a Roman sepulchral interment between Hellange and Zouftgen, in the Grand Duchy of Luxembourg.[1] Two, of a purple colour, were similar in form to those found in London: others, also ribbed, were somewhat deeper and not so wide. The latter were of a greenish white streaked with grey; and brown with opaque white. Another was a tall, narrow-necked vase, with a circular mouth and two handles, formed of a transparent blue spotted with opaque white, similar to fig. 11, pl. xxxii. With these and various other objects was a circular glass bowl, perfectly plain, composed of at least six colours, blue, rose, yellow, transparent white, opaque white, and

[1] "Publications de la Société pour la recherche et la conservation des Monuments Historiques, année 1853;" Luxembourg, 1854.

purple. The entire surface of the bowl is divided into four rectangular triangles by two bands of rose colour and opaque white, crossing each other : at the point of intersection, in the centre of the bowl, is a purple square with five pellets in opaque white placed in quincunx. The four divisions are filled with bands of different colours, one of which, perhaps the most remarkable, is of transparent white with incrustations of spiral tubes of opaque white, as in Venetian glass. In Great Britain but few examples even of fragments of the ribbed bowls have been discovered ; and perfect specimens are still more rarely to be met with. One, in transparent bluish green glass, is in the possession of Mr.

Joseph Clarke, F.S.A.[1] It was found in a funereal deposit at Takeley, in Essex, placed in a patera of the red glazed pottery, together with three middle brass coins of Vespasian, which, as they had not suffered by circulation, give an approximate date to the interment ; and show that at this comparatively early period choice works in glass were

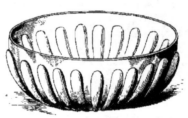

Depth, 3 inches: across the mouth, 6 inches.

imported into Britain. Another, very similar, was found among the extraordinary sepulchral remains excavated by the late Mr. Inskip, near Shefford, in Bedfordshire, with other elegant and rare glass vessels, among which is a blue bottle with narrow neck and handle, ornamented with very narrow ribs ; and an amber-coloured vase, with ribbed globular body and wide mouth.[2]

In pl. xxxii, figs. 7, 9, 10, 11, are fragments which have formed parts of bowls or vases of a peculiar compound glass, which was produced by mixing small coloured beads or particles of glass with masses of fused glass of various colours : indeed the whole of the specimens in this plate are of this class, with the exception of figs. 1 and 4, which are of a simple and semi-transparent blue. A far more difficult manipulatory process is indicated in one of the three fragments of a flat glass, one-sixth of an inch thick, which were obtained from among the ruins of a Roman house near Great Tower Street. The filaments of coloured glass which are worked into the dark ground are arranged so as to form a regular pattern. The whole was then fused and cut into plates at right angles, so that all the

[1] By the kindness of Mr. Clarke I am enabled to give an engraving of this bowl.

[2] Engraved in colours in the publications of the Cambridge Antiquarian Society. See also the "Graphic and Historical Illustrator," pp. 343 and 378.

R 2

sections would present the design on both sides in proportion to the depth of
the filaments and beads. The delicacy of the work, and the skill required in
the manipulation, may be conceived from the fragment here represented ; but a

perfect estimation of the elegance and beauty of
the glass and of the combination of the colours
can only be obtained by an inspection of the
originals, now in the British Museum. A slight
oxidation prevents the peculiarities from being
at first sight fully appreciated ; but this could
be removed by a polisher, and then the full
extent of the colours could be estimated.

Among other remarkable examples of Roman
glass found in London may be particularised the
drinking cup, pl. xxxi, fig. 7, in colourless glass,
three inches and a half in height, and covered
with a pattern formed of incuse hexagons : a
drinking cup, also in white glass, with a pattern

Actual size.

of incuse ovals and hexagons ; and a fragment of a globular cup of white glass
entirely covered with a net-work pattern.

Glass was also used for personal ornaments such as beads, studs, and armlets ;
and for imitations of gems. Examples of beads will be found in pl. xxxi ; and also
two of the smaller ampullæ, used for unguents and perfumes.

PERSONAL ORNAMENTS; AND IMPLEMENTS OF THE TOILET.

THE jewels and personal ornaments of the Anglo-Saxons which have survived to the present day are of a far more costly and elegant description, and also more varied, than those of the Romano-Britons. The reason is that the former owe their preservation to the seclusion of the cemeteries in which they were deposited, as well as to the general custom of burying with the body the more valuable ornaments of the deceased. Thus many a Saxon burial-place of very limited extent has supplied more striking and costly objects of personal costume than most of the sites of flourishing Roman towns ; and the tumuli of Kingston Down, in Kent, of Chessel Down, in the Isle of Wight, and other remote localities, have, in this department of our national antiquities, exceeded in richness all that remains of the decorations of the inhabitants of the populous and wealthy Londinium.

The fibulæ are among the most conspicuous of the ornaments discovered in London ; but they are such only as were commonly worn, and convey no notion of the more complex and expensive kinds worn by the wealthier classes, the character of which is represented by the circular jewelled Saxon brooches. All of the latter show more or less a Roman influence ; and they better illustrate the rich fibulæ frequently mentioned by ancient writers, than the numerous varieties in brass which are to be met with in collections of Roman antiquities. The Emperor Hadrian, Spartian states, wore neither gold in his belt nor gems in his fibulæ.[1] Trebellius Pollio mentions, among the gifts bestowed by Valerian upon Claudius Gothicus, when military tribune, two silver-gilt fibulæ, and a gold fibula with a copper *acus* or pin ;[2] and Vopiscus informs us, that the Emperor Aurelian, among other regulations which he introduced into the Roman army, ordered that the common soldiers should wear golden fibulæ instead of silver, alleging that nature had made gold more plentiful than silver.[3] Golden fibulæ set with precious stones are often mentioned among gifts conferred for military valour or as tokens of affection ; but these are

[1] Sine auro balteum sumeret, sine gemmis fibulas stringeret.—*In Hadriano*, 10.

[2] Fibulas argenteas inauratas duas, fibulam auream cum acu Cyprea unam. — *In Claudio*, 14. The pins of fibulæ in the precious metals were

usually of iron or copper : those discovered in this country are more frequently of iron.

[3] Et ut fibulas aureas gregarii milites haberent, idem primus concessit ; quum antea argenteas habuissent.—*In Aureliano*, 46.

now so rare, that it is difficult to point to examples; and the Saxon fibulæ, as before observed, must be considered as the nearest approach to them.

Most of the Roman fibulæ found in England, in France, and in Germany, are bow-shaped and in bronze, such as figs. 7, 9, 12, 13, 16, and 17 of pl. xxxiii; and of this class there is an almost infinite variety. There is a rare example in the British Museum, in gold, resembling fig. 9 of those found in London, which was dug up at Odiham, in Hampshire. Several of this form have been found in England and in France. One of the most remarkable was discovered in a Roman cemetery at Anières, on the Seine. It is inscribed on one side of the bow, DOMINE MARTI VIVAS; and on the other, VTERE FELIX, indicative of the good wishes of the donor towards the person to whom it had been presented. They were usually worn upon the shoulders by males and upon the breast by females; but upon the effigy of a Roman lady in a sepulchral monument at Mayence, no less than five fibulæ are represented, three in front, upon the bosom, one upon the right shoulder, and one fastening drapery upon the left arm. That upon the breast is of circular shape, precisely like the Anglo-Saxon: the others somewhat resemble the large, flat, silver-gilt varieties.

Figs. 4 and 6 of pl. xxxiii are enamelled. They belong to a class containing a

Actual size.

great variety of forms, and set with coloured glass and pastes. The compartments of fig. 4 are filled with blue and green glass. Others are enamelled with green, blue, yellow, and red; and are not unfrequently in the form of animals as well as of objects of art. One of the London examples is in the form of a sandal, and filled with a deep blue enamel. One found upon the breast of a skeleton, at Great Waldingfield, in Suffolk, and preserved in the collection of Mr. Warren, is of this type, with a red enamel. A fibula of very peculiar shape is shown in the annexed cut. It is in bronze; and bears traces of having been silvered and enamelled with projecting bosses.[1]

The *armillæ* or armlets found in London are chiefly in bronze, although some are in glass, in jet, and in a bituminous shale, an extensive bed of which

Actual size.

[1] Some notion may be obtained of the almost endless variety of form of the Roman fibulæ by consulting the plates of the Publications of the Archæological Society of Luxembourg, 1853-5, which contain a great number discovered upon the site of the castrum at Dalheim.

at Kimmeridge, near Purbeck, was worked by the Romans for the manufacture of beads, rings, armlets, and other articles. A pair of gold armillæ were dug up in Queen Street, Cheapside, in 1839, which are very remarkable. They are of thin gold, fourteen inches in length and nearly an inch in width at the centre, from which they taper towards the ends, each of which is perforated with three holes; and they weigh one hundred and six grains each. The holes were for fastening filets. Many of the ancient armillæ in gold and in silver are often elaborately ornamented and of elegant forms, in volutes or coils, or in a single circle; and both kinds are often chased to represent serpents, as are the London examples given in the subjoined cut; and the beautiful and more characteristic pair in silver, found

In bronze. Three-fourths of the actual size.

in Buckinghamshire, and now in the museum of Mr. Bateman, of Youlgrave.[1] Another, in bronze, from the Thames, is almost a counterpart of one in gold, in the British Museum, found also in this country;[2] and the small specimen in bronze, fig. 3, pl. xxxiii, in form likewise resembles well-known specimens in gold. Fig. 5 of the same plate has, apparently, served either as a bracelet or a necklace. It bears a head in low relief, before which is the Greek φ, probably for φιλία, indicative of its being a keepsake, or love token.

Armillæ are very frequently mentioned by ancient writers, and in inscriptions,

Bead in Jet.

among gifts conferred upon soldiers for distinguished valour. In such cases they are sometimes specified as being in gold, and associated with torques, phaleræ, and golden wreaths or chaplets; and occasionally they appear upon the sculptured effigies of distinguished soldiers, as upon the monument of M. Cælius, at Bonn, who is covered with military decorations.

Jet was used, not only for armillæ, but for a variety of personal ornaments, such as bullæ, beads, hair-pins, and

---

[1] They are engraved in the "Descriptive Catalogue" of his museum, p. 130.

[2] Engraved in the "Archæological Journal," vol. v, p. 341.

necklaces; many of which, found in this country, are of excellent workmanship; and as jet was one of the articles of British commercial
exportation, it is probable they are chiefly of home manufacture.[1]

Fig. 1, pl. xxxiii, is a finger ring, in gold, and fig. 2, a bulla,
or pendent neck ornament in gold.

Hair-pins, of a considerable variety of form, are represented in
plates xxxiv and xxxvi. Those in pl. xxxiv, figs. 14 to 20; 22 to
26; 28 and 29, are in bone. Figs. 14 to 27, pl. xxxvi, are in
bronze. The most curious is fig. 15, pl. xxxiv, in the form of a
hand holding *tabellæ* or writing tablets. Figs. 17, 19, and 20
of the same plate, are ornamented with busts, which time or rough
usage has rendered decapitated. Figs. 26 and 28 are remarkable
for the crosses with which they are surmounted; and figs. 20 and 21,
pl. xxxvi, as appears from examples found in Saxon tumuli, were
worn united by chains like the modern "union pin."[2] Fig. 25, pl.
xxxiv, is tipt with gold; and a small piece of the
same metal was attached to the lower end when it
was received from one of the excavators. Further
examples, in bronze, are given on the sides of this
page. The perfect pin has for its top a circular
coin-like ornament with a bust in armour, and a
cross, to which the attention of the helmeted
personage seems directed. It is not improbable
that this was executed in allusion to the well-
known story of Constantine, seeing a cross in
the sky previous to the battle in which he con-
quered Maxentius. The design and workmanship indicate it
of the fourth or fifth century. Towards the lower extremity
is an eye, intended for a fillet, to aid in securing the hair which
was wound round the pin at the back of the head, precisely as at
the present day in Germany and Italy, where the pin forms a
prominent feature in the head attire, especially when of gold
or silver. The mode of using it is illustrated by an epigram of
Martial:[3]

Actual size.

Actual size.

[1] Solinus, cap. 22.—Bede, "Hist. Eccl.," lib. i, cap. 1.
[2] Two are figured in Mr. Akerman's "Archæological Index," pl. xviii.   [3] Lib. xiv, 24.

Acus aurea.

Tænia ne madidos violet bombycina crines,
Figat acus tortas sustineatque comas.

A very elegant bronze gilt hair-pin, of Roman workmanship, was found in a Saxon grave, at Gilton, near Sandwich.[1] Hair-pins in jet are not unfrequently met with. Some very beautiful examples, found in Germany, are engraved in the publications of the Rhenish Antiquarian Society.[2] In one instance, in our own country, glass hair-pins were found in a Roman grave.[3]

Figs. 14 and 15, pl. xxxiii, are small enamelled bronze boxes on lockets, very much resembling in construction the modern vinaigrettes. They are heart-shaped, circular, and square. One, of a circular form, found at Richborough, is figured in page 84 of the *Antiquities of Richborough, Reculver, and Lymne;* and a heart-shaped variety, found at Reculver, is engraved in pl. vii of the same work. They appear to have been used for perfumes, and to have been worn or carried upon the person. Fig. 8 is a pair of tweezers and a nail cleaner; fig. 10, tweezers and ear pick; and fig. 11, tweezers, ear pick, and nail cleaner combined. Combs, in bone and in wood, have also been found; but usually in a very fragmentary state. In form, they resemble those found in a more perfect state of preservation in Saxon graves.[4] Pieces of metallic mirrors have also been found; but the only perfect one was discovered in the ancient cemetery at Deveril Street, on the Dover road. It is engraved in the *Archæologia,* vol. xxvi, p. 467.

One of the most interesting of the toilette implements of the inhabitants of Londinium, is a strigil or bath-scraper, found upon the site of the New Royal Exchange, and now in the library at Guildhall. It is in bronze, and ten inches and

Strigil. In bronze.

three quarters in length; but the bowl appears to have been broken at the extremity, so that, originally, it was probably from two to three inches longer. Its form will be rendered more intelligible from the engraving which is half the size of the original. A strigil, found at Reculver, and now preserved in the library of

[1] "Collectanea Antiqua,", vol. ii, pl. xxxvii, fig. 3. A silver-gilt Frankish hair-pin is figured in pl. xlix of the same volume.

[2] "Jahrbücher des Vereins von Alterthums- freunden im Rheinlande" xiv, taf. iv-v.

[3] "Collectanea Antiqua," vol. iii, pl. ix.

[4] See "Inventorium Sepulchrale," pl. xiii.

Trinity College, Cambridge,[1] has a bowl, curved considerably more, and, towards the extremity, more shallow, and inclined slightly outwards. The handle of that is solid, and covered with small knobs, to enable it to be held firmly. The London example seems more closely to resemble some found at Pompeii, into the handles of which the hand could be inserted. The two strigils found in the sepulchre of the Great Hill, at Bartlow, in Essex, resemble that found at Reculver ; but the handles are open : it is therefore impossible to say whether this was simply curved inwards, like a sickle, as those of Pompeii, or whether it resembled the others alluded to, which were discovered in this country.

The strigil was employed by the Greeks and Romans in scraping off the perspiration which flowed from the skin in gymnastic exercises, and the impurities loosened by the bath, the edges being lubricated by oil, upon precisely the same principle as the scraper is used at the present day, for the coats of horses, the channel receiving and carrying off the perspiration and the impurities detached by the edge. Its peculiar features are combined in an enigma of the poet Symposius,[2] the solution to which is the strigil itself.

> Rubida, curva, capax, alienis humida guttis,
> Luminibus falsis auri mentita colorem,
> Dedita sudori, modico succumbo labori.

The colour counterfeiting gold is characteristic of the bronze, of which strigils were often made, especially when kept bright by oil and constant use. Equally clear is the description of Apuleius, making one end straight, that it might be held in the hand, and the other end curved and hollow, for the perspiration to flow through.[3] Martial also describes them of curved iron, as fabricated at Pergamus in Asia Minor; and he recommends their use as tending to save the wear and tear of the clothes at the fuller's :[4]

Strigiles.
> "Pergamus has misit, curvo distringere ferro :
> Non tam sæpe teret lintea fullo tibi."

Persius[5] has an allusion to their common use in the bath:

> "I puer, et strigiles Crispini ad balnea defer";

and numerous other passages in ancient writers might be cited in illustration of this useful implement, which might be reproduced at the present day with benefit to the speculator and advantage to personal cleanliness and health.

The application of the strigil was usually allotted to slaves by those who could

---

[1] Engraved in the "Antiquities of Rich-borough, Reculver, and Lymne," pl. vii.

[2] "Poetæ Latini Minores," tom. vi, p. 561.

[3] "Honestam strigileculam, recta fastigiatione clausulæ, flexa tubulatione ligulæ, ut et ipsa in manu capulo moraretur, et sudor ex ea rivulo laberetur." *Floridorum,* lib. ii.

[4] Epig., lib. xiv, 51.

[5] Satyr., v, l. 126.

afford to keep or to pay for them. This is illustrated by an anecdote related of Hadrian.[1] The emperor was accustomed to bathe frequently at the public baths, among the common people, with whom he would freely chat and joke. One day he noticed a veteran soldier whom he knew, rubbing his back and the other parts of his body against some projections of the building, and inquired why he used the marble for a scraper. When the emperor found he had no slave for the purpose, he gave him one, and an allowance to keep him. This liberality of the prince provoked several other old men, shortly after, to exhibit themselves in like manner; but he directed them to be called to him, and then ordered them to rub one another.

The vignette to this section is a bronze enamelled girdle-clasp, nearly four inches in diameter. The enamels are red and yellow. On the under side are two fastenings for attaching it to the girdle at one end, and for a hook on the other. The buckles in bronze do not call for especial notice; but two in bone, not of common occurrence, are given in pl. xxxiv, figs. 9 and 12, half the actual size.

SANDALS.

One portion of the costume of the inhabitants of Londinium has been revealed to us in the most satisfactory of all ways, namely, by examples almost as perfect as when in use, and quite sufficiently so to understand their forms and mode of manufacture. The least perishable part of the human clothing is leather; but under ordinary circumstances it yields to the destructive action of the atmospheric air and moisture: and thus throughout the extensive excavations in London not a particle was found,

[1] Spartian, "In Hadriano," c. 17.

except in certain localities where the air had been excluded. These were the neighbourhood of Lothbury and Prince's-street, the site of the New Royal Exchange, and
the bed of the Thames. The first was in the course of the stream which flowed
from Moorfields, by Walbrook, to the Thames; the second was a pit of great depth;
and both, to a considerable extent, were filled with a moist, tenacious soil, impervious
to the air; and the beds of rivers, from the same cause, are particularly favourable
to the preservation of animal and vegetable as well as metallic substances. Oil
having been applied to the sandals before the water with which they were saturated
had evaporated, the leather is now preserved with much of its original pliability and
general character. We can, then, look upon these sandals as being nearly in the
same condition as when they covered feet which trod the streets of Roman London.;
and probably they are the only specimens extant; for although much has been
written upon the various coverings of the feet of the ancients, the illustrations have
been supplied from representations, and not from existing remains.

A selection from the sandals formerly in my own collection is here given. They
present some of the best preserved forms
and patterns, but by no means shew
the entire variety of the ornamented
open work. They were formed, judging from fig. 3, of four layers of
leather; the outside, or lowermost, being
the thickest, and the innermost the
thinnest; and are, in every instance,
made right and left. These layers are

Fig. 1.
Length, 7 inches; width, 8 inches.

held together, without any appearance of stitching, by nails clenched on the inside
of the sole. The nails have heads rather broad and projecting, and slender strigs
sharply pointed for clenching. On some of the soles they are placed in a single
row round the edge; five rows in the broadest part, and three at the heel: on
others they are still more thickly set. Fig. 3 shews the heads of the nails; but in
some instances they are not quite so
pointed. The upper part of the sandals was formed out of one piece of
leather, the middle making a layer
of the sole and the sides; the entire
upper portions cut or punched into
elegant patterns, and looped to receive strings for drawing them tight

Fig. 2.
Length, 10 inches; width, 3½ inches.

together, and tying over the instep or across the leg. Figs. 1, 2, and 4, will fully explain how this important part of the sandals was made. They were then sewn at the toe and heel, as in fig. 1, or at the heel only, as in fig. 2. Fig. 1, with the exception of one latchet on either side of the fore part, and the lower part of the sole, is perfect. Fig. 2 shews the long loops or latchets of the fore part adapted for lapping over, beyond the centre of the foot, to join the loops on the opposite side, which are much shorter. Fig. 3 has all the layers of the sole quite perfect. It is constructed differently from the others in the upper part; the latchets being intended

to tie over the instep, and not fastened with a thong, like the others. Enough remains of fig. 4 to shew its arrangement and tasteful design.

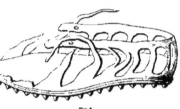

Fig. 3.
Length, 9 inches; width, 3 inches.

Most of the sandals found in London are of small size; the greater number appear to have belonged to youths or women; and many were children's. Those of eleven to thirteen inches in length, we may suppose were men's. Some of very small size were similar in character to the examples described; and all appear to have been nailed. Thus, it is clear, that although Juvenal speaks of the nails in the soldiers' *caliga*,[1] and Pliny[2] compares the scales of a certain kind of fish with its thick and pointed nails, they were by no means confined to the military caliga. The sandals found in London, so far as can be judged from less perfect specimens, seem to resemble those found in other parts of this country. In some of the military stations in the north of Britain, the soles of sandals

Fig. 4.
Length, 11 inches; width, 5½ inches.

thickly studded with nails, have been met with;[3] but, unfortunately, no example is afforded us to judge of the construction of the upper part. The nailed soles, alone, have been also found in sepulchral cists;[4] but with the upper leather entirely

[1] Cum duo crura habes, offendere tot caligatos Millia clavorum.—"Sat." xvi, 24.
[2] Squamis conspicui crebris atque præacutis, cla- vorum caligarum effigie.—*Nat. Hist.*, lib. ix, c. 18.
[3] Dr. Bruce's "Roman Wall," 2nd edit., p. 442, and pl. xviii.
[4] "Col. Ant.," vol. i, pl. xliv.

perished. The close shoes worked with gold found in a Roman cist at Southfleet,[1] in Kent, belong to a very different class of sandals, frequently mentioned by ancient writers as used by wealthy persons of luxurious habits.

Writers on the costume of the ancients, have found a fertile field of discussion in the shoes and boots worn by the Greeks and Romans, and in explaining the various kinds ; but as it seldom came within the objects of historians and poets to describe minutely personal costume, and as terms are sometimes used arbitrarily, the subject has proved to be one of considerable difficulty ; and the caprice of fashion at different periods of time, and other causes, must be taken into account whenever the nomenclature of ancient dress is attempted to be strictly defined and interpreted. By the aid, however, of the representations in various works of ancient art which have come down to us, the terms used to designate the leathern attire of the feet, can be understood with tolerable certainty ; and the sandals found in London, furnish an important addition to other sources of information on this point. The *caliga* was almost essentially military : it is constantly used in reference to the sandal worn by common soldiers, who, from it, were called *caligati*.[2] The *crepida*, on the other hand, was one of the sandals worn by civilians. It was distinguished from the complete close shoe *(calceus)*, by its open work of loops and eyes, through which passed the thong or strap *(amentum)*, for fastening it. Thus Pliny, in telling the anecdote of the shoemaker who criticised one of the paintings of Apelles, says he found fault with the artist for not making enough *ansæ*, or eyes, on the inner side of a man's *crepida*.[3] Caligula, Suetonius states, was so whimsical in his dress, that he would use alternately, the *crepidæ*, the *cothurni* (boots), the soldier's *caligæ*, and the women's *socci* (a loose kind of shoes). Aulus Gellius[4] devotes a chapter to the proper application of the names of certain kinds of shoes, from which we gather, that, shortly after the time of Hadrian (when he wrote), *gallicæ* (probably the origin of our galoshes), *crepidæ*, and *crepidulæ*, were in common use by civilians, and that they correctly belonged to the same class as the *soleæ*, (the most simple and primitive kind), because they left the upper part of the foot almost naked, or bound only with slender straps *(teretibus habenis)* ; contrary to the *calcei*, which were close-fitting, and covered the ankle. In the edict of Diocletian and Maximian, published by Colonel Leake,[5] several sorts of shoes are mentioned, chiefly of two classes, the *caligæ*, and the *soleæ* and *gallicæ*. This valuable document, preserved in an inscription, fixed

[1] "Engraved in "Costume in England," by F. W. Fairholt, p. 30.
[2] *Feruntque a sutore reprehensum, quod in crepidis una intus pauciores fecisset ansas.*— "Hist. Nat.," xxxv, 10.
[3] Suetonius, "Aug.," c. xxv; "Vital.," c. vii.
[4] "Noctes Atticæ," lib. xiii, c. 20.
[5] "Journal of a Tour in Asia Minor," London, 1824; and "Transactions of the Royal Society of Literature," vol. i, 1829.

a maximum of prices throughout the Roman empire ; and it enumerates a vast number of articles of commerce, among which were lasts for two kinds of men's caligæ, and for those of women and children. Then we have the caligæ themselves distinguished, as country caligæ without nails ; military caligæ without nails ; and patrician, senatorial, equestrian, and women's ; this division closes with *campagi*.[1] Then follows a list of various kinds of shoes, made under the head of *soleæ* and *gallicæ*, including single-soled and double-soled countrymen's *gallicæ* ; the same for women ; others of various colours ; and coloured *socci*, or slippers.

From these citations it will be seen there is some little difficulty in saying positively to which class of the Roman shoe those found in London may be referred. While they may not be improperly called *crepidæ*, and probably with more certainty belonged to this class, they seem in some respects to bear affinity to the *caliga* which, from the edict of Diocletian, seemed, under that form, towards the close of the third century, to include a rather wide range of shoes in very general use.   At the same time, it may be noticed that upon the sepulchral monument of a maker of caligæ (*sutor caligarius*) at Milan, there is a representation of a pair of caligæ, which appear to be close-fitting shoes, contrary to what is generally supposed.[2]

It has been observed that in some of the ancient military stations in the north of England, soles of Roman sandals have frequently been found.   In Mr. Mayer's museum is a pair discovered in the moss, near Port Carlisle, on the line of the Roman Wall, at the depth of eight feet.   They are of a very different pattern from those found in London, approaching more to the *calceus* or perfect shoe, covering the heel and toes in close leather ; but open down the front as far as the toes, with long narrow slashes cut on each side.

[1] *Ca(m)pagi militares.* The campagi appear to have been of foreign origin, and more amply furnished with intersecting cords, or network, than the caligæ, as we may infer from a passage in Trebellius Pollio : " Caligas gemmatas annexuit, quum campagos reticulos appellaret."—*In Gallieno*, 16.

[2] Rich's " Illustrated Companion to the Latin Dictionary and Greek Lexicon," p. 101.

IMPLEMENTS AND UTENSILS.

IN pl. xxxv, and in this page, are brought together examples of almost every variety of numerous little implements in steel, in which we recognise the *stilus* or *stylus*, called also *graphium*, used by the Greeks and Romans for writing upon tablets of wood in their ordinary epistolary correspondence. They amount to nearly or quite a hundred; but although so large a number has been found in London, they are elsewhere of the highest rarity, if not altogether unknown; and although from the frequent allusions to the stilus in ancient writers its form and character were sufficiently well understood, there is, as in other matters of antiquity, a complete assurance we are fully comprehending passages in ancient writers, when we look upon the objects themselves, upon a proper conception of which a perfect comprehension of such passages depends. When the poet Horace advises the *stile* to be often turned in order that what is badly or inelegantly written may be amended:—

> " Sæpe stilum vertas, iterum, quæ dignæ legi sint,
> Scripturus :"[1]

the literal meaning is understood when we look upon the stilus itself, with its sharp point for writing, and its flat end for smoothing the incised wax upon the tablet : at the same time we may see clearly the derivation of the modern word *style*, originally restricted to the character of a person's writing, and the expression of writing with *acumen*, or point. With his graphium, or stilus, Suetonius[2] states, Julius Cæsar wounded Cassius; and it will be readily seen that some of these stili, in the hands of a desperate man, could almost serve for daggers : indeed they often were used as weapons; and the name is yet reflected in the Italian *stiletto*.

Actual size.

[1] " Sat.," lib. i, x, 72.   [2] " D. Jul. Cæs.," c. lxxxii.

Symposius, one of the minor Latin poets, has bequeathed us a riddle on the stylus, which will not require an Œdipus to solve :

Graphium sive *stylus.*

"De summo planus, sed non ego planus in imo ;
Versor utrinque manu, diversa et munera fungor ;
Altera pars revocat, quidquid pars altera fecit."[1]

It is obvious the stylus could only be used for certain kinds of writing, or, rather, for writing upon soft substances, such as wax, which would require protection. Wax was commonly employed for this purpose ; and it was applied, when melted, to thin tablets of wood, called *tabellæ,* or *pugillaria,* surrounded by a rim which shielded the waxen surface and prevented friction. Two, or more, of these were joined together by wires or string, bound with a filet or cord and sealed, the outsides being perfectly plain. The apparatus and process of writing a letter are clearly indicated by the following passages in a play of Plautus :

—— "Effer cito stilum, ceram, et tabellas, et linum.

Ch. Cape stilum propere et tabellas tu has tibi. *Mn.* Quid postea?
Ch. Quod jubeo scribito istic. . . .

Mn. Ne interturba: jam imperatum in cera inest."[2]

The tabellæ are also illustrated by specimens yet extant, discovered with the

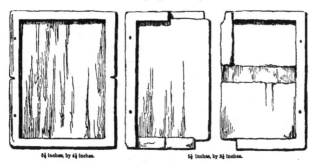

5½ inches, by 4½ inches.   5½ inches, by 3½ inches.

styli, three of which form the annexed cut : that on the extreme left, an outside cover, is indented by the marks of the string which tied it : the other is an inner leaf

---

[1] "Poetæ Latini Minores," tom. vi, p. 478.   [2] "Bacchides," iv, 4, 6, 64, 76, 91.

T

shewn on both sides : they belonged, as their dimensions shew, to separate tabellæ.[1]

Aulus Gellius tells us that in affairs requiring great secresy letters were written upon the wood itself : the pugillaria were then covered with wax, so that if the messenger were intercepted and the letter opened, it would appear quite blank ; but the right owner would understand that by removing the wax he would disclose the epistle.[2]

A wall-painting in Herculaneum gives a representation of a lady holding the tablets in one hand, and a stylus in the other, both resembling the examples in our engravings ; and at Sens, in the collection which supplied the illustration in p. 61, is the sepulchral effigy of a man who, from similar implements of writing which he carries, appears to have been a notary.

The use of the style and wooden tablets was continued through the middle ages down to a comparatively recent time, as may be exemplified by the versification of an anonymous writer of the fourteenth century :

> " Les uns se prennent à escrire
> De greffes en tables de cire ;
> Les autres suivent le coustume
> De fourmer lettres à la plume ;[3]

and Shakspeare making Hamlet exclaim :

> " My tables,—meet it is I set it down.[4]

The long bronze spoons (*ligulæ*) in pl. xxxvi, figs. 2, 4, 8, 9, 10, 11, 12, with narrow bowls and oval or oblong heads, appear to have been used for unguents, and other preparations kept in the long-necked ampullæ and other bottles.   Two of the same kind were in a metal case, with a box of colours and a variety of implements and glass bottles, discovered in the grave of a female painter near Fontenay (Vendée) ;[5] and as the whole of the minor objects clearly appertained to the profession of the defunct, the spoons were doubtless used for extracting liquids from the bottles for mixing and preparing the colours, in which process the oblong terminations were probably also of service.   The stems of some are tastefully ornamented, studded with silver, and inlaid with silver wire.   Another kind of spoon, the *cochleare*, is shewn in fig. 21, pl. xxxiv ; and in figs. 11, 12, 13, pl. xxxvii, the first being in bone, the others in bronze : the bowl of fig. 13 is

---

[1] The former of these is in the Guildhall library ; the latter, in the British Museum.

[2] " Noctes Atticæ," lib. xvii, cap. ix.

[3] Du Cange, " Gloss.," *sub voce* " Graphium."

[4] " Hamlet," Act I, sc. iv.

[5] " Description de la Villa et du Tombeau d'une femme artiste Gallo-Romaine," par B. Fillon, Fontenay, 1849.

constructed with a hinge to fold back upon the handle, the lower part of which is in the figure of a crouching animal. Fig. iv, pl. xxxvii, flat at one end and pointed at the other, seems intended to be used as the others and to combine the fork and spoon, as in eating eggs and shell-fish, explained by Martial :

> " Sum cochleis habilis, sed nec minus utilis ovis,
> Numquid scis potius cur cochleare vocer ?"[1]

One, in silver, found at Reculver,[2] presents a slight variation in form from those here engraved. Connected with the *cochleare*, an old superstition, which, like many others, has survived to our own times, may be mentioned. Pliny, in speaking of spells and incantations, and the remedies by which their evil influences were counteracted, states that the shells of eggs, as soon as the meat was swallowed, were broken by the bowls or pierced by the points of the spoons.[3] At the present day it is a very general habit in many parts of England, particularly in the eastern counties, and probably not confined to the lower orders, to break the bottom of the shell, after the egg is eaten, in order that the witches might not have it to sail in, a popular belief alluded to by Beaumont and Fletcher in their play of *Women Pleased :*

> " The devil should think of purchasing that egg-shell,
> To victual out a witch for the Burmoothes."

The union of the fork with a double point or prong, and the spoon, was also probably of Roman origin, although, as yet, examples have only been found with Saxon remains.[4] Forks were certainly known to the Romans, although but few specimens have come down to us. There are two, of very different pattern, found in London, preserved in the British Museum ; and several are figured in M. Grivaud de la Vincelle's *Arts et Metiers des Anciens,* pl. xxxii.[5]

Actual size.

---

[1] "Epigram.," lib. xiv, 51.

[2] "Antiquities of Richborough, Reculver, and Lymne," pl. vii, fig. 18.

[3] Defigi quidem diris deprecationibus nemo non metuit. Huc pertinet ovorum, ut exorbuerit quisque, calices cochlearumque protinus frangi, aut eosdem cochlearibus perforari.—"Nat. Hist.," lib. xxviii, cap. ii.

[4] "Archæologia," vol. xxvii, pl. xxiv; and "Col. Ant.," vol. iv, pl. xvi.

[5] This work is chiefly founded upon antiquities discovered on the site of a Romano-Gaulish town in the department of the Haute-Marne. Paris, 1819.

T 2

Figs. 17, 18, 19, pl. xxxv; figs. 1, 3, 6, pl. xxxvi, and probably one or two more in those plates, do not come under the particular classes of implements already described. They are such as, it may be conceived, were used for various purposes in the arts. There is also a class of tools which seem more adapted for modelling than for any other purpose. They are all in iron, and, like the styli, almost quite free from rust. They will be understood by the specimen on the side of the previous page.

A rather considerable quantity of small knives form a very remarkable section in the antiquities of London, because they are totally different in form and other peculiarities from any yet published. Those of types well known it has not been thought necessary to engrave on the present occasion. Plate xxxvii, figs. 2, 3, 5, 6, and another slightly varying in pattern, shewn in this page, represent knives in steel with bone handles, and rings for suspension upon the person. From the number which have been found it may be inferred they were such as almost every person carried about with him. Ivory was much used by the higher orders for various domestic implements, including knives; and Juvenal, in contrasting the furniture of his own villa with that of the houses of the more wealthy and luxurious, mentions his bone-handled knives:

"   .   .   Adeo nulla uncia nobis
Est eboris, nec tessellæ, nec calculus ex hac
Materia; quin ipsa manubria cultellorum
Ossea.[1]

Clasp-knives seem, also, to have been not uncommon, if we may judge from some which have been found at Reculver and at Hadstock.[2] The handles of these are of bronze and ornamented with the figures of a dog and a hare. But still more remarkable are the knives, figs. 8 and 9, stamped with the makers' names. The former of these is in excellent preservation, the steel being free from rust, and, with the help of a whetstone, still fit for service. The stamp upon this is OLONDVS.F: upon the other, which, in addition, bears a minute figure of a man, standing, P.PASILI.F.,

Actual size.

---

[1] "Sat.," xi, l. 131.
[2] "Antiquities of Richborough, Reculver, and Lymne," pl. vii, and p. 207.

or P.PASIL.FE. The handle of this knife has been cased with wood, traces of which are still apparent. The handles and blades of the slender knives, such as fig. 14, are wholly of iron. Among other uncommon kinds of knives found in London may be noted one, seven inches in length, and two inches in width at the haft, the blade curved upwards, almost to a semicircle, and adapted for cutting both ways ; and a strait knife, the blade of which resembles that of the table knives of the present day : the handle was encased with bone or wood and ornamented with bronze tubes, forming, when the handle was complete, rosettes along each side, and two at the top, which takes the form of a double semicircle. It is probable that these tubes were filled with enamel; and it is impossible to determine whether this knife is Roman or early Saxon. One very similar was found with Roman and Frankish remains in Germany.[1]

The ordinary implement used by the Romans for sharpening knives was the whetstone (cotis), of which several have been found in London and elsewhere resembling those used at the present day, with a hole at one end of the smaller ones for suspension. The steel was generally considered of more recent invention, until a very perfect one was found in Princes Street. The implement itself is of steel : the handle, in the form of a horse's head springing from leaves of the lotus, is in bronze ; and a brass ring is attached for hanging it to the girdle. It is shewn, of the full size, on the side of this page.

The scissors, or shears, fig. 7, pl. xxxvii, are in iron, with a thin plate of brass to strengthen the handle. The form, that of our sheep-shears, resembles that of shears found in Saxon graves,[2] and with mortuary urns in North Germany ;[3] and also Roman, as represented in a wall-painting at Pompeii and upon a bas-relief at Sens, in France, some of the former being of very small size, the last of large dimensions. A pair of scissors from the Thames, originally nearly or quite fourteen

Actual size.

[1] "Denkmaeler von Castra Vetera und Colonia Trajana, tab. xlvi, No. 7.

[2] "Inventorium Sepulchrale," pl. xv, fig. 20.
"Archæologia," vol. xxxvi, p. 278.

inches in length, is upon the lever principle, like those in common use at the present day. It is in iron, with a square brass plate on each side, the loops of the handle being tipped with brass knobs.

Among the few implements which can positively be identified as used for agricultural purposes, are a weed hook, and a sickle in iron. The latter, found in Southwark, is rather thinner and smaller than those now used. It resembles one found in Pompeii ; and one which I picked up in the river running by the side of the Roman station at Catterick, in Yorkshire, and deposited in the collection of Sir W. Lawson, of Brough Hall. The weed-hook is shown in fig. 3, in the annexed group, together with a bronze fish-hook (fig. 4), from the Thames, and a bucket-

1. 13½ inches wide at bottom.   2. 9½ inches high.
3. 5 inches long.   4. Half the actual size.

handle and large hook, figs. 1 and 2, both in iron. The last two implements were found during the excavations made for Moorgate Street, on the Coleman Street side, near a public house called the Swan's Nest, in a pit or well. This pit was about three feet square, and boarded on every side with narrow planks about two feet in length, and an inch and a half to two inches thick. Towards the bottom this framework was discontinued, and the pit contracted from a square into an oval form. Its entire depth was upwards of thirty feet. It had been carefully planked over with thick boards, and, at first, appeared to contain nothing but the gravelly soil of the district ; but at a considerable depth numerous earthen vessels were found, pre-senting the appearance of having been regularly

packed in the sandy and gravelly soil, which had settled so closely round them that many were broken in being extricated. Some of them are engraved in page 80 of this volume. At the bottom of the pit were found the bucket-handle and the hook, a small red patera, a few fragments of the embossed red pottery, and a small brass coin of Allectus.

Among the various objects found in the gravel pit which in the earlier days of Roman London occupied the site of the New Royal Exchange (see p. 12), were a considerable number of small wooden implements, which had evidently been cut and fashioned upon a certain principle for some purpose connected with the indus-trial arts. I suspected this might be for spinning or weaving ; and the remains of wool still twisted round a few of them convinced me that my conjecture was correct; but, probably, without this evidence of their use, they might have been passed over disregarded. They vary from about six to eight inches in length; but were probably somewhat longer originally, as the ends of most of them are worn or broken off. Their form will be understood by two here represented, one of which has some filaments left by the Roman spinster. They perfectly agree in character with some representations of the Roman *fusus* or spindle, as used with the distaff for twisting or spinning wool and flax into thread by means of the forefinger and thumb. The lower extremity was inserted into a wheel, or whorl (*vorticellum*), formed of stone, bone, or of baked clay. A great number of these whorls have been found in all parts of London. An example of the spindle fully charged will be found in an interesting sculpture at Mayence, which represents a Roman lady seated with balls of wool in her lap and the spindle hanging from her left hand.[1]

Half the actual size.

These traces of the domestic employment of the women in Londinium, are the earliest evidence, from existing remains, of weaving in Britain, which in the course of time, became one of the leading staple manufactures in England. There is early historical evidence of the abundance of sheep, as well as other cattle, goats included; and also of a factory, in which women were employed for weaving, and which was under the imperial jurisdiction, being superintended by a *procurator:* this shews that the establishment was of importance, and formed a prominent part of the revenue of the province. It is probable it furnished a material portion of the woollen clothing of the army in Britain; and that the surplus, (if any), was sold or exported. The "Notitia Dignitatum," gives us this information under the division specifying the public establishments of the western empire confided to the "Comes Sacrarum Largitionum," wherein appears the *Procurator Gynæcii Bentensis in Britannis.* The town which possessed this *gynæcium*, or factory, was *Venta Belgarum*, Winchester, reading, as we are warranted, the word *Bentensis* as *Ventensis.* Winchester, it is well known, was distinguished very early in the middle ages for its manufactory of woollen cloth. The corporation of weavers at London is the earliest

[1] "Collectanea Antiqua," vol. ii, pl. xxx. A representation of a woman spinning, taken from a bas-relief at Rome, which well explains the entire operation, is given in Mr. Yates's "Textrinum Antiquorum;" and still more ancient, as well as medieval examples, will be found in Mr Akerman's paper on the Distaff and the Spindle, in the "Archæ-logia," vol. xxxvii.

[2] The horns and bones of cattle among Roman remains found in London, are chiefly those of sheep, goats, deer, swine, and oxen; of the last, many are of the *bos longifrons*, an extinct species of ox. See "Antiquities of Richborough, Reculver, and Lymne," p. 105-111.

of the civic companies of which records have reached us ; and there is every reason to believe that both were of Roman origin.

Plate xxxviii is devoted to examples of small portable bronze balances, weights, and keys. Examples of the *statera*, or steel-yard used with sliding weights suspended by chains, such as fig. 1. pl. xxiii, and the dog's head in p. 75, have not, so far as I know, been found in London. The specimens of the balance (*libra*) figs. 1, 2, 3, are of the simplest kind, being composed of a beam with a pair of scales, such as figs. 4, 4, which show the two sides of a small, ornamented variety. Fig. 6 is a handle, at the lower part of which is a rivet for the tongue or index, such as appears on figs. 10 and 13, to mark the weight precisely, as in the modern scales, which closely resemble the Roman without any important alteration or improvement. Figs. 10 and 13 are folding balances, examples of which are not so common as the others. A very remarkable small portable balance was found in the Roman villa at Hartlip, in Kent.[1] It has two hinges, one of which also forms a foot or stand when the balance is prepared for weighing, and is constructed precisely upon the same principle as the scales intended for weighing letters sent through the post, or for testing the correct weight of known quantities of precious objects, such as gold coins and jewellery. On the side of this page is the beam of a balance graduated to serve also as a foot measure. The weights, figs. 5, 7, 8, 9, are the two ounce, the ounce, and the half and quarter ounce.

The keys found in London are numerous and of great variety of pattern, as may be conceived from the seventeen different specimens selected for our plate. The exceedingly modern look of some will strike the reader who is not familiar with the character of the keys of the ancients. Modern ingenuity in the construction of locks and keys has achieved but little, if anything, beyond what the inventive genius of the ancients had accomplished, as one of our most eminent locksmiths admitted when he examined these keys and found among them clear evidence that the principle of some of his patent keys was only a revival of what was perfectly understood by the Romans and commonly used in London sixteen or seventeen hundred years ago. Unfortunately the locks have not come down

Actual size.

[1] It is figured in p. 19, vol. ii. of the " Collectanea Antiqua."

to us except in a very mutilated state, from having been made chiefly in iron ; but, so far as their construction can be understood, they resemble the modern.

The bells of the ancients, as is evident from the numerous representations in sculpture as well as from existing remains, present no material difference from those in use at the present day ; and all the purposes for which they were used are also identical. Three varieties, found in London, are given in the annexed cut, the smallest of which is quite perfect and retains its original sharp, clear sound.

Two-thirds of the actual size.

Very many of the remains of antiquity which come before the practical archæologist speak for themselves, and are recognised from an unmistakeable resemblance to their modern representatives, although they themselves may possibly be presented to us for the first time, such as the butcher's steel, and the bronze cock (*epistomium*) of a fountain (fig. 1), found in Philpot Lane ; but there are others which are difficult to be understood from their bearing no particular analogy to anything in use at the present day ; and which have not been found under circumstances which decidedly explain them.

To this class of antiquities belong some implements in iron found in London,

Fig. 1.
Length, 5 inches.

Fig. 2.
Length, 6 inches.

one of which is here represented (fig. 2), and will give a fair notion of their general form, although scarcely two, of a considerable number now recorded as found in different parts of this country and on the continent, are precisely alike. One, of several in the Evreux Museum, is figured in the third volume of the *Collectanea*

U

Antiqua : another, found in repairing the bridge at Blackwater, in Essex, illustrates
a paper by the Rev. E. Cutts, in the first volume of the *Proceedings* of the Essex
Archæological Society ; and M. Namur has published examples found in the Roman
camp at Dalheim, near Luxembourg.[1] They have been found at Stony Stratford,
at Springhead near Gravesend, and at other places in this country ; and at Autun,
Dijon, and other localities in France. The most reasonable explanation that has
been suggested is, that they were used for temporary purposes for the feet of horses
and oxen, either in the case of disease or in journeys where the roads were particularly bad. Supposing they were so used, they were probably lined with leather or
wool and bound round the hoofs and legs with straps. When Catullus (xvii, 25)
speaks of a mule leaving its iron *solea*, or shoe, in the mud :

> " —— In gravi derelinquere cœno,
> Ferream ut soleam tenaci in voragine mula ;"

it is certain he could not have meant a shoe fixed to the foot with nails, but a shoe
not permanently bound on ; and, from the context, one apparently used for soft or
quaggy land. At the present day, in Holland, it is usual to bind long flat iron
shoes to the horses' feet. They are fastened with a strap of leather ; and are somewhat in the form of an ordinary horse-shoe, but much longer and wider ; and, did
we not know they are commonly used, would seem almost as unsuitable as the
iron shoes under consideration. Singular as the shape of these iron implements
certainly is, we shall probably not be wrong in explaining them as veritable iron
horse-shoes such as Catullus refers to ; and it is worthy of notice, that at Springhead, where some were dug up, at the same time and place, horse-shoes of the
modern fashion were also found, as well as other objects in iron. It has been often
asserted that the shoeing of horses with nails was not practised by the Greeks and
Romans ; and that when ancient writers speak of horse-shoeing, they mean shoes
strapped on and not nailed. This is one of those minor points in archæology so
difficult to decide upon without some unquestionable evidence. Horse-shoes with
holes for nails have been found in London with Roman remains ; and likewise at
Springhead : they have also been found, in one instance at least, with Roman and
Saxon Remains in a cemetery used by people of both nations. But what seems to
settle the question is a Roman bas-relief discovered at Vaicon, and now preserved
in the museum of Avignon, in which is represented a carriage drawn by two mules.
With that attention to minute details often observable upon Roman works of
art, the sculptor has introduced the nails of the shoe upon one of the feet of the

---

[1] "Publications of the Luxembourg Archæological Society" for the year 1855,
pl. iii, figs. 21, 24.

mules, in a manner so marked as to leave no doubt of his intention to show the animal shod with an iron-nailed shoe made to the shape of the foot precisely as those now in use.

In some of our plates have been introduced a few small implements which, from their resemblance to well-known objects in use at the present day, cannot fail to be understood. Such are fig. 18, pl. xxxiv ; fig. 19, pl. xxxv ; figs. 3, 6, 7, and 13, pl. xxxvi ; and fig. 1, pl. xxxvii. The shoemaker's awl, here delineated, is

Length, 5¼ inches.

remarkably well preserved : it is of wood, bound, at the lower part, with bronze, the point being of iron. Figs. 6 and 8, pl. xxxiv, are perforated pieces of bone, such as are often found in the ruins of Roman buildings. From their constant recurrence it may be considered that they appertained to the machinery of some domestic art ; and it has been conjectured that they were used in weaving. Figs. 1, 3, and 7, of the same plate, are pommels of daggers. The dice, fig. 10, is identical with those now in use. Fig. 13 is a pipe or fife, made from the shin bone of a bird. It is engraved half the actual size, as are all in pl. xxxiv, from fig. 1 to 13 inclusive. The remainder are of the full size.

In the course of removing the foundations of walls in various parts of the City, many fragments of mill-stones have been found. They are chiefly of two kinds; for turning with the hand, and for working with mules and asses. Some of the latter, had been originally of large size ; but, having been broken up for building purposes, in no instance has it been possible to restore them so as to complete either of the two stones of which a Roman mill was formed. The fragments, however, were quite sufficient, from comparison with perfect mills found at Pompeii and elsewhere, to shew clearly that they were made precisely upon the same principle. The lower stone, forming the base, is of a conical shape, with a pivot upon the top. The upper stone, somewhat in shape of an hour-glass, fits over the conical part of the lower, and has a socket which fits its pivot ; while its other hollow cone received the corn which passed through perforations at the bottom, and was ground between the two stones, the upper one rapidly revolving by means of a handle or bar inserted in each side. For an excellent illustration of the larger kind of hand-mill

I must refer to one at Orléans, etched in the fourth volume of the *Collectanea Antiqua.* The design upon the lamp in fig. 4, pl. xxx, of the *Roman London* illustration, gives a good idea of their general character, so far as it can be shewn upon so small a scale. They varied in diameter from two to five feet : those of London were chiefly of an intermediate size. They were imported into Britain from Germany, where they were manufactured in large quantities from the dark porous lava of the Eifel and the neighbourhood of Andernach on the Rhine. Wherever in England or in France we meet with these hand-mills, they are invariably of this volcanic stone, which explains the term *puniceæ* applied to them by Ovid :[1]

"Et quæ puniceas versat asella rotas."

The only perfect hand-millstone found in London belonged to the smaller

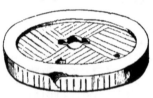

16 inches in diameter : 3½ inches thick.

The above stone reversed.

description of mills. It was worked with an iron handle upon the lower stone, which was convex, with an iron pivot at apex.

Smaller hand-mills, made from the native conglomerate called pudding-stone, are also found in all parts of the country where Roman buildings existed.[2] In some parts of Greece this primitive mode of grinding corn, mentioned by Homer, is still commonly used; and in Scotland and Wales, not long since, the quern usually formed part of the peasant's domestic utensils. At Abbeville, in France, I noticed one in use. It was fixed in a stand, and turned by an iron handle, just as the smaller ancient hand-mills were worked,

which it resembles in form.[3]

The cuts on the opposite page represent a small stone mortar (fig. 1), used for grinding and preparing colours for painting ; a stone mortar (fig. 3), for pounding hard substances ; and a fragment of a shallow clay vessel (fig. 2), which appears to have been used, like fig. 1, for some purpose connected with the fine arts. Fig. 1 is stained red, apparently with an oxide of lead ; and its use is further identified

[1] "Fasti," vi, 318.
[2] See "Col. Ant.," vol. i, pl. xli, for some
found at Springhead, in Kent.
[3] "It is figured in p. 130, vol. iii, "Col. Ant."

from its resemblance to a mortar for colours found with the implements and utensils of a painter before referred to (p. 138). To the same class of utensils we

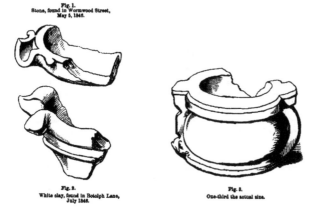

Fig. 1.
Stone, found in Wormwood Street,
May 5, 1846.

Fig. 2.
White clay, found in Botolph Lane,
July 1846.

Fig. 3.
One-third the actual size.

may assign the vessel in pale red terra-cotta, which supplies the last wood-cut to our volume.

7¼ in. in diameter; 4 in. in height.

COINS.

MEDALLIONS IN BRASS.

MARCUS AURELIUS.

Obv. M. ANTONINVS. AVG. TR. P...... Laureated head to the right: bust in armour. *Rev.* .... COS. III. In the exergue, ... RM. (*Vict. Germ.*), Victory, in a quadriga   1

FAUSTINA, THE YOUNGER.

Obr. FAVSTINA AVGVSTA. Head of Faustina to the left. *Rev.* VENVS. Venus, standing between a Cupid and a Triton   -   -   -   -   -   -   -   1

Plate xxxix, *fig.* 2.

COMMODUS.

Obv. M. COMMODVS ANTONINVS PIVS FELIX AVG. BRIT. Laureated head to the right. *Rev.* COS. VI. P. P., in the exergue. The Sun driving a chariot of four horses upon clouds: below, a figure representing the Earth, reclining, with the right arm raised, and holding in the left a cornucopia   -   -   -   -   -   -   1

Plate xxxix, *fig.* 1.

CARACALLA.

Obv. AVT. K. M. AVP. CEOVIP. ANTΩNHIOC. (*sic*) AVT. Head, radiated and laureated, to the right. *Rev.* ΠEPINΘIΩN NEΩKOPΩN. A galley of four rowers with sail set   -   -   1
This coin, struck at Perinthus, in Thrace, is the only Greek coin, so far as I am aware, discovered in London. It was found within the precincts of the Tower.

TRAJANUS DECIUS.

A much corroded piece.

GOLD.

MAXIMIANUS.

Obv. MAXIMIANVS P. F. AVG. Laureated head to the right. *Rev.* SALVS. AVGGG. The goddess Salus standing and feeding a serpent from a patera. In the exergue, M.L. (*Moneta Londinensis*).
This exceeding rare coin, although bearing the name and effigies of Maximian, was, unquestionably, struck by Carausius, together with numerous other coins, chiefly in brass, with a view to imply that his usurpation of the imperial titles and power was sanctioned by Diocletian and Maximian, who, with himself, are indicated by the three G's, denoting *three* Augusti. This coin is engraved in the *Numismatic Chronicle*, vol. xiv, p. 159. (1) ——[1] COMITATVS AVGG. Diocletian and Maximian on horseback   2

[1] The reverses only, except in a few cases, are here given.

CRISPUS.

GAVDIVM ROMANORVM. In the exergue, ALAMANNIA. A female captive, seated by a trophy - 1

SILVER.

CONSULAR.

Considia.—C. CONSIDI. Victory in a quadriga (1). *Fonteia.*—Cupid on a goat. *Furia.*—
L. FVRI CN. F. Curule chair and fasces (1). *Petronia.*—CAESAR AVGVSTVS SIGN. RECE
A kneeling figure presenting a standard - - - - - - 4
  Two of these are of base silver. There are also a few specimens of family denarii in
  lead, some of which bear evident marks of having been plated.

CNAEIUS POMPEIUS.

..... CLAS ET ORAE MARIT. EX. S. C. Anapius and Amphinomus; Neptune standing between
  them - - - - - - - - - 1

JULIUS.

L. Æ.... BVCA. Venus standing, holding the hasta - - - - - 1

MARCVS ANTONIVS.

LEG.... Military standard. (Much worn) - - - - - - - 1

AUGUSTUS.

AVGVSTI. A candelabrum within a wreath - - - - - - 1

NERO.

IVPITER CVSTOS. Jupiter seated. (Much defaced) - - - - - 1

VITELLIUS.

CONCORDIA P. R. A female figure, seated - - - - - - 2

VESPASIANUS.

IVDAEA (1). AVGVR. TRI. POT. Sacrificial vessels (1) - - - - 2

TITUS.

PRINCIPI IVVENTVTIS. Standard, with two hands joined across it - - - 1

DOMITIANUS.

Titles. Pallas, standing - - - - - - - - 1

NERVA.

COS. III. PATER. PATRIAE. Sacrificial instruments (1). CONCORDIA EXERCITVVM. Hands
  joined across a standard, upon the prow of a galley (1) - - - 2

TRAJANUS.

S. P. Q. R. OPTIMO PRINCIPI. Victory inscribing, on a shield affixed to a tree, DACICA (1).
  Titles: type of Felicity (1) - - - - - - - 2

HADRIANUS.

AEGYPTOS (1). ALEXANDRIA (1). RESTITVTORI HISPANIAE (1). Titles, with common types (2) 5

ANTONINUS PIUS.

APOLLINI AVGVSTO (1). FORTVNA OPSEQVENS (*sic*) (1). TRANQVILLITAS AVG. (1). Titles (2) 5

152   ILLUSTRATIONS OF ROMAN LONDON.

Marcus Aurelius.
FELIC. AVG. IMP. VI. COS. III.   Mercury (1).   Titles; Victory on a globe, holding a wreath and
trophy (1).   *Idem;* common types (2)   -   -   -   -   -   -   4

Faustina, the Younger.
FECVND. AVGVSTAE.   A female figure with four children (1).   IVNO (1)   -   -   -   2

Verus.
Titles; Soldier marching with trophy and a victory (1).   A warrior standing (1).   Type of
Equity (1)   -   -   -   -   -   -   -   -   -   3

Lucilla.
VESTA (1).   IVNO REGINA (1)   -   -   -   -   -   -   -   2

Commodus.
Titles; Victory marching; and other common types   -   -   -   -   -   3

Clodius Albinus.
(Miner. Pa)CIF. COS. II.   Minerva standing.

Severus.
PROVID. DEORVM (2).   VICTORIAE AVGG. FEL. (1).   BONAE SPEI (1).   LEG. XI. CL. TR. P. COS.
Eagle between two standards (1).   FVNDATOR PACIS. (1).   ARAB. ADIAB. (1).   SALVS
AVGVSTI (1).   Titles (1)   -   -   -   -   -   -   -   9

Julia Domna.
MATER AVGG.   Cybele in a car, drawn by four lions (1).   HILARITAS (1).   CERERI. FRVGIF. (1)
FELICITAS (2).   IVNO REGINA (1).   SAECVLI FELICITAS (1).   DIANA LVCIFERA (3)   -   10

Caracalla.
SPEI PERPETVAE (1).   PROVIDENTIA DEORVM (1).   FELICITAS AVGG (1).   Titles; Trophy,
and captives (2)   -   -   -   -   -   -   -   -   5

Plautilla.
CONCORDIAE.   Female figure seated (1).   CONCORDIAE AETERNAE.   Caracalla and Plautilla
joining hands (1)   -   -   -   -   -   -   -   -   2

Geta.
PRINCIPI IVVENTVTIS.   A military figure and a trophy (1).   PIETAS AVGG.   Sacrificial vessels (1)   2

Macrinus.
SALVS PVBLICA.   Type of Salus seated (1).   PM. TR. P. II. COS. P. P.   The Emperor seated (1)   2

Aquilia Severa.
CONCORDIA.   Female figure standing to the left before an altar; in the right hand, a patera; in
the left, a cornucopia; in the field, a star   -   -   -   -   -   -   1

Julia Soaemias.
VENVS CAELESTIS.   Venus standing; in the field, a star   -   -   -   -   1

Julia Maesa.
FECVNDITAS AVG.   Female figure with a cornucopia: at her feet, a child

JULIA MAMMAEA.

IVNO CONSERVATRIX (1). VENVS VICTRIX (1). VESTA (1)   -   -   -   -   3

SEVERUS ALEXANDER.

SPES PVBLICA (2). P.M.TR.P. II. COS. P.P. Type of Salus (2). Titles; the Sun standing (1)   5

MAXIMINUS.

PAX AVGVSTI. Type of Peace (1). FIDES MILITVM. A female, standing, holding two standards   2

BALBINUS.

PROVIDENTIA DEORVM. Type of Providence   -   -   -   -   -   1

GORDIANUS THE THIRD.

PAX AVGVSTI (1). VIRTVTI AVGVSTI. Hercules (2)   -   -   -   -   3

SALONINA.

PIETAS AVGG. A female figure, holding the hasta; before her, two children   -   1

TREBONIANVS GALLUS.

VOTIS DECENNALIBVS, in a wreath (1). IVNO MARTIALIS; Juno seated (1)   -   2

VOLUSIANUS.

VIRTVS AVGG. Mars standing   -   -   -   -   -   -   1

VALERIANUS.

PIETAS AVGG. Two figures joining hands (1). APOLLINI CONSERVAT (1). Others in billon, badly preserved   -   -   -   -   -   6

VALERIANUS JUNIOR.

PIETAS AVGG. Sacrificial vessels (1). CONSECRATIO (2)   -   -   -   3

SALONINA.

PIETAS AVGG. A female with two children (1). IVNO VICTRIX. Juno, standing (1)   -   2

POSTUMUS.

DIANAE LVCIFERAE. Diana standing. *Plate* xli, *fig.* 13   -   -   -   1

CARAVSIUS.

VBERITAS AVG. A woman milking a cow   -   -   -   -   1

JULIANUS.

VOT. X. MVLT. XX. in a wreath   -   -   -   -   1

URBS ROMA.

Half a denarius of the type of the well-known little brass coin of the time of Constantine, with a helmeted female head and VRBS ROMA; on the reverse, the Wolf and Twins; in the exergue, L. C. It is remarkable for being in silver. Halves of denarii of Caracalla and of Otacilia, in good silver, occur among coins found in the Thames at London. They appear to have been intentionally divided, probably for the convenience of commerce   -   -   -   -   -   -   -   1

VALENS.

VRBS ROMA: in the exergue, TRPS. A personification of Rome, seated   -   -   1

THEODOSIUS.

CONCORDIA AVGGG. A woman wearing a turreted crown, seated; her foot on the prow of a galley   1

ANCIENT FORGED DENARII.

By far the larger portion of denarii found in the Thames consist of lead and brass plated with silver. Of lead, we have specimens of the Consular, Mark Antony (*reverse*, Octavius), Plautilla, Vespasian, Nerva, Trajan, Plotina, Hadrian, Pius (*reverse*, Aurelius), Aurelius, Faustina, Verus, Lucilla, Didius Julianus, Caracalla, Geta, and Severus Alexander. There are, also, two leaden consular quinarii. Of brass, plated with silver, there are examples of Augustus, Trajan, Hadrian, Aurelius, Severus, Julia Domna, and Soaemias. Of Severus and Julia Domna they are very abundant.

An interesting proof of the immense quantity of base silver coins sent into the provinces was afforded by a discovery made in the City. During excavations for the Club House at the corner of Swithin's Lane, several hundred denarii were found, packed in layers in some enclosing material, such as a box, which had perished. They are of iron, plated with silver so ingeniously, that, when new, it must have been difficult to detect the fraud. The plating is so thick that, in some instances, the iron has entirely vanished while the casing of the coin remains. Many of the coins, from the oxidation of the iron, are conglomerated into large masses; others are still well preserved. An examination of nearly a hundred of the latter shows that the latest is of Claudius, in whose reign it may be considered they were sent into Britain. They consist of Family and Imperial denarii, the latter being of Mark Antony, Augustus, Tiberius, Caligula, and Claudius.

LARGE BRASS.

NERO.

Rev. ROMA. Rome, seated (1). ANNONA AVGVSTI CERES. As the reverse of *fig.* 4, *pl.* xxxix (1). DECVRSIO. Two horsemen. *Plate* xxxix, *fig.* 3.   -   -   -   -   -   3

GALBA.

ROMA, across the field (1). The other quite illegible   -   -   -   -   -   2

VESPASIANUS.

ROMA (1). . . . COS. DES. II. CAESAR. DOMIT. COS. DES. Titus and Domitian standing. *Plate* xxxix, *fig.* 6. ANNONA AVGVSTI CERES. Ceres seated before an altar; in front of her a female carrying a cornucopia: in the back ground the prow of a galley. *Plate* xxxix, *fig.* 4   -   -   -   -   -   -   -   -   -

TITUS.

ROMA (1). ANNONA AVG. (1). IVDAEA CAPTA. S. C. A female seated in a dejected attitude upon arms beneath a palm tree; behind her a bearded male figure with his hands bound. *Plate* xxxix, *fig.* 5   -   -   -   -   -   -   -   3

DOMITIANUS.

GERMANIA. (Capta) (1). IOVI VICTORI, *Plate* xxxix, *fig.* 8 (3). S. C. The Emperor sacrificing at an altar before a temple (1). S. C. The Emperor standing with his right foot on a recumbent river god. *Plate* xxxix, *fig.* 7. S. C. The Emperor and two

soldiers, with one of whom he is joining hands over an altar (1).   s. c.   The Emperor
crowned by Victory   -   -   -   -   -   -   -   8

NERVA.

FORTVNA AVGVST (1).   CONCORDIA EXERCITVVM.   Two hands joined across a standard (1)   -   2

TRAJANUS.

s. p. q. r. OPTIMO PRINCIPI; in exergue: ARAB. ADQ. (6).   s. p. q. r. &c.   The Emperor on
horseback, riding over a prostrate figure (2).   s. p. q. r. &c.   Various types of Peace,
Abundance, &c. (8).   FORTVNAE REDVCI (3).   A badly preserved specimen of the
Rex Parthis Datus type (1)   -   -   -   -   -   -   20

HADRIANUS.

RESTITVTORI ORBIS TERRARVM (1).   NEP. RED. (1).   FORTVNA (2).   FELICITATI AVG. COS.
III. P. P.   A galley with five rowers (1).   CONCORDIA EXERCITVVM (2).   FELICITAS
AVG. (2).   MONETA AVGVSTI (1).   Titles, with types of Peace, Abundance, &c.   -   20

SABINA.

Illegible; and much worn   -   -   -   -   -   -   -   2

ANTONINUS PIUS.

SALVS (2).   VOTA SVSCEPTA DECENN. IIII. COS. III. (2).   ANNONA AVG. (3).   ROMA (2).   s. c.
Type of Hope (1).   APOLLINI AVGVSTO (1).   ABVNDANTIA AVG. (2).   CONCORDIA
EXERCITVVM (2).   TR. POT. COS. IIII.   Wolf and Twins (1).   FELICITAS AVG. (2).
PIETATI AVG. (2).   INDVLGENTIA AVG. (1).   CONSECRATIO (1).   COS. IIII.   s. c.   The
Emperor in a quadriga (1).   With titles; and the more common types (17)   -   -   40

FAUSTINA THE ELDER.

s. c.   A figure standing (1).   AVGVSTA (2).   AETERNITAS (2)   -   -   -   -   5

MARCUS AURELIUS.

VICT. AVG. &c.   Titles: in the exergue, RELIG. AVG.   Temple of Mercury (1).   IMP. VI. COS. III.
Victory inscribing on a shield VIC. GER. (2).   SALVTI AVGVSTOR. &c. (2).   Titles: A
figure with four standards (1).   GERMANIA SVBACTA (1).   VOTA SVSCEPTA DECEN-
NALIVM (2).   s. c.   Pallas throwing a javelin (1).   Titles: Victory inscribing on a
shield VIC. PAR. (2).   Idem, in the exergue, FORT. RED. (2).   VICT. GERM. IMP. VI.
COS. III. in a wreath (1).   Titles: chiefly common types (25)   -   -   -   40

FAUSTINA THE YOUNGER.

CERES; a female figure, standing (1).   Defaced (3)   -   -   -   -   -   -   4

VERUS.

CONCORDIA AVGVSTOR. TR. P. COS. II. (1).   Titles: a captive beneath a trophy (2).   Idem,
Victory standing; beside her, a shield inscribed VICT. PART. suspended from a tree (1).
REX. ARMEN. DAT.   Verus and attendants, upon an estrade; below, the king of
Armenia, standing (1)   -   -   -   -   -   -   -   5

LUCILLA.

IVNO (1).   VENVS (1).   Reverses illegible (3)   -   -   -   -   -   5

CONCORDIA AVGGG. A wom— ... and crowned by Victory (1). - - - - 7

By far '

... *Claudius Albinus.*

... badly preserved - - - - 1

Severus.

... *standing (1).* A female figure seated, holding a patera (1) 2

Julia Domna.

... Defaced (2) - - - - 3

Venus, standing (1). *Geta.*

Fortune seated - - - - 2

PORT. RED. TR. P. III. COS. II. P. P. *Julia Mammaea.*

VENVS VICTRIX. *(1).* FECVNDITAS AVGVSTAE. Type of Fecundity - - - 2

Gordianus.

SECVRITAS AVG. Security personified, seated - - - 1

Postumus.

Victory, marching. Much detrited - - - - 1

MIDDLE BRASS.

Augustus.

.. M. MACCILIVS TVLLVS III. VIR. A. A. A. F. F. (1). PROVIDENT (1). ROM. ET AVG. Altar (1) 3

Agrippa.

S. C. Neptune, standing - - - - 10

Claudius.

S. C. Pallas (30). CERES AVGVSTA. *Plate* xl, *fig.* 1 —LIBERTAS AVGVSTA (3). CONSTANTIAE AVGVSTI (1). There are also a number of the first type of very barbarous work, apparently provincial imitations - - - - 40

Antonia.

TI. CLAVDIVS CAESAR. P. M. TR. P. IMP. - - - - 4

Germanicvs.

C. CAESAR AVG. GERMANICVS PON. M. TR. P. POT. In the field, S. C. - - 1

Caligvla.

Legend gone. Vesta, seated - - - - 1

Nero.

PACE P. R., etc. Temple of Janus (1). S. C. Triumphal arch (1). MAC. AVG., the *Macellum,* or market-house, at Rome. *Plate* xl, *fig.* 2 (1). ARA PACIS (4). GENIO AVGVSTI (3). PONTIF. MAX. &c. Nero playing on a harp (3). SECVRITAS AVG. (20). VICTORIA AVG. (20). S. C. Victory with a shield inscribed S. P. Q. R. (30) - - - 83

VESPASIANUS.

s. c. Temple of six columns (1). ROMA (2). FELICITAS AVG. (4). FIDES PVBLICA (8). VICTORIA AVGVSTI (6). s. c. Victory with shield inscribed s. p. q. r. (12). PROVIDENT. Altar (16). PAX. AVG. (20). PAX. AVGVST. A woman leaning upon a column (1). IVDAEA CAPTA. *Plate* xl, *fig.* 4 (4). AEQVITAS AVG. (20). FORTVNAE REDVCI (20). s. c. Eagle on a globe (30). SECVRITAS AVGVSTI (15). VICTORIA NAVALIS (3)   162

TITUS.

ROMA (2). IVDAEA CAPTA, *plate* xl, *fig.* 3 (5). AEQVITAS AVGVSTI (10). VICTORIA AVGVSTI (8). VICTORIA NAVALIS (20). s. c. An altar (8). FELICITAS PVBLICA (8). s. c. Type of Hope (20). SALVTI AVGVSTI. An altar (1) -   -   -   -   -   82

DOMITIANUS.

s. c. The emperor on horseback (1). s. c. Soldier with trophy (1). s. c. Heap of arms, *plate* xl, *fig.* 5 (2). ANNONA AVG. (3). AEQVITAS AVGVSTI (10). FORTVNAE AVGVSTAE (15). VIRTVTI AVGVSTI (30). MONETA AVGVSTI (30). FIDEI PVBLICAE (12). IOVI CONSERVATORI (1). s. c. Type of Hope (30)   -   -   -   -   135

NERVA.

LIBERTAS AVG. (3). CONCORDIA EXERCITVVM; two hands joined across a standard ; *plate* xl, *fig.* 6 (5). AEQVITAS AVGVSTI (2). FORTVNAE AVGVSTI (5). NEPTVNO . . (*Circens. Restit.*)—Neptune standing to the right, his left hand grasping a trident; behind him a river god, the Tiber (1)   -   -   -   -   -   16

TRAJANUS.

s. p. q. r. OPTIMO PRINCIPI. The emperor in a quadriga (1). Column (1). Soldiers with two trophies (1). Three standards (1). Captive seated on arms before a trophy (5). TR. POT. COS. II. Abundantia, seated upon a chair formed of two cornucopias ; *plate* xl, *fig.* 7 (1). Female figure, standing; in exergue, ARAB. ADQVIS (6). Victory, standing; on a shield suspended from a tree, VIC. DAC. (2). Victory standing by a trophy (2). s. p. q. r., etc. A horseman riding over a prostrate figure, *plate* xl, *fig.* 8 (2). Titles; Victory with shield inscribed s. p. q. r. (10). Fortune seated (8). Types of Piety, Abundance, etc. (10) -   -   -   -   -   -   -   50

HADRIANUS.

COS. III. Pegasus (1). PONT. MAX. TR. POT. COS. III. In the exergue, BRITANNIA. The province of Britain seated on a rock, with spear and shield. Three varieties are given in *plate* xl, *figs.* 9, 10, 11 (12). Titles; three standards; Modius; Types of Fortune, Piety, etc. (20). FELICIT . . . . . . Two figures joining hands (1). COS. III. Varieties of the galley type (4). ANNONA (3). s. c. in wreath (1). s. c. Pallas (1). HILARITAS P. R. COS III. (2). AFRICA (1). FIDES PVBLICA (4)   -   -   -   50

SABINA.

s. c. Ceres, seated on a modius ; in her right hand flowers, in her left a torch   -   -   4

ANTONINUS PIUS.

IMPERATOR II. In the exergue, ANCILIA (2). GENIO SENATVS (1). BONO EVENTVI (1). ANNONA AVG. (3). CONCORD. COS. IIII. Three hands joined (1). PIETAS. AVG. (4). CONCORDIA

EXERCITVVM (1). BRITANNIA COS. IIII. (10). S. C. A figure holding a lyre and a patera (1). PM...COS. DES. II. Abundantia, standing; *plate* xl, *fig.* 12 (1). Titles; Pallas, standing (1). TR...... The Tiber, reclining; below, TIBERIS—S. C. *Plate* xl, *fig.* 13 (1). Types of Piety, Fortune, Liberty, Felicity, etc. (15) - - - 42

FAUSTINA THE ELDER.

AETERNITAS. Female figure, standing (2). Idem. A seated figure holding a globe, on which is a phœnix (1). PIETAS AVG (4). FELICITAS (3). VENERI AVGVSTAE (1). IVNONI REGINAE (2). AVGVSTA (1). S. C. Diana standing - - - - - 14

MARCUS AURELIUS.

PIETAS (1). CONCORDIA (2). IVVENTAS (1). CONCORDIA EXERC....(1). IMP. VIII....; in the area, FELICIT... Galley, with rowers (1). Titles; Types of Equity, etc. (10). CONSECRATIO. An eagle (1) - - - - - - - 17

FAUSTINA THE YOUNGER.

S. C. DIANA (1). SALVS AVGVSTA (2). FELICITAS (2) - - - - - 5

VERUS.

LIBERALITAS TR. P. V. IMP. COS. Type of Liberality (1). CONCORDIA AVGVSTORVM. Two figures joining hands (1) - - - - - - 2

COMMODUS.

HERC. COMMODIANO P. M. TR. P. XVI. COS. VI. A figure sacrificing on an altar before a tree, upon which is a lion's skin; *plate* xli, *fig.* 2 (1). HERC. ROMAN. AVG. Club in a wreath. The head of Commodus, on the obverse, is covered with a lion's skin; *plate* xli, *fig.* 1 (1). S. C. Minerva standing (1). ....TR. P. XV. IMP. VIII. COS. VI. A ploughman driving two oxen (1). Titles; female figure with cornucopia (1). SAL. GEN. HVM. COS. VI. P.P. Salus raising a kneeling figure (1) - - - - 6

SEVERUS.

P. M. TR. P. XVI. COS. III. P.P. Victory, seated on arms before a trophy; in right hand a palm, in left a shield (1). ROMAE AETERNAE. Rome seated upon arms (1) - - 2

JULIA DOMNA.

FORTVNAE FELICI. Fortune, seated, with rudder and cornucopia; before her a child; behind, a column with a statue; *plate* xli, *fig.* 5 (1) - - - - - - 1

CARACALLA.

VIRTVS AVGVSTORVM. An armed female seated on a helmet, and holding a victory; her left arm upon a shield; *plate* xli, *fig.* 3 (1). PONTIF. TR. P. XI. COS. III. In the exergue, PROF. AVGG. The emperor on horseback, galloping over a fallen figure (1). PONT. TR. P. XIII. COS. III. A soldier standing before a trophy and captive; *plate* xli, *fig.* 4

GETA.

VICT. BRIT. TR. P. III. COS... A winged Victory seated on arms (1). FORT. RED., etc. (1) - 2

MACRINUS.

ANNONA AVG. (1). PONTIF. MAX. TR. P. II. COS. II. P. P. Security leaning upon a pillar, *plate* xli, *fig.* 6 (1). Idem. The emperor in a quadriga (1) - - - - - 3

SEVERUS ALEXANDER.

LIBERALITAS AVG. III. (1). FIDES MILITVM (1). P. M. TR. P. X. COS. III. P. P. A female figure holding ears of corn over a modius; in her left hand a ploughshare (1) - - 3

MAXIMINUS.

PAX AVGVSTA. Peace personified - - - - - - - - 1

MAXIMUS.

PIETAS AVG. Sacrificial vessels, *plate* xli, *fig.* 7 - - - - - - 1

GORDIANUS.

LAETITIA AVG. N. (1) Titles; a soldier standing (1) - - - - - 2

PHILIPPUS.

AEQVITAS AVG. Type of Equity (1). FELICITAS TEMP. Type of Felicity (1) - - - 2

TRAJANUS DECIUS.

A woman holding a military standard - - - - - - - 1

DIOCLETIANUS.

GENIO POPVLI ROMANI. In the exergue, P. TR. (3). Idem; in the exergue, PL., etc. (4) - 7

MAXIMIANUS.

GENIO POPVLI ROMANI. In the exergue, P. L. C. (5). HERCVLI CONSERVATORI (1) - 6

CONSTANTIUS.

GENIO POPVLI ROMANI. In the exergue, P. T. R. - - - - - - 2

FL. VAL. SEVERUS.

GENIO POPVLI ROMANI. Genius standing by an altar - - - - - 1

CONSTANTINUS.

PRINCIPI IVVENTVTIS. The Emperor standing between and holding two standards; in the field, on the left, C. I.: on the right, H. S.: in the exergue, P. L. C. *Plate* xli, *fig.* 8 (1). A similar type with P. T. R. in the exergue (1) - - - - 2

SMALL BRASS.

NERO.

CER. QVINQ. ROM. CON. S. C. (1). GENIO AVGVSTI. S. C. (1). PONTIF. MAX. TR. P. IMP. P.P. S. C. An armed female figure seated upon arms (2). MAX. TRIB.......S. C. similar (1) 5

TRAJANUS.

S. C. A vase and wreath, upon a table - - - - - - - 1

POSTUMUS.

PAX. AVGG. (1). MONETA AVG. (1). VICTORIA AVG. (1). CONCORD. EQVIT. (1) IOVI VICTORI (1)   5
A silver coin of Postumus is given in *Plate* xli, *fig.* 13.

VALERIANVS.

PIETAS AVGG.: in the exergue, KAR. Mercury, holding the purse and caduceus. *Plate* xli, *fig.* 9
    (1). CONSERVAT......Apollo (1)   .   -   -   .   -   -   2

GALLIENVS.

IOVI CONSERVATORI (1). VICTORIA AVG. (3). SALVS AVG. (3). NEPTVNO CONS. AVG. A
    sea-horse (2). SOLI. CONS. AVG. Pegasus (3). APOLLINI. CONS. AVG. Centaur (2).
    DIANAE. CONS. AVG. A stag (1). LIBERO. P. CONS. Panther (3). Various (20)   -   38

VICTORINVS.

PAX. AVG. (5). INVICTVS. (1). VIRTVS AVG. (6). SALVS AVG. (5). LAETITIA AVG. (3).
    AEQVITAS AVG. (3). Various (20)   -   -   -   -   -   -   .   43

MARIVS.

VICTORIA AVG. (1). CONCORDIA MILITVM (2)   -   -   .   -   -   3

CLAUDIUS GOTHICUS.

GENIVS EXERCITVS. (2). SECVRIT. AVG. (3). FORTVNA AVG. (2). LIBERT. AVG. (2). DIANA
    LVCIF. (1). IOVI VICTORI. (2). CONSECRATIO. (6). Various, badly struck (20)   -   38

QVINTILLVS.

MARTI PACIF. (2). CONCORD. EXER. (1). CONCORD. MILITVM. (1). FORTVNA. AVG. (1)   -   5

AVRELIANVS.

RESTITVTORI. EXERCITVS (1). CONCORDIA MILITVM. The Emperor and Concordia joining hands.
    Plate xli, *fig.* 10 (1). VICTORIA AVG. (1). APOLLINI CONS. (1)   -   -   4

SEVERINA.

CONCORDIA MILITVM. A female figure holding two standards   -   -   -   1

THE TETRICI.

PAX AVG. (6). VIRTVS. AVGG. (4). HILARITAS. AVGG. (6). SPES PVBLICA. (5). Various, badly
    struck (20)   -   -   .   -   -   -   -   -   41

TACITVS.

LAETITIA FVND. In the exergue, XXI. (1). TEMPORVM FELICITAS (1). PAX PVBLICA (1)   -   3

PROBUS.

VIRTVS PROBI. AVG. (1). PAX AVG. (2). CONCORD. MILIT. (1). PROVIDENT. AVG. (1) -   5

NVMERIANVS.

VNDIQVE VICTORES. In the exergue, KAS. A male figure standing; in his right hand a globe;
    in his left the hasta pura   -   -   -   -   -   -   -   -   1

CARINUS.

AEQVITAS AVGG. In the field, A. In the exergue, K. A. z. - • - - - 1

DIOCLETIANUS.

IOVI CONSERVATORI (2). PAX. AVGGG. In the field, S.P. In the exergue, MLXXI. (2). GENIO. POP. ROM. (1) - - - - - - - - - 5

MAXIMIANUS.

PAX AVG. (1). PAX AVGGG. In the field, S. P. In the exergue, MLXXI. (3). VIRTVS AVGG. (1). GENIO. POP. ROM. (2) - - - - - - - 7

CARAUSIUS.

EXP......ENI (Expectate Veni). Two figures (1). FORTVNA AVG. (2). FIDES MILITVM. (1). MART....R. (1). MONETA AVG. In exergue, C. (1). Idem, in field, S. P. (1). PAX AVG.; in the field, the letters B. R., or B. E., or F. O., or F. R., or S. C., or S. P.; and in exergue, M. L., or MLXXI, or C. Type of Peace, standing; in right hand, a flower, in left, the hasta held transversely on some specimens, on others, erect (30). PAX AVGGG. In field, S. P.; in exergue, C. or MLXXI. (8). PIETAS AVGGG. In field, L. P.; in exergue, M. C. Mercury (a unique type) (1). PROVID. AVG. In field, S. P. or S. C.; in exergue, C. Types of Providence (7). LAETITIA AVG. (5). SEC....PER.. Security leaning on a column, in right hand a garland (an unpublished variety) (1). SPES PVBLICA (1). SALVS AVG. (3). TEMP. FELICITAS. The four seasons personified. *Plate* xli, *fig.* 11 (1). IOVI....SER. (1). VIRTVS. AVG. (3). VICTORIA AVG. Victory, on a globe, holding a wreath and palm branch; at her feet two captives (unique) (1). ROMA RENO .. Wolf and Twins (1). LEG.... A bull (1). LEG..II. A ram (1). ...... Legend defaced; a capricorn (1) - - - - - 72

ALLECTUS.

LAETITIA AVG. In field, S. A. or S. P.; in exergue, ML or C. A female figure, standing (2). The same legend. A galley; in exergue, Q. C. or Q. L. (3). MONETA AVG. In field, S. A.; in exergue, ML. (1). PAX AVG. In field, S. or S. P., or S. H.; in exergue, ML, MLXX, or M.S.L., or C. Peace, standing. *Plate* xli, *fig.* 12 (12). PIETAS AVG. (1). PROVID. AVG. In field, S. P.; in exergue, C. (4). Idem; the obverse reading IMP. C. ALLECTVS PIV. FEL. AVG. (1). PROVIDE. AVG. (1). PROVIDENTIA AVG. In field, S. A.; in exergue, ML. (3). TEMPORVM FELICITAS. Female figure, standing (2). VIRTVS AVG. In field, S. A.; in exergue, ML. Mars, standing (1). Idem; varieties of the Galley type (8) - - - - - - - - 40

HELENA.

PAX PVBLICA; in exergue, TR. P. (5). SECVRITAS REIPVBLICAE; in exergue, P. LON. A female standing, holding in her right hand, a branch. *Plate* xli, *fig.* 16 (1). A similar type, struck at Treves (1) - - - • - - - 7

THEODORA.

PIETAS ROMANA; in exergue, T. R. (2). A woman suckling two children - - - 2

Y

GAL. VAL. MAXIMIANUS.

PRINCIPI IVVENTVT; in exergue, XXI. T. A military figure holding a standard and hasta (1).
    CONCORDIA MILITVM (1)   -   -   -   -   -   -   2

C. GAL. VAL. MAXIMINUS.

GENIO POP. ROM.; in the exergue, P.L.N.   -   -   -   -   -   -   -

MAXENTIUS.

VICTORIA DD. NN. AVGG.   -   -   -   -   -   -   -   -   1

THE LICINII.

GENIO POP. ROM. (2). LICINI AVGVSTI VOTIS. XX. (1). SOLI INVICTO COMITI (2). VOT. V.
    MVLT. X. CAESS. T. S. A. (1). D. N. LICIN. AVGVSTI; within a wreath, VOT. XX. (1)   7

CONSTANTINUS.

BEATA TRANQVILLITAS; in exergue, S. TR. (3). VICTORIAE LAETAE, &c. (6). VIRTVS EXERCIT.
(4). SARMATIA DEVICTA; in the exergue, P. LON. (4); Idem; in exergue, P. L. C. (4).
ROMAE AETERNAE (2). PROVIDENTIAE AVGG.; in exergue, P. LON.: the gate of a
castrum. *Plate* xli, *fig.* 14 (3). VIRTVS AVG.; in the exergue, S. CONS. (2). MARTI
CONSERVATORI. Head of Mars (1). Idem; in exergue, P. T. R. Mars, standing (1).
SOLI. INVICTO COMITI (3). CONCORDIA MILIT (1). The Emperor ascending in a
quadriga; from above, an outstretched hand (2). Various (12)   -   -   -   48

[POPULUS ROMANUS.]

Obv.—POP. ROMANVS. Youthful laureated bust, with cornucopia. *Rev.*—CONS. B. A star,
within a wreath   -   -   -   -   -   -   -   -   -   1

[URBS ROMA.]

Obv.—VRBS ROMA. Head of Rome. *Rev.*—Wolf and Twins; various letters in the exergues (10)   10

[CONSTANTINOPOLIS.]

Obv.—Personified head of the city of Constantinople. *Rev.*—Genius, with shield and hasta;
her foot upon the prow of a galley   -   -   -   -   -   -   -   5

FAUSTA.

SPES REIPUBLICAE; in exergue, P. TR. A female with two children (2)   -   -   -   2

CRISPUS.

PRINCIPI IVVENTVTIS; in exergue, P. L. N. (2). BEATA TRANQVILLITAS; an altar inscribed
VOTIS XX; in exergue, P. LON. *Plate* xli, *fig.* 15 (5), or P. L. C. (4). PROVIDENTIA
CAESS. (2). VIRTVS EXERCIT. In the exergue, P. LON (3). CAESARVM NOSTRORVM
VOT. X.; in exergue, A. SIS.; or P. LON; or S. TR (4). Various (8)   -   -   -   29

CONSTANTINUS JUNIOR.

BEATA TRANQVILLITAS; in exergue, P. LON. (3); or S. TR. (3). CLARITAS REIPVB. (2). CAESARVM
NOSTORVM VOTIS V.; in exergue, P. LON. (2). VIRTVS CAESS (2). Various (12)   -   24

CONSTANS.

VICTORIAE DD. AVGG. Q. NN. (3). FEL. TEMP. REPARATIO. A phœnix (3)   -   -   -   6

CONSTANTIUS II.

FEL. TEMP. REPARATIO; in the exergue, AQ. S; and varieties   -   -   -   -   4

MAGNENTIUS.

FELICITAS REIPVBLICAE; in the exergue, TR. P. (1).   FEL. TEMP. REPARATIO; in the exergue,
    TR. S.   The Emperor in a galley rowed by a Victory (1)   -   -   -   -   2

DECENTIUS.

VICT. DD. NN. AVGG. ET. CAESS. (1).   Idem; in the exergue, TR. P.   Two Victories, holding a
    shield inscribed VOT. V. MVLT. X.   -   -   -   -   -   -   -   2

JULIANUS.

VOT. X. MVLT. XX., within a wreath   -   -   -   -   -   -   -   1

VALENTINIANUS.

RESTITVTOR REIPVBLICAE (2).   SALVS REIPVB (1)   -   -   -   -   -   -   3

VALENS.

SECVRITAS REIPVBLICAE (4).   GLORIA ROMANORVM (3)   -   -   -   -   -   7

GRATIANUS.

GLORIA ROMANORVM (2).   VICTORIA AVGG. (1)   -   -   -   -   -   3

VICTOR.

SPES ROMANORVM; in the exergue, S.M.R.Q.S.   The camp gate   -   -   -   -   1

HONORIUS.

GLORIA ROMANORVM.   The emperor standing between two captives   -   -   -   -   2

Minimi, or very small coins struck by the Romans or Romano-Britons, in late times; but too
    rudely executed to be classified   -   -   -   -   -   -   -   200

This list of Roman coins found in London amounts to upwards of two thousand.
It gives only those which, for about the last twenty years, passed under my own
eye, chiefly from the bed of the Thames. A much larger number, within that
period of time, must have been found. Six hundred or more, picked up from gravel
dredged from the Thames, and strewed along the bank of the Surrey Canal, were
collected by the late Mr. R. Pimm, of Deptford. It is well to record this fact,
because the gravel taken from the bed of the Thames, below London Bridge, has
been extensively used for repairing the banks of the river at Barnes and other

places ; and this gravel contained large quantities of coins, the finding of which in some future day may puzzle and deceive persons ignorant of their history. A hoard of denarii of the Higher Empire was found in the City, which, the Corporation having declined purchasing, was bought by Mr. Mark Boyd.[1] Vast quantities are said to have been found in removing the piers of old London Bridge and in excavating the approaches to the new bridge. Of these, and of those exhumed in the City in former times, scarcely a record has been preserved. The list here presented will not give more than an imperfect notion of the number actually brought to light; but it will serve to convey a faint idea of the incalculable quantity which must have been met with both in modern times and in past ages.

Coins from the Thames constitute the bulk of this catalogue. They were dredged up at a considerable depth beneath the surface of the bed of the river, along the line of the old bridge and opposite what is now the Adelaide wharf ; but by far the greater number came from about twenty yards below the second arch of the new bridge. Some facts in connexion with their discovery and considerations deduced therefrom, have been given in the first part of this volume.

Many of them are of considerable individual interest and of great rarity. The Roman medallions, though few, are an unusual feature in collections of coins made upon the sites of ancient towns ; and the Greek Caracalla, found in the precincts of the Tower, is the only authenticated instance of a Greek coin procured from excavations in London. From Claudius to Trajan the coins in middle brass are particularly numerous. Of large brass those of Trajan, Hadrian, Antoninus Pius, Marcus Aurelius, the Faustinas, and Commodus, are the most plentiful. Of the family of Severus base denarii are very common, as are in the small brass series the coins of Carausius, Allectus, and the Constantine family. Relatively, they mark important epochs in the history of Roman Britain, pointing to periods when history sheds a faint light on the prosperity and vicissitudes of the province, as the illegible, and inartistic little pieces called *minimi* reflect the decline and fall of the Roman domination. In the three plates devoted to this department of the London antiquities, the first contains medallions and large brass coin : the second, middle brass : the third, chiefly second and third brass coins, including three, of Constantine, Crispus, and Helena, struck in Londinium, as certified by the exergual P. LON.

The coins of Vespasian and Titus relating to the subjugation of Judæa are monuments of peculiar interest, and equally so are the coins relating to Britain. Examples of these two series are given in plates xxxix and xl. Upon the large

---

[1] Mr. Boyd informs me they were stolen from his house, a few years since, with other valuable property.

brass coin of Titus, in the former of these plates, the national features of the Jewish male captive can be recognized, while the Syrian costume of the seated female beneath the palm tree, is equally truthful and in keeping with the propriety of detail so remarkable in the Roman coins.

The middle brass coin of Nerva reading NEPTVNO (*Circens. Restit.* or *Constit.*) is of the highest rarity. A similar coin is the subject of a paper, by Ashby, in the third volume of the *Archæologia* : a variety is mentioned by Eckhel.[1] It was struck on the occasion of some extraordinary patronage conferred by the emperor on the Circensian games.

The personification of our own island upon a rather extensive series of Roman coins, furnishes a subject for historical investigation which, to Englishmen, cannot fail to be exciting and pleasurable. In the London list the coins relating to Britain are of Hadrian, Antoninus Pius, Commodus, and Geta. It is remarkable that the coins of Carausius and Allectus, although they were struck in this country, do not, in any one instance, bear the name of the province. Of Hadrian, at least fifteen of the Britannia type; and of Antoninus Pius, more than twenty, have been obtained from the Thames. Three varieties of the former are given in pl. xl, figs. 9, 10, 11. Britain is represented as a female, armed, and in the attitude of watchfulness, her right foot upon a rock, emblematical of the protection and repose ensured to the province by the visit of Hadrian and the erection of the great wall across the north of Britain. Upon the coins of Antoninus Pius the genius of Britain is depicted as a youthful male figure, seated upon a rock and accompanied by a large oval shield, and a standard. The coins of Commodus and Geta relate to victories gained in Britain.[2]

The state of Britain under Carausius and Allectus, when the province, chiefly by the aid of a powerful navy, was raised to the rank and independence of an empire, is more fully understood from the coins of the period than from the brief notices of historians and contemporary writers; and the dredging of the Thames has contributed to increase these numismatic materials in several new types. The unique coin in small brass, reading GENIVS EXERCIT(*us*), is unfortunately lost : it was in the possession of the late Mr. R. F. Newman when I made the sketch engraved in Mr. Akerman's *Coins of the Romans relating to Britain*, pl. v, fig. 36. The PIETAS AVGGG., with Mercury standing; and the VICTORIA AVG., Victory upon a globe between two captives, were hitherto unknown. The rare gold coin of Maximian, SALVS AVGGG., as well as the small brass of that emperor and of Diocletian, inscribed PAX

---

[1] "Doct. Num. Vet.," tom. vi, p. 406.

[2] The entire series will be found, well illus-

trated, in Mr. Akerman's "Coins of the Romans relating to Britain," Lond., 1844, J. Russell Smith.

AVGGG., PROVID. AVGGG., etc., were struck by Carausius to impress upon the people of Britain the belief that his imperial authority was fully recognized by the emperors at Rome. The legend VBERITAS AVG., with the design, a woman milking a cow, and also TEMP(ORVM) FELICITAS, the four seasons personified, pl. xli, fig. 11, are typical of the fruitfulness of Britain and of its prosperity under the sway of Carausius. The list includes one of inferior workmanship, as if hurriedly engraved and struck, of the type presenting two figures joining hands, and reading *Expectate veni.* Whether, or not, this remarkable legend may have been suggested by the lines in Virgil :[1]

> *quibus Hector ab oris*
> *Exspectate venis ?*

there can be no doubt that upon the coins it is meant to express the wishes of Britain for the advent of Carausius ; and that the two figures are intended for Carausius himself, and Britain who welcomes him.

Three of the coins of the Constantine family minted in Londinium are given in pl. xli, figs. 14, 15, 16. That of Helena, the mother of Constantine, with the letters P. LON., in the exergue, is very uncommon. Engravings of other coins of this period, of the mint of Londinium, not particularized in this volume, because not actually found in London, may be consulted in pl. vi of Mr. Akerman's work before referred to. To these may now be added a new type which has lately come into my possession. It is of Constantine, the father, reverse VIRTVS EXERCIT., a trophy, beneath which are two captives : in the exergue, P. LON.

---

[1] " Æneid.," lib. ii, 1. 282.

INDEX.

INDEX TO THE PLATES.

Drawn & Engraved by F W Fairholt.

The Wall at Tower Hill.

Plate II

1

2

3

4

Inscriptions and Sculpture

Plate. III

2

DIS
ANIBVS
B·ALPINI·CLASSICIANI

3

A·ALFID·POMP
O·IVSSAIX·TES
TAMENT·HER
POS·ANNOR·LXX
NA·ALLINI
H·S·EST

4

5

Fragments of Tombs. etc.

J.G.W. del.

Plate III

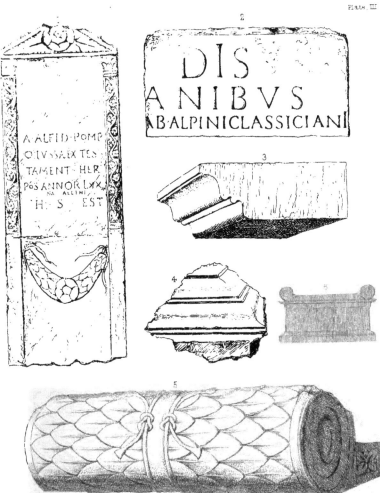

Fragments of Tombs. etc.

J.G.W. del.

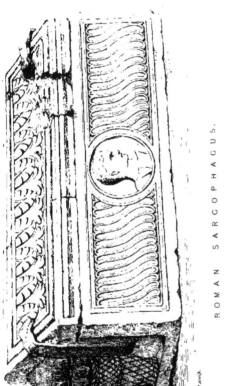

ROMAN SARCOPHAGUS.

LONDON.

Plate 7

In Stone. Height 25 Inches.

DISCOVERED AT BEVIS MARKS, CITY.

Drawn & Engraved by F W Fairholt

Tessellated Pavement.

discovered under the S.E. area of the Excise Office.

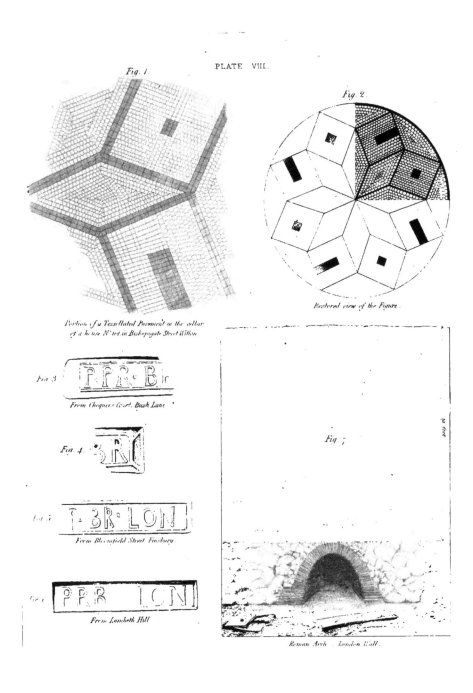

PLATE VIII.

Fig. 1.

Fig. 2.

Restored view of the Figure.

Portion of a Tessellated Pavement in the cellar
of a house N° 101 in Bishopsgate Street Within.

Fig. 3

From Chequers Court, Bush Lane.

Fig. 4.

Fig. 5

From Bloomfield Street Finsbury.

Fig. 6

From Lambeth Hill.

Fig. 7

Roman Arch, London Wall.

PLATE IX.

FRAGMENT OF ROMAN TESSELLATED PAVEMENT

DISCOVERED AT THE DEPTH OF 14 FEET

UNDER THE FRENCH PROTESTANT CHURCH

IN THREADNEEDLE STREET.

APRIL 1841.

PLATE X.

J.Basire lith.

THE CENTRE OF A ROMAN PAVEMENT DISCOVERED IN THREADNEEDLE STREET
UNDER THE LATE FRENCH CHURCH, 1841.

ROMAN TESSELLATED PAVEMENT.

PLATE XII.

ROMAN TESSELLATED PAVEMENT.

Plate XIV.

Wall Paintings.

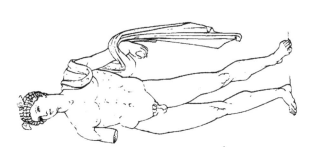

Bronze Figure of Mercury, found in the bed of the Thames 1837.

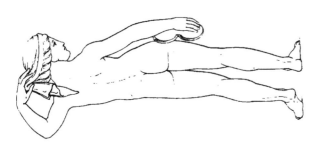

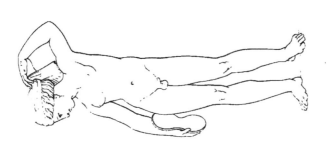

...the blood at the head of the Thames 1837

PLATE XVIII.

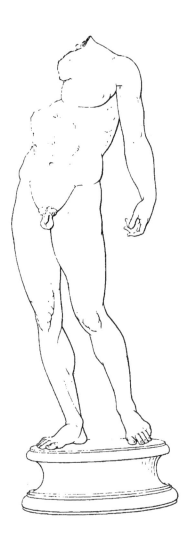

Bronze, supposed to represent Jupiter, found in the bed of the Thames. 1837.

Published by the Society of Antiquaries of London April 23rd 1838.

H. Moses.

Ld. Sct.

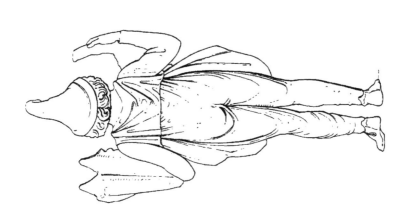

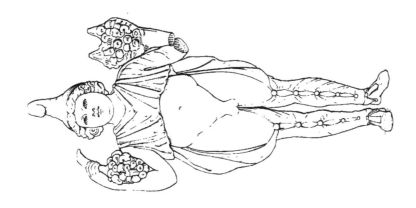

PLATE XXI.

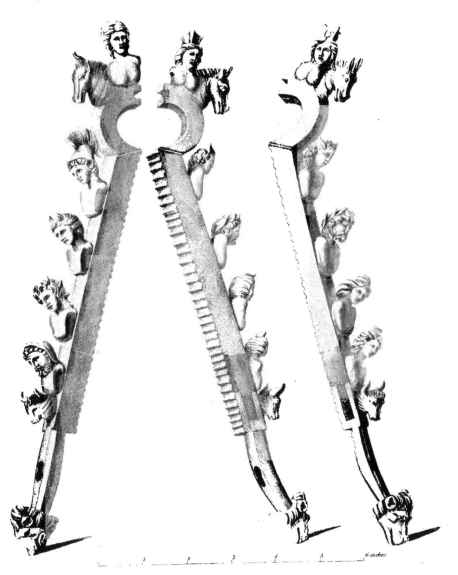

Bronze Forceps found in the Bed of the Thames, 1840.

Published by the Society of Antiquaries of London April 4.th 1851

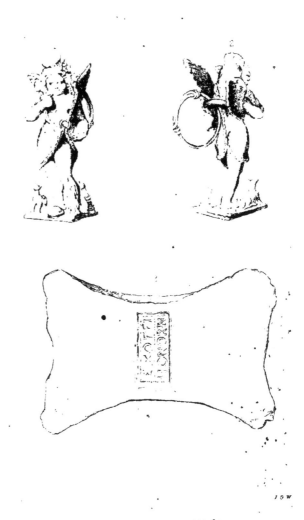

Statue of Harpocrates &c.

Plate X

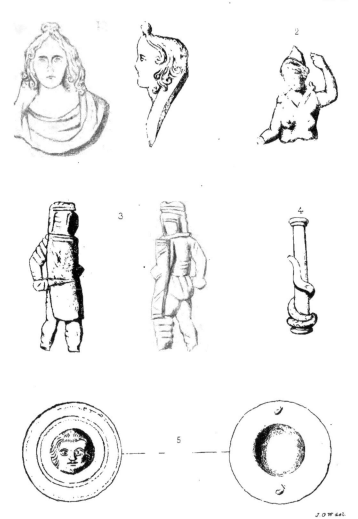

2

3

4

5

J.G.W del.

Weight, Statuettes, etc.

Red Glazed Pottery

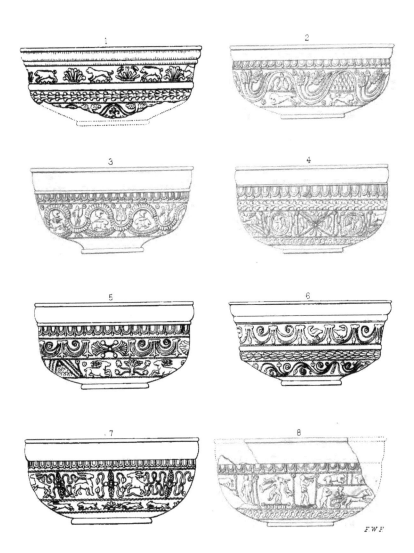

1   2

3   4

5   6

7   8

F.W.F.

Red Glazed Pottery

Plate XXVI

Red Glazed Pottery

F W F

Plate XI

Red Glazed Pottery

FWF

Plate XXVIII

Red Glazed Pottery

Plate

Red Glazed Pottery

F.W.F.

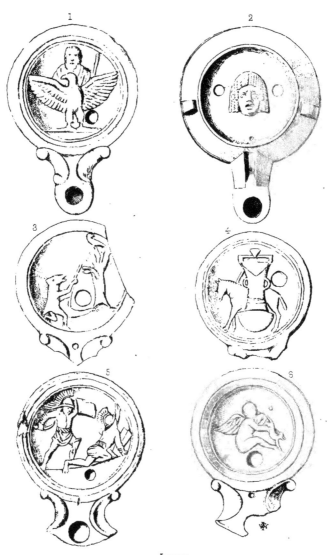

Lamps.

Plate XX

Glass

Plate I.

Personal Ornaments & Toilette Implements.

Plate XXXII

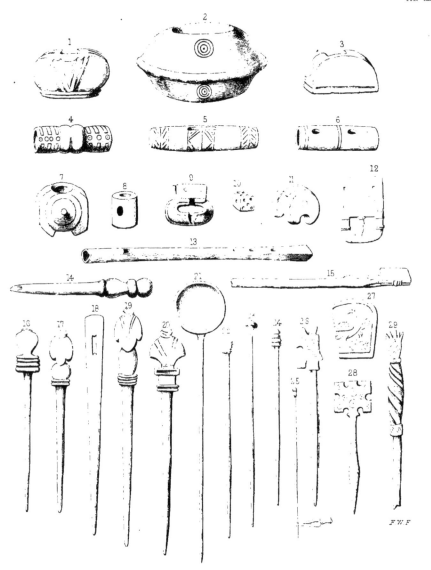

Personal Ornaments & other objects.
in Bone

Plate X

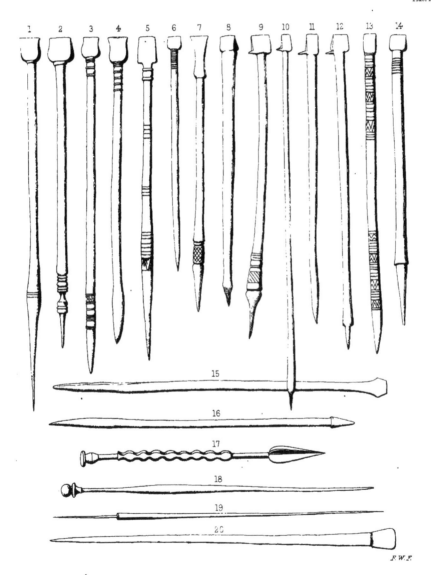

Styli.

F.W.F.

Plate XXV.

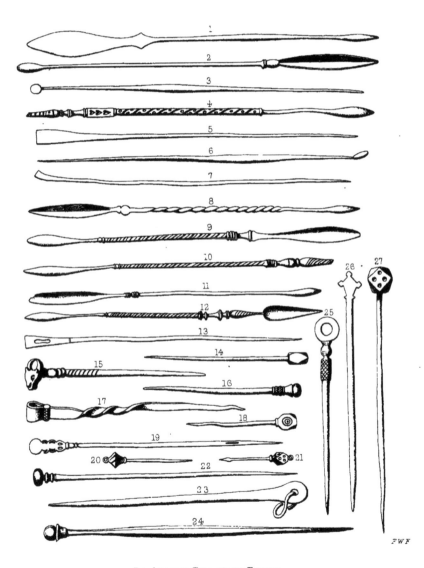

Implements, Pins, etc in Bronze.

FWF

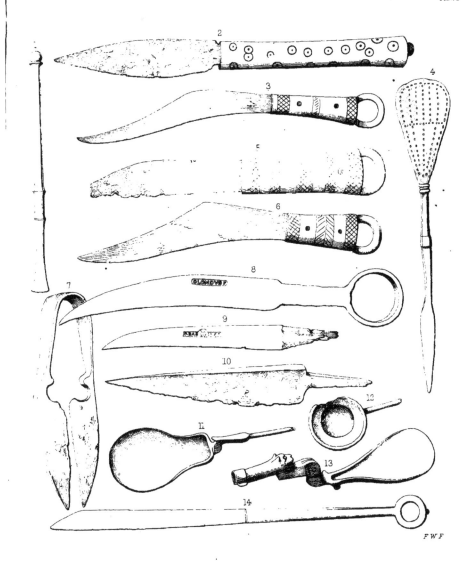

Plate 2

Knives. Spoons. etc

F W F

Plate XXXVIII

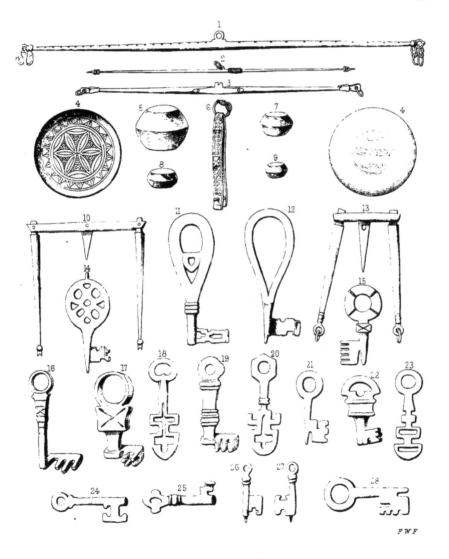

Scales, Weights. & Keys

F W F

Plate

F.W.F.

Plate X

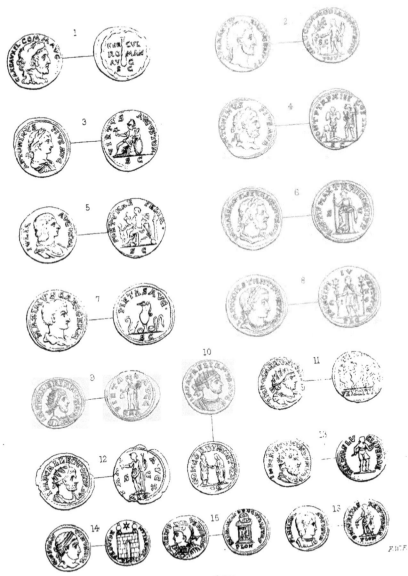

Coins.

LIST OF SUBSCRIBERS.

The Academy of Sciences, Arts, and Belles Lettres, of Caen

The Royal Scottish Academy of Painting, Sculpture, and Architecture, Edinburgh

The Society of Antiquaries of Normandy, Caen

The Society of Antiquaries of Picardy, Amiens

The Imperial Society of Emulation of Abbeville

The Society of Antiquaries of Newcastle-upon-Tyne

George Brindley Acworth, Esq., Star Hill, Rochester

J. Yonge Akerman, Esq., Sec. Soc. Ant. Lond., Somerset House

William Allen, Esq., 24, Stoke Newington Green

James Anderton, Esq., 20, New Bridge-street, Blackfriars

Joseph Arden, Esq., F.S.A., 27, Cavendish-square, and Rickmansworth Park, Herts

The Rev. Charles John Armistead, F.S.A., Chaplain, R.N., Hong Kong

George Atherley, Esq., Southampton, *deceased*

The Bank of England Library and Literary Association

The Birmingham Architectural Society

C. C. Babington, Esq., M.A., F.R.S., St. John's College, Cambridge

John Church Backhouse, Esq., Blackwell, Darlington

Charles Baily, Esq., 72, Gracechurch-street

C. A. Bannister, Esq., Mayor of Kingston-upon-Hull

John Barnard, Esq., F.S.A., Sawbridgeworth

John Barrow, Esq., F.R.S., F.S.A., 7, New-street, Spring Gardens

Benjamin Barrow, Esq., M.R.C.S., Ryde, Isle of Wight

Frederick Lowry Barnwell, esq., F.S.A., 60, Russell-square

Thomas Bateman, Esq., Youlgrave House, Bakewell

Thomas Battam, Esq., F.S.A., 5, Aubrey Villas, Notting Hill

John Adkins Barton, Esq., Bournemouth

Thomas Barton, Esq., Threxton House, Watton, Norfolk

The Bedfordshire Archæological Society, Bedford

John Bell, Esq., Gateshead

Robert Bell, Esq., Irthington, Cumberland, *deceased*

Professor Thomas Bell, V.P.R.S., P.L.S., 17, New Broad-street, City

Monsieur Temblaire de Belloquet, Homme de Lettres, Officier de la Legion d'Honneur, 8, Boulevard d'Argenson, Neuilly, Paris

Francis Bennoch, Esq., F.S.A., M.R.S.L., Blackheath

W. Harding Bensted, Esq., Maidstone

Miss Bicknell, 6, Clarendon Crescent, Leamington Spa

Mrs. Frances Biscoe, Holton Park, Wheatley, Oxon

Mrs. Sarah Blackett, Hill Green, Stockbury, Sittingbourne

William Madox Blackwood, Esq., F.S.A., Rother House, Rotherfield, Sussex

Wm. Bland, Esq., Hartlip Place, Sittingbourne

z 2

172

Thomas Leigh Blundell, Esq., M.D., 29, New Broad-street, City

Sir John Boileau, Bart., V.P.S.A., Ketteringham Park, Norfolk

Frederick Boöcke, Esq., 5, South-street, Alexander-square, Brompton

Francis S. Bolton, Esq., Edgbaston, Birmingham

The Baron de Bonstetten, Eichenbühl, Thoune, Suisse

Beriah Botfield, Esq., M.P., F.R.S., F.S.A., Norton Hall, Daventry

Mrs.Boyle,SeabridgeHall,Newcastle-under-Lyne

Charles Bradbury, Esq., 23, Crescent, Salford

J. G. Breach, Esq., Pavilion, Folkstone

J. W. Northway Brewer, Esq., 5, Liverpool-street, City

E. Kynaston Bridger, Esq., 4, Prince's-place, Kennington-road

William Bridger, Esq., Shide-house, Isle of Wight

John Britton, Esq., *deceased*

The Rev. J. Collingwood Bruce, LL.D., F.S.A., Hon. Sec. Society of Antiquaries of Newcastle-upon-Tyne

Department of Antiquities, British Museum

W. H. Brockett, Esq., Gateshead

John Brown, Esq., F.G.S., F.R.S.N.A., 3, Newcastle-place, Clerkenwell

John Buchanan, Esq., F.S.A., Scot. Glasgow

His Grace the Duke of Buccleuch, Montague House, Whitehall

The Rev. James Bulwer, Hunworth Rectory, Holt, Norfolk

Edward H. Bunbury, Esq., 15, Jermyn-street, St. James's

John Burder, Esq., Cliff Point, Higher Broughton, Manchester

James Burrell, Esq , 42, Manchester-street, Manchester-square

The Ven. Archdeacon Burney, D.D., F.R.S., F.S.A., M.R.S.L., Wickham Bishops, Essex

The Cambridge University Library

The Free Library, Cambridge

Benjamin Bond Cabbell, Esq., F.R.S., F.S.A., 52, Portland-place

Mrs. Campbell, Kilravock Castle, Nairn, Scotland

William George Carter, Esq., F.S.A., 6, Raymond's Buildings, Gray's Inn

Richard Redmond Caton, Esq., F.S.A., Union Club

William Chaffers, Esq., F.S.A., 1, Bolton Wood, Abbey Wood, St. John's Wood

David Noble Chambers, Esq., F.S.A., 47, Paternoster-row

Monsieur A. Charma, President of the Academy of Sciences, Arts, and Belles Lettres, of Caen

John A. Chidley, Esq., 10, Basinghall-street, City

The Rev. Professor Christmas, M.A., F.R.S., F.S.A., 5, Lark Hall Rise, Clapham

Hyde Clarke, Esq., D.C.L., 42, Basinghall-street

Joseph Clarke, Esq., F.S.A., The Roos, Saffron Walden

John Clayton, Esq., V.P. Soc. Ant. of Newcastle-upon-Tyne, The Chesters, Hexham

Andrew Coates, Esq., Philadelphia, N. America

George Coates, Esq., Glasgow

Peter Coates, Esq., Paisley

Thomas Coates, Esq., Paisley

The Rev. R. P. Coates, Precincts, Rochester

William Wise Cobb, Esq., Toronto

The Abbé Cochet, F.S.A., Dieppe

Thomas Somers Cocks, Esq., M.P., 15, Hereford-street, May Fair

Robert Cole, Esq., F.L.S., Hollybourne Lodge, Alton, Hants

The Rev. J. N. Coleman, Ryde, Isle of Wight

Charles Henry Cooper, Esq., F.S.A., Town Clerk, Cambridge

Joseph Sidney Cooper, Esq., Château de Brébant, St. Leonards-on-Sea

George Richard Corner, Esq., F.S.A.,3, Paragon, New Kent-road

The Rev.Tullie Cornthwaite, M.A., Walthamstow

John Ross Coulthart, Esq., F.S.A. Scot., Mayor of the Manor of Ashton-under-Lyne

James Gibson Craig, Esq., 24, York-place, Edinburgh

Messrs. Crossley and Clarke, Leicester

Mrs. Culverwell, Argyle-place, Regent-street

The Rev. George Henry Dashwood, F.S.A., Stow Bardolph, Downham Market

Thomas Dashwood, jun., Esq., Ryde, Isle of Wight

The Lord Bishop of St. David's, Abergwala Palace, Carmarthen

Robert Davies, Esq., F.S.A., The Mount, York

Pudsey Dawson, Esq., Hornby Castle, Lancaster

James Dearden, Esq., F.S.A., Rochdale Manor, Lancashire

His Grace the Duke of Devonshire, Holkar, Kendall

The Rev. J. Bathurst Deane, M.A., F.S.A., Sionplace, Sion Hill, Bath

Charles Dickens, Esq., Tavistock House, Tavistock-square

John Disney, Esq., LL.D., D.C.L., F.S.A., The Hyde, Ingatestone, Essex, deceased

C. Wentworth Dilke, Esq., 76, Sloane-street

Henry Dodd, Esq., City Wharf, Hoxton

Samuel Dodd, Esq., Hartland-terrace, Kentish Town-road

Sir Henry E. L. Dryden, Bart., Canons Ashby, Daventry

Mrs. Dunkin, Dartford, Kent

John Dunn, Esq., 2, County-place, Paisley

Monsieur Antoine Durand, Member of the Société d'Histoire et d'Archéologie de Genève, aux Courtillet, Lançy, Suisse

Thomas William Eady, Esq., Hornsey

Sir William Earle, 4, Park-crescent

The Lord Ellesmere, Bridgwater House, deceased

Richard Ellison, Esq., F.S.A., Sudbrook Holme, Lincoln, two copies

George Eastwood, Esq., 27, Haymarket

W. Philpott Elsted, Esq., Dover

Charles H. Elt, Esq., Myddelton Hall, Islington

The Right Hon. Thomas Erskine, Fir Grove, Eversley, Winchfield

John Evans, Esq., F.S.A., Hon. Sec. Num. Soc., Nash Mills, Hemel Hempstead

William Euing, Esq., 209, West George-street, Glasgow

Frederick William Fairholt, Esq., F.S.A., 11, Montpelier-square, Brompton

Edward Falkener, Esq., 61, Gracechurch-street

Henry Farrer, Esq., 106, New Bond-street

Thomas Faulkner, Esq., F S.A., Shide Hill House, Isle of Wight

James Fenton, Esq., M.A., Barrister-at-Law, Norton-Hall, Gloucestershire

John Fenwick, Esq., F S.A., Treasurer of the Society of Antiquaries of Newcastle-upon-Tyne

The Rev. Fred. C. Finch, St. Botolph, Bishopsgate

Robert Fitch, Esq., F.G.S., Norwich

W. Stevenson Fitch, Esq., Ipswich

The Earl Fitzwilliam, Milton, Peterborough, deceased; two copies

John Wickham Flower, Esq., Park Hill, Croydon

William Henry Forman, Esq., Union Club

W. Wynne Ffoulkes, Esq., M.A., Barrister-at-Law, Local Sec. Soc. Ant. Lond., 7, Stanley-place, Chester

Augustus Wollaston Franks, Esq., M.A., Dir. S.A., 55, Upper Seymour-street

Mrs. Garner, Queen-street, London

Richard Gibbs, Esq., Cedar Lodge, Stockwell Park

Charles Gill, Esq., Tiverton

John Godefroy, Esq., 5, Eleanor-road, Hackney

Mrs. Goreham, Cakeham, West Wittering, Sussex

W. C. Grant, Esq., Hillersden House, Cullompton

The Guildhall Library

Mrs. Gunn, Irstead, Norfolk

Miss Anna Gurney, North Repps, Cromer, deceased

Daniel Gurney, Esq., F.R.S., F.S.A., North Runckton, Norfolk

Hudson Gurney, Esq., F.R.S., F.S.A., Keswick Hall, Norwich

George Gwilt, Esq., F.S.A., Southwark, deceased

Miss Hackett, 26, Clapton-square

Chas. Hall, Esq., Osmington, Weymouth, *deceased*

John Hampden, Esq., Mem. Num. Soc. Lond., Leamington Priors

Mrs. Hannington, St. George's, Hurstpierpoint, Sussex

Colonel Francis Vernon Harcourt, M.P., Ryde, Isle of Wight

The Rev. L. Vernon Harcourt, Newsell's Park, Royston, Essex

The Rev. C. Hardwick, M.A., Christian Advocate in the University of Cambridge, St. Katharine's Hall

Frederick Harford, Esq., 9, Rutland Gate, Hyde Park; *two copies*

William Hargrove, Esq., author of *The History of York*, York

John Harris, Esq., Essendon Villa, Belvedere, Erith, Kent

Mrs. Harrison, Dacre Park, Cheshire

William Harrison, Esq., Galligreaves House, Blackburn

Henry Harrod, Esq., F.S A., Aylsham, Norfolk

James Smyth Hartley, Esq., East Parade, Colne

William Hawkes, Esq., Edgbaston, Birmingham, *two copies*

Edward Hawkins, Esq., V.P.S.A., F.L.S., British Museum

Walter Hawkins, Esq., F.S.A., 5, Leonard-place, Kensington, *two copies*

The Rev. Professor Henslow, Hitcham, Bildeston

Thomas Hewitt, Esq., Summerdale House, Cork

The Rev. John Harwood Hill, B.A., Cranoe Rectory, Market Harborough

George Hillier, Esq., Ryde, Isle of Wight

John Hodgson Hinde, Esq., V.P. Soc. Ant. of Newcastle-upon-Tyne

Fred. Hindmarsh, Esq., F.G.S., 17, Bucklersbury

Francis Hodson, Esq., Lee-road, Blackheath

A. J. Beresford Hope, Esq., M.P., F.S.A., 1, Connaught-place

Lucas Houghton, Esq., 30, Poultry

The Rev. Thomas Hugo, M.A., F.S.A., M.R.S.L., F.L.S., 57, Bishopsgate-street Within

James Hunt, Esq., Ph.D., F.S.A., M.R.S.L., Exmouth House, Hastings

The Rev. Arthur Hussey, M.A., Rottingdean, Sussex

Henry Hussey, Esq., 7, Hyde Park-square, and Wellington-crescent, Ramsgate

John Huxtable, Esq., Stoke Newington, *deceased*

The Archæological Institute of Great Britain and Britain and Ireland, Suffolk-street, Pall Mall East

James James, Esq., F.S.A., Halton Cottage, Wendover

J. Livingston Jay, Esq., Royal Hospital, Greenwich

Llewellynn Jewitt, Esq., F.S.A., Derby

Goddard Johnson, Esq., East Dereham, Norfolk

James Cove Jones, Esq., Loxley, Wellesbourne, Warwick

John Jolliffe, Esq., Surgeon R.N.; H.M.S. *Buzzard*, South America

William Kell, Esq., F.S.A., Newcastle-upon-Tyne, *two copies*

Edwin Keet, Esq., 13, Park-place South, Chelsea

Miss Kenrick, Stone House, Canterbury

John Whitefoord M'Kenzie, Esq., 16, Royal Circus, Edinburgh

Henry William King, Esq., 54, Tredegar-square, Bow-road

Jesse King, Esq., Appleford, Abingdon

William Warwick King, Esq., 25, College-hill, Cannon-street West

George Kirkpatrick, Esq., Newport, Isle of Wight

John Knowles, Esq., Croydon

Herr Conrad Kraus, Architect, Mayence

Edward Law, Esq., 23, Douglas-road, Canonbury

Colonel W. Martin Leake, F.R.S., M.R.S.L., etc., 30, Queen Ann-st., Cavendish-square

Mrs. W. Martin Leake, ditto

John Edward Lee, Esq., The Priory, Caerleon

Joseph Frederick Ledsam, Esq., Chad Hall, Edgbaston, Birmingham

The Permanent Library, Leicester

J. Lister, Esq., F.G.S., Shibden Hall, West Riding, Yorkshire

Edward Litchfield, Esq., Cambridge

Mrs. Locke, Fring Hall, Docking, Norfolk

The Right Hon. Lord Londesborough, K.C.H., F.R.S., F.S.A., Grimston, Tadcaster

R. Grove Lowe, Esq., St. Albans

Mark Antony Lower, Esq., F.S.A., St. Ann's House, Lewes

The Rev. W. C. Lukis, M.A., F.S.A., Collingbourne Ducis, Marlborough

Harry Lupton, Esq., Thame

D. Albert, Duc de Luynes, Dampierre par Chevreuse, Seine et Oise, France

H. B. Mackeson, Esq., F.G.S., Hythe, Kent

Stewart Macnaghten, Esq., Bittern Manor, Southampton

The Corporation of Manchester

Charles Wykeham Martin, Esq., M.P., F.S.A., Leeds Castle, Kent

John Mather, Esq., Liverpool, *deceased*

John May, Esq., Hyde-lane, Battersea

Joseph Mayer, Esq., F.S.A., F.R.A.S., F.R.S.N.A., Liverpool, *two copies*

John Mayer, Esq., Statten Island, New York

Jos Mayer, Esq., Brown Hills, Burslem

Samuel Mayer, Esq., Newcastle-under-Lyne

Miss Mayer, Thistleberry House, Staffordshire

Miss Meteyard, 20, Carlton-road-villas, Kentish-town

Captain James Middleton, F.S.A., Liverpool

Keith Milnes, Esq., South Audley-street, *deceased*

Frank J. Mitchell, Esq., Newport, Monmouthshire

Mrs. Moncreiff, Pitcaithley House, Bridge of Earn, Perth

Hugh E. Montgomerie, Esq., F.S.A., Ashley House, Wickham-terrace, Upper Lewisham-road

Sir Oswald Mosley, Bart., D.C.L., Rolleston Hall, Staffordshire

C. Octavius Swinnerton Morgan, Esq., M.P., V.P.S.A , F.R.S., Newport, Monmouthshire

G. G. Mounsey, Esq., Castletown, Carlisle

Sir Henry Muggeridge, Alderman, 16, Earl-street, Blackfriars

The Museum of Science and Art, South Kensington, *two copies*

Charles C. Nelson, Esq., 30, Hyde-park-gardens

The Rev. G. M. Nelson, Bodicote Grange, Banbury

G. H. Nevinson, Southfields, Leicester

His Grace the Duke of Newcastle, Clumber

William Newton, Esq., 42, Queen-square

John Gough Nichols, Esq., F.S.A., 28, Upper Harley-street

Henry Norris, Esq., F.R.C.S., Charmouth, Dorsetshire

George Warde Norman, Esq., Bromley, Kent

His Grace the Duke of Northumberland, Alnwick Castle

Colonel the Hon. M. E. Onslow, Woodbridge House, Guildford

Robert Ormston, Esq., Newcastle-upon-Tyne

Benj. Brogden Orridge, Esq., 30, Bucklersbury

Frederick Ouvry, Esq., Treas. S.A., 29, Upper Gower-street

The Lord Overstone, Carlton Gardens, *two copies*

The Rev. John Papillon, B.A., F.S.A., Lexden, Essex

J. Noël Paton, Esq., Wover's Alley Cottage, Dunfermline

Apsley Pellatt, Esq., M.P., Staines

Frederick Perkins, Esq., F.S.A., Chipstead-park, Sevenoaks

M. J. Boucher de Crevecœur de Perthes, President of the Imp. Society of Emulation of Abbeville

The Rev. John Lewis Petit, M.A., F.S.A., 9, New-square, Lincoln's-inn

Sir Thomas Phillipps, Bart., M.A., F.S.A., Middle Hill, Broadway, Worcestershire

Herr Gustav Pietsch, Architect, Mayence

H. C. Pidgeon, Esq., 3, Westbourne-villas, Harrow-road

R. Plant, Esq., Canonbury-park

John Henry Plowes, Esq., 89, York-terrace, Regent's-park

The Rev. Beale Poste, Bydews-place, Maidstone

Henry Glasford Potter, Esq., F.S.A., Acacia-cottage, Hampton

Edward Pretty, Esq., F.S.A., Chillington-house, Maidstone

William Proctor, Esq., M.R.C.S., York

Alfred Pryer, Esq., Hollingbourne, Kent

Purnell B. Purnell, Esq., Stancombe-park, Dursley

Sir John Ratcliff, F.S.A., Wyddrington, Edgbaston

Lovell Reeve, Esq., Wandsworth

The Rev. G. C. Renouard, Swanscombe, Kent

A. Henry Rhind, Esq., F.S.A., Sibster, Wick, Caithness

Charles Rivaz, Esq., 3, Craven-hill-gardens, Hyde-park

Frederick Roach, Esq., Arreton-manor, Isle of Wight

The Rev. Canon Rogers, Exeter, *deceased*

William Henry Rolfe, Esq., Sandwich, *two copies*

Henry William Rolfe, Esq., 3, Punderson-place, Bethnal Green

The Bibliothèque de Rouen

John B. Rudd, Esq., Tollesby Hall, Middlesbro'-on-Tees

Dr. Russell, New Hall-street, Birmingham

The Sandwich Book Society

Joseph Sams, Esq., Darlington

Miss Saul, Bow Lodge, Bow-road

J. B. Scott, Esq., Chelsea

J. R. Scott, Esq., Coal Exchange, Thames-street

Major Sheppard, Kingston-upon-Thames, *deceased*

Major Henry Smith, R.M., Wish-street, Southsea, Hants

Mr. John Russell Smith, Publisher, 36, Soho-square, *three copies*

Vice-Admiral W. H. Smyth, K.S.F., D.C.L., F.R.S., F.S.A., St. John's-lodge, Aylesbury

S. Reynolds Solly, Esq., F.R.S., F.S.A., Serge Hill, King's Langley

Messrs. Sotheby and Wilkinson, Wellington-street, Strand

The Lord Southampton, Whittlebury, Towcester

Charles Spence, Esq., Admiralty

The Rev. John Stacye, Shrewsbury Hospital, Sheffield

The Rev. Edward W. Stillingfleet, Hotham Brough, East Yorkshire

Miss Strutt, Derwent Bank, Derby

Colonel Sykes, F.R.S., India House

The Lord Talbot de Malahide, F.S.A., Malahide Castle, Dublin

W. J. Taylor, Esq., M. Num. Soc., 33, Little Queen-street, Holborn

James Thompson, Esq., Leicester

Joseph Thompson, Esq., Pin Mill, Ardwick, Manchester

Samuel Thornton, Esq., The Elms, Highgate, Birmingham

John Timbs, Esq., F.S.A., 88, Sloane-street, Chelsea

Edward Tindall, Esq., Old Guildhall, Bridlington

Sir Walter C. Trevelyan, Bart., M.A., F.S.A., Wallington, Morpeth

The Rev. Edward Trollope, B.A., F.S.A., Leasingham, Sleaford

Messrs. Trübner and Co., Publishers, 12, Paternoster-row, *two copies*

Dawson Turner, Esq., F.R.S., F.S.A., M.R.S.L., etc., Lee Cottage, Old Brompton, *deceased, three copies*

Miss Turner, Great Yarmouth

Mrs. Turner, Newcastle-under-Lyne

George Unwin, Esq., 31, Bucklersbury

Sylvanus Urban, Gent., 377, Strand

Thomas B. Uttermare, Esq., Langport, Somerset

George Virtue, Esq., F.S.A., Paternoster-row

Monsignor Virtue, Chaplain to the Forces, Aldershott

Sir Edward S. Walker, Berry Hill, Mansfield

The Rev. H. Aston Walker, Enfield

Miss H. Walne, Norwich, *two copies*

John Green Waller, Esq., 68, Bolsover-street, Portland-place

James Wardell, Esq., Deputy Town Clerk, Leeds

Charles Warne, Esq , F.S.A., Sydenham

Mr. Joseph Warren, Ixworth

Albert Way, Esq., M.A., F.S.A., Hon. Sec. Archæological Institute, Wonham Manor, Reigate

G. Bish Webb, Esq., Hon. Sec. Surrey Archæological Society, 6, Southampton-street, Covent-garden

William Webster, Esq., M. Num. Soc., 17, Great Russell-street

Richard Weekes, Esq., F.R.C.S., Hampton-lodge, Hurstpierpoint

Augustus Wetter, Esq., Architect, Savannah, Georgia, United States, America

Herr Carolus Wetter, Oppenheim, Architect to the Grand Ducal Government of Rhenish Hessia

Herr Conrad Wetter, 67, Myddleton-square

Herr Johann Wetter, Archæologist, Mayence, Rhenish Hessia

Alfred White, Esq., West Drayton

Humphrey Wickham, Esq., Strood, Kent

J. G. De Wilde, Esq., Northampton

The Rev. David Williams, D.C.L., Warden of New College, Oxford

William Wills, Esq., Edgbaston, Birmingham

Henry Wilson, Esq., Stowlangtoft Hall, Suffolk

James H. Wilson, Esq., 19, Onslow-square, Brompton

Sir Thomas Maryon Wilson, Bart., Charlton House, Blackheath

Charles Wynn, Esq., Nostel Priory, Wakefield

Richard Windle, Esq., 6, Osborn-street, Whitechapel

John Wodderspoon, Esq., the Lower Close, Norwich

J. G. Woodhouse, Esq., Bronte House, Liverpool

The Rev. G. H. Woods, Shopwyke House, Chichester

Richard Waugh Wright, Esq., Manchester

Thomas Wright, Esq., M.A., F.S.A., Member of the Institute of France, 14, Sydney-street, Brompton

The Rev. C. F. Wyatt, Forest Hill, Wheatley, Oxon

James Wyatt, Esq., Bedford

W. Michael Wylie, Esq., F.S.A., Blackwater, Hants

James Yates, Esq., M.A., F.R.S., Lauderdale House, Highgate

William Yewd, Esq., 20, Devereux-court, Temple

Miss Zornlin, Warwick Villa, Kenilworth

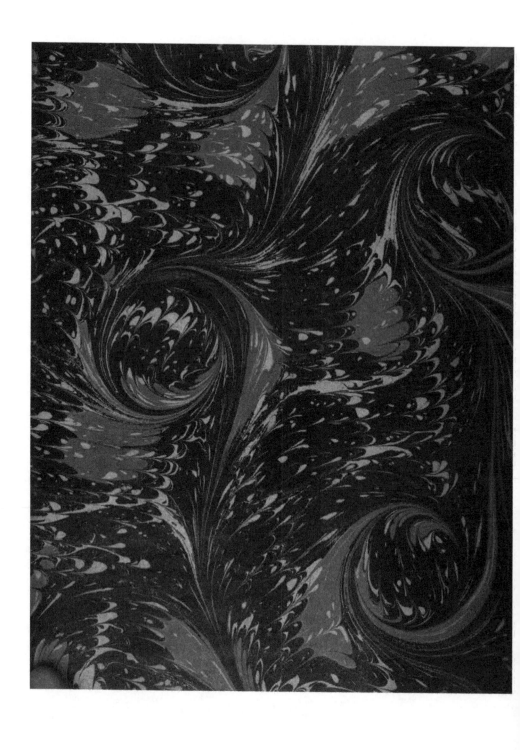

Lightning Source UK Ltd.
Milton Keynes UK
UKHW020612130123
415268UK00005B/77